GETTING

BACK TO

BUSINESS

GETTING

BACK TO BUSINESS

WHY MODERN PORTFOLIO THEORY FAILS
INVESTORS AND HOW YOU CAN BRING
COMMON SENSE TO YOUR PORTFOLIO

DANIEL PERIS

New York   Chicago   San Francisco   Athens   London   Madrid
Mexico City   Milan   New Delhi   Singapore   Sydney   Toronto

1 2 3 4 5 6 7 8 9   LCR   23 22 21 20 19 18

ISBN   978-1-260-13532-9
MHID   1-260-13532-2

e-ISBN   978-1-260-13533-6
e-MHID   1-260-13533-0

This publication is designed to provide accurate and authoritative information in regard to the subject matter covered. It is sold with the understanding that neither the author nor the publisher is engaged in rendering legal, accounting, securities trading, or other professional services. If legal advice or other expert assistance is required, the services of a competent professional person should be sought.

> —*From a Declaration of Principles Jointly Adopted*
> *by a Committee of the American Bar Association*
> *and a Committee of Publishers and Associations*

The views and opinions expressed in this publication are those of the author and do not necessarily reflect the views or opinions of Federated Investors, Inc., or its affiliates.

McGraw-Hill Education books are available at special quantity discounts to use as premiums and sales promotions or for use in corporate training programs. To contact a representative, please visit the Contact Us pages at www.mhprofessional.com.

Library of Congress Cataloging-in-Publication Data

Names: Peris, Daniel, author.
Title: Getting back to business : why modern portfolio theory fails investors and how you can bring common sense to your portfolio / Daniel Peris.
Description: New York : McGraw-Hill, [2018]
Identifiers: LCCN 2018009919| ISBN 9781260135329 (alk. paper) | ISBN 1260135322
Subjects: LCSH: Portfolio management. | Investments.
Classification: LCC HG4529.5 .P464 2018 | DDC 332.6—dc23
LC record available at https://lccn.loc.gov/2018009919

Contents

Preface

A number of years ago, I found myself in a somewhat awkward position at work. I had been employed as a stock analyst and portfolio manager for about 15 years, had passed the grueling, three-part CFA® (Chartered Financial Analyst) exam, was part of a group managing a multibillion-dollar portfolio of client assets, and had already authored two books on investing. Yet something did not seem right. The traditional "rules" of investing struck me as arbitrary and often contributed to worse rather than better investor outcomes. And my team's approach (focused on dividends) was at odds with how just about everyone else in the industry operated (focused on share prices). As my own investing experience was in stark contrast with the existing theory and most practice, it seemed like a good time to back up and review the basics.

It would have been easy enough to criticize the prevailing investment framework for its obvious flaws—all large, complex systems have weaknesses, particularly those that incorporate human behavior. Throughout my career, I had encountered critiques of the existing system—usually narrow academic articles or asides from practitioners—but I didn't find them satisfying or comprehensive. Here my background as a historian proved helpful. To understand why things are done today in a certain manner, my first instinct is to look at how *they came to be done that way.* A child of the later Cold War, I spent my college and young adult years studying the Soviet Union, trying to figure out how we had come to our Dr. Strangelovian state of affairs. I completed my training in the early 1990s, just as the Soviet Union collapsed—along with funding for careers in that area. I eventually made my way to financial research. My poor sense of timing intact, I joined the investment profession just in time to experience the tech bubble and the stock market sell-off of 2000–2001. The following decade was spent working my way through the stock research thickets, and I encountered the next major market "correction," the financial crisis of 2008, as a portfolio manager. The stock market has recovered nicely since then and moved on to new highs. This book is, in part, about how to think about investing in general, but also how to think about the stock market when and if the "other shoe" drops.

Throughout this up-and-down and up-again market ride, I have been increasingly struck by what I thought were self-defeating forms of behavior, not only by retail investors, who are well known to succumb to bad timing and often emotional impulses, but also by investment professionals and the gatekeepers supposedly well schooled in the "science" of investment. That puzzled me. My response was to turn back the clock to figure out how we got to the industry's current set of practices and assumptions, known as Modern Portfolio Theory (MPT). Just about everyone in the investment management industry uses some form of MPT—whether people admit it or not. The emergence of MPT is well documented, but as I reviewed the materials, I found that the "history of the history"—the conditions at the time MPT was developed—was more pertinent to understanding why it was so readily adopted and why it has created so many problems for investors today. As I'll argue here, the circumstances surrounding MPT's appearance in the middle of the last century go a long way to explaining the system's profound shortcomings and the desirability of an alternative. In a profession (and a society) utterly lacking a historical sensibility, one periodically needs to ask why we do things the way we do, how we got here, and whether perhaps there is a better way.

Although I was trained as a historian, at the end of the day, I am a practitioner. So I have attempted to sketch out what I consider an improvement on the existing assumptions and procedures, particularly in regard to stocks, but more generally in regard to all financial or publicly traded investments. Moreover, I argue that this better way is within easy reach of most investors, particularly those who are active in their own businesses or familiar with the businesses of friends or family members. I don't have a stand on evolution versus revolution other than to note that revolutions usually fail. (Please recall my earlier career in Soviet studies . . .) In contrast, I've come to the view that incremental improvement over time is preferable. My hope is that this modest volume contributes to movement in that direction.

Acknowledgments

Over the past five years, I have discussed the issues raised in this book and shared early drafts with numerous practitioners, academics, and individual investors. I am grateful to all of them for helping me work out and refine my propositions. Some were sympathetic to my agenda; others challenged it energetically. I want to call out two readers in particular, one from each camp. Pierre Schell shares many of my views, but our exchanges allowed me to see points that I might otherwise have overlooked. My colleague, Mike Granito, took the other side and interpreted the orthodox finance model in a number of very stimulating back-and-forth sessions. At McGraw-Hill, Noah Schwartzberg has been an excellent partner in this venture. Finally, the members of my family have had to endure my being occupied with investment theory and history for too long. *Getting Back to Business* is dedicated to them. It is now time for me to get back to them.

Introduction: The Need for Rules

People need to believe in a "system." Whether in regard to morals and the hereafter (organized religion), the management of our societies (government), or the search for our daily bread (economic systems), people want to believe in a stable set of rules. This belief in an overriding, chaos-vanquishing order is very comforting, so much so that it appears to be built into the human psyche and has been a prominent part of social life since the beginning of civilization 5,000 years ago. I will defer to the anthropologists and the sociologists, as well as the religious philosophers, as to why this is the case. The important point is that humans want order, full stop.

Just consider a few commonsense examples. Why does everyone in a given geography drive on the same side of the road and understand yellow to mean caution and red to mean stop? Imagine what would happen if these simple conventions in modern society were not followed. Suffice it here to note that in regard to more complex pursuits, such as the accumulation and disposition of financial capital—the world of investments—the same basic impulse to have a governing paradigm applies. People take comfort in the existence of a set of rules; it suggests that there is a right answer to every question, whether or not one really exists. Particularly when strongly stated, and better yet when stated in a mathematical formula, the resulting answers make us feel safe, even when, as it turns out, we may not be. Decision making under conditions of uncertainty is the profoundly human condition that all these paradigms seek to address. They are laudable and necessary efforts to vanquish the chaos that would exist without them. But not every convention is perfect. And these rules can and should be constantly under review.

Modern Portfolio Theory (MPT) is not a top-tier economic, political, or religious system, but it is an internally coherent set of trusted assumptions and practices. As a narrative, it is comforting. It tells a story that appears reasonable and logical. And it affects just about everyone with financial investments. It is not only a matter of direct ownership of stocks and bonds by individuals. These rules are right under the surface of many of the tools that do-it-yourselfers see in their online brokerage accounts and in the 401(k) statements that have become ubiquitous in middle-class American households. How your financial advisor manages your account is a direct outcome of Modern Portfolio Theory, whether you or the advisor knows it or not. During your first visit, the advisor will put you through a review process that determines your financial goals and your tolerance for risk. After that conversation, the firm's asset allocation model spits out a combination of stock and bond products (and perhaps "alternatives") that is a direct result of MPT. The products offered are supposed to perform and interact in a particular manner. You are encouraged to view the entire exercise as a well-designed mechanical system at work.

The pension funds of old economy companies, as well as the retirement assets for public sector employees and trade unions, are invested strictly according to the dictates of MPT. To do otherwise could get the trustees fired or sued for not following so-called industry "best practices." The slavish use of MPT, however, may be the reason so many of those plans are seriously underfunded and have no realistic chance of ever meeting their obligations in full. If you are one of those employees or retirees and are wondering why the outlook for your pension is so grim, you probably want to know how your twice-monthly contributions are invested. That "how" is MPT. If you send your child to a private school with an endowment that helps offset some of the tuition cost, what you end up paying is, in effect, dependent on how the endowment is invested. That "how" is MPT. If you work at a school or a cultural enterprise with its own endowment, your job may depend on how the endowment is invested. That "how" is MPT. Even if you don't own any financial instruments, you've been affected by MPT. Believe it or not, your monthly utility bill is calculated in part by one of the key formulas that emerged to apply MPT. So unless you have no financial investments, don't ever plan to have any, and don't use electricity from the grid, MPT affects your life. You may want to read on.

Despite the fact that investing touches the lives of so many people, only a relatively small percentage of the population spends much time thinking about the overarching system that guides those activities. The vast majority of us are too busy living our lives, and for those of us of working age, too busy trying to make enough money to invest in the first place. So we buy into the system without too much questioning. We assume that there must be some time-tested logic to investing. Because if there weren't a good set of rules by which our hard-earned dollars are being invested, why would we even bother to build up a retirement nest egg? And it is not just individual investors who have (mostly unknowingly) bought into MPT. The underlying assumptions and directives of

MPT are widely treated as accepted wisdom by most invest-ment professionals, even if they do not explicitly embrace it. Investment management and consulting businesses are built around its core concepts. The system is perpetuated through extensive education and accreditation programs for newcom-ers to the financial services industry.

So what is MPT? It is a complex system, and it is nonca-nonical—that is, there are disagreements, outgrowths, vari-ants, and changing elements. But the core beliefs to which almost all the academics and practitioners subscribe can be reduced to two basic assertions. I will cover them in greater detail later, but the first (developed by Harry Markowitz in the 1950s) defines "risk" and "return" and elevates diversifica-tion of one's portfolio—having a larger rather than a smaller number of separate investments—to the primary means of managing the former (risk) and achieving the latter (return). Markowitz then argued that rational investors with good information at their disposal will naturally prefer the highest possible return for a given degree of risk. Alternatively, for any given amount of expected return, investors will naturally choose the portfolio that has the lowest risk. Those portfolios that have the optimal amount of risk and return are deemed to be "efficient." When put on a graph, those portfolios form a nice-looking curve that has been called the "efficient fron-tier." It sounds great. Who wouldn't want to be invested right where the formulas say they should be?

The second foundational belief came a decade later from William Sharpe, Jack Treynor, and several others. Their "cap-ital asset pricing model"(CAPM) also achieved two goals. First, it dramatically simplified Markowitz by measuring risk vis-à-vis a single market index as opposed to individual security versus individual security, as had been the case in Markowitz's original work. That shift made the necessary calculations a lot fewer and much easier to do. Second, it offered an elegant, easy-to-understand formula to determine the "expected return" from any given security. A decade earlier, Markowitz had left that important input essentially unspecified, in the sense of not being easily predictable through a simple mathematical formula.

Modern investment management rests on these two foundations, and the "stuff" of almost all current investment practice is a consequence of these two intellectual breakthroughs and the further work done by other academics and some practitioners. They include the basic measurement of professional investment, expressed in industry jargon: relative benchmark performance, the generation of alpha, the factor exposures to get investor portfolios on the aforementioned efficient frontier, etc. These terms will be defined in later chapters, but you should know that your money is being managed with these lofty goals in mind. And for those of you who have gone down the rabbit hole of so-called passive investing through index funds and exchange-traded funds (ETFs), you should know that although passive investing and MPT might seem at first glance to be polar opposites, they are very much outgrowths from the same rootstock, and they overlap historically and intellectually. There are, to be fair, numerous professional investors who share my doubts about the usefulness of MPT and therefore manage client assets in a way to distinguish themselves from the norm. Those efforts, as I'll argue here, are to be encouraged. But in many of those cases, their approaches serve to highlight how far and wide MPT remains the standard approach. That is, the exceptions can be seen as proving the rule.

As far as paradigms go, MPT is not particularly old; it arose in response to developments almost a century ago and emerged about 50 years ago as a more or less coherent system. To appreciate its strengths and identify its weaknesses, we need to understand the investing climate of those prior periods. My goal is to place MPT in historical context, to show how some very clever and necessary ideas coming from academia (1950s–1960s) became a practical and functioning doctrine (1970s–1980s) and then degenerated into a heavy dogma (1990s–2000s) that is now a material hindrance to making successful business decisions through the stock market. To assert that MPT has become a failed orthodoxy is hardly a radical claim. All things that rise eventually fall, and history books are filled with examples of high-belief systems and more mundane operational frameworks that came and went. For instance, some of the smartest people in medieval Europe fervently believed that the sun revolved around the Earth. When their own observations suggested otherwise, these leading intellects of the day either ignored those observations or tried by various twists and turns to make them fit their existing worldview. Generation after generation was taught that geocentrism was true beyond any doubt. While my challenge to MPT does not rise to that of Copernicus, Galileo, Brahe, and Bruno, rejecting a dominant paradigm can be hard to do when you are in the very midst of it. And to most investment professionals, MPT still seems "right." But after 50 years of this particular way of seeing things, it's time for a refresh, or at the very least a major review of where this framework came from and whether it still works.

Challenging MPT as a practitioner is not convenient. The narrative supporting it is broad and deep. The entire investment industry is set up around it, and it would be much easier for a mid-career portfolio manager such as myself just to accept its tenets and to operate within its confines. To paraphrase a quip from acclaimed economist Paul Samuelson, it is difficult to persuade people to go against something they are paid to support. But the truth is the truth: after half a century and despite constant tweaking, MPT is not helping investors achieve their financial goals; investor returns are mediocre at best, retirement accounts are far from where they need to be, and most pension funds are not even remotely able to meet their future obligations. Not surprisingly, few people hold the investment industry in high regard, and most people actively dislike Wall Street.

In *The Strategic Dividend Investor* (2011), I identified a prolonged decline in interest rates as contributing to the retreat from stock market investments focused on generating cash streams, that is, dividend payments, and turning the stock market into a grand betting parlor. In *The Dividend Imperative* (2013), I focused on the harm done by share repurchase programs. In this volume, however, I am suggesting that although falling interest rates and share buybacks are manifestations of a problem, they would not have done the damage that they did without the underlying paradigm of MPT, which gave a green light to speculating in prices rather than investing in businesses. That intellectual narrative— the time-honored set of comforting MPT rules by which we invest—is itself the problem. Nearly a decade into a market rally, and with a large portion of the population of an age where the condition of their retirement accounts really matters, it is a good time to double-check the story that we have been taught.

What's at stake is not just the health of your 401(k) or the publication records of academics. For better or worse, investment in publicly traded equities—the stock market—is closely associated in the popular imagination with capitalism, and with the mostly free market–based system of exchange and investment that is a distinctive characteristic of our society. Stock market volatility and poor returns run the risk of creating discontent that could spill over into the "big" issues about how our society is structured. That would be unfortunate. As a historian, I would argue that our market-based system for the raising and deployment of capital has worked remarkably well over the past two centuries. It would be a shame to let a flawed subset of that system—the current theory of stock market investment—tarnish the overall enterprise or imperil its future.

As it has aged, MPT has garnered its share of critics, and their work will be duly acknowledged here. It is not my goal, however, to publish yet another litany of complaints—most industry participants are already familiar with the basic criticisms. Fortunately, one of the fundamental aspects of our market-based economy is that it is open to evolution and alteration as circumstances warrant. When there is a will, there is a way. So in the final part of this book, I propose a different approach to portfolio theory, particularly in regard to investment in stocks. The answer—or at least the starting point for an ultimate replacement for MPT—turns out to be hiding in plain sight of businesspeople everywhere but stubbornly invisible to the academics. And that is to construct, manage, and measure investment portfolios as one might an actual business, with a focus on the distributable cashflows to the owners of the businesses. It is a shockingly simple solution: judge investments first and foremost by how much money—real cash money—they generate.

Some might wonder whether I am just talking my own investment "book of business" as a portfolio manager. *This is precisely the case.* The alternative portfolio approach outlined here substantially mirrors how the team I work with manages the assets of our clients, taking seriously the business ownership that is equity investing, and focusing on the cashflows received by company owners. At the same time, we try to step back from the daily share price changes and the existing system built on trying to guess what those share prices might be six months or a year out. Our cash-based proposition has garnered substantial support from individual investors and their financial advisors—the ones closest to actual businesses. But we have made less progress with institutional consultants, big pension funds, and endowments whose guardians remain in the thrall of MPT. These gatekeepers risk losing their jobs by not playing by the existing rules. This book is especially for them, and for all of those affected by their decisions, that is, the rest of us.

One might assume that those individuals who are currently benefiting from the current system would not be interested in a new one. Perhaps. And those practitioners in their fifties and sixties can do a quick calculation in their head and conclude that it may be wiser to profit from the last decade of a decaying system rather than to start anew. It's hard to argue with that view, but I would point out that the forward-thinking among those in the investment industry should welcome a discussion of ways to improve overall strategy. Or to put it in simpler hockey terms, courtesy of Wayne Gretzky, "A good hockey player plays where the puck is. A great hockey player plays where the puck is going to be." The investment puck may still be in the MPT "blue zone," but everyone who works in the system, not to mention all investors, have an interest in knowing where it's going. The "getting-back-to-business" approach advocated here is one possibility; there will be others. But the more important point cannot be denied: the current system needs a thorough overhaul.

As a practitioner, I don't much care for the reigning standards of the investment industry, and I am driven to come up with a better alternative. My background as a historian informs my method—looking to the past to understand how this situation developed and then to come up with a different approach. This sequence of thought corresponds to the layout of this book. Chapter 1 describes stock market investing prior to the Crash of 1929. It highlights both the chaotic, catch-as-catch-can practices that characterized investment up to that point and the genuine need for a more coherent approach. To set the context for the reader, the text will go back and forth comparing current practices and what went on prior to 1929. It presents two snapshots, one of yesteryear and one of today. A more traditional historical narrative begins in Chapter 2, which focuses on the key academics and practitioners who went to work after 1929 seeking to figure out what had happened and how it could be prevented in the future. They set the stage for all that was to follow.

Chapter 3 continues the linear story as it explores the work of Harry Markowitz and the other postwar figures who developed MPT as we know it today. It also explains MPT's achievement of "accepted wisdom" status among the investment establishment. By the time MPT began hitting investor accounts, it had been forged into a comprehensive narrative, a way of talking about investments, with its own terminology and manner of expression. That undoubtedly contributed to its appeal. Parts of this story—the key articles published by the leading academics—are already well known to many market participants. What is different is the provisioning of context: not what the developments within MPT were, but why they would come to be seen as the nearly inevitable and exclusive solution to a pressing problem. Professionals need to know where their profession came from. We are all taught the MPT formulas that are supposed to deliver "certain" outcomes, but few understand why and how those rules came about and why that context matters. As I will argue, and the state of your retirement account likely demonstrates, it matters a lot.

Chapter 4 is set in the present time and argues that MPT no longer works. In practice, MPT fails to achieve its own stated goal of maximizing return for a given amount of risk, and it has led to too many other unintended consequences that have cost investors. The proof of the pudding is in the eating, and MPT, as we'll see, looks great as a recipe, but it just doesn't work out well when put in practice in the real-world kitchens of most investors. There have been meaningful efforts at improvement over the years, and those advances are highlighted, but on balance, the paradigm is found wanting.

Chapter 5 outlines an alternative approach to constructing and managing investment portfolios. The proposal I offer is not meant to be comprehensive. Rather it is meant to start a discussion—to reframe the narrative—about how we describe and analyze investment in publicly traded assets. Readers content with the current system will find plenty to nitpick in this final chapter, no doubt. They are welcome to make their own suggestions, but I hope they will agree with me that the investment framework cannot be left as it is. We can, like the "Earth-does-not-move" crowd, continue to cling to our comforting illusions despite all evidence to the contrary. But we do so at the expense of our clients, and ultimately at the expense of our entire enterprise. We must have the courage to admit change is needed and the conviction to act.

This book has been written with investment professionals and engaged individual investors in mind. The former would generally like to see any duel fought with extended equations and definitive mathematical proofs. The latter generally just want to know which side wins and what they should do about it. This account leans toward the latter, with a bare minimum of equations. That is part of the argument. Too many market participants, and most of the market's guardians, have gotten lost somewhere around the third decimal point, their t-statistics, and the correlation coefficients. They have lost sight of the big picture, rendered mostly in words. This work focuses on that underlying idea of a sensible, businesslike approach to financial investments. What-should-I-do-today investors will look in vain, however, for specific stock recommendations. They need to consult their financial advisors. It is my hope that when they do, they will have been empowered to ask why their portfolio is not run in a businesslike manner and what changes can be made to get it there.

GETTING

BACK TO
BUSINESS

1

What Chaos Looks Like

*October. This is one of the peculiarly dangerous
months to speculate in stocks. The others are July,
January, September, April, November, May, March,
June, December, August and February.*
>   —Mark Twain, *Pudd'nhead Wilson*, 1894

Groucho Asks a Question

In 1929, Groucho Marx was riding high. He and his brothers Harpo, Chico, and Zeppo had made the transition from
vaudeville to Broadway to Hollywood. They had just completed their first talking picture, *The Cocoanuts*, based on
their Broadway musical comedy from 1925. And they were
starring on Broadway in a new musical comedy, *Animal
Crackers*. (It would be filmed the following year.) Groucho
was raking in the cash, $2,000 each week, a fabulous sum in
those days. Marx had come from the modest financial means
of recent immigrants, and he took a particular interest in his
new wealth. He watched the pennies, turned off the lights,
and worried about the future. But Groucho was not without
contradictions. He also loved to speculate in stocks, seeking

and acting on hot tips. The year 1929 was just right for him. Like most of his acquaintances who had also been sucked into the market, Groucho quickly went beyond his original capital and began investing on margin, putting just 10% down. During the late 1920s, stocks were going one way—up—and you could shell out just $1,000 to buy $10,000 in stock. If your $50 stock rose to $55, and surely it would, you had doubled your original investment. How could you lose?

At the time, Groucho and his family were living in Great Neck, a Long Island suburb that offered him and his showbiz neighbors an easy commute to their jobs in New York City. In this congenial setting, Groucho found himself frequently doing what lots of other men were doing at that time, hanging out at the local brokerage office. In Groucho's case, it was the Great Neck branch of the Wall Street brokerage firm of Newman Brothers & Worms. One day, the branch manager, a certain Mr. Green, was pointing out to him that RCA—one of the most popular stocks of the time—was up yet again, to $535 per share. Groucho replied, "There's just one thing I don't understand, Mr. Green. I own RCA, too. But how can it be selling for five hundred and thirty-five a share and never declare a dividend? If a company's sound and making money, it should declare a dividend once in a while. Doesn't that seem strange to you?" The branch manager assured his client that it was a new world out there and that stocks would continue to rise, even if they did not pay dividends. But Groucho insisted: "Well, I think I know what you're talking about, but I still don't understand why RCA doesn't declare any dividends."[1] A short time later—in Twain's ill-fated month of October—RCA wasn't selling at $535 anymore, and Groucho, who had bought RCA and other stocks on margin, found himself ruined, without savings and deep in debt. Fortunately for

Groucho, he still had his "day" job and several decades of a productive and profitable career ahead of him.

Groucho's moment of lucidity occurred against the backdrop of a crazed investment world, one seemingly with no rules. Given this environment, the fact that Modern Portfolio Theory (MPT) became the dominant investment paradigm in the postwar period, and its continued use since, is striking, but perhaps not surprising. One academic has characterized 1952, the date of the origin of MPT, as the Big Bang of finance.[2] Before that, there was utter darkness. How does one explain the sudden appearance and remarkable spread of MPT? In this chapter, I argue that the substance of MPT and the investment practices it entailed filled what was essentially an intellectual vacuum, a void so wide and deep that any comprehensive, internally coherent system to direct investments had a good chance of enjoying widespread acceptance. MPT did not succeed because it was the *best* investment strategy; it succeeded because it was the *first* systematic investment strategy to emerge from the carnage of the 1929 Crash and the Great Depression that followed.

To appreciate this act of intellectual creation, you need to turn back the clock, forget everything you know about the stock market, and imagine what investment was like prior to the current system. Forget the idea that risk and reward can be quantified; forget the notion of a market that can be measured easily. Forget investment policy statements, the style box, benchmarks, relative performance, and portfolio rebalancing. Forget Seeking Alpha, CNBC, and Jim Cramer. Scratch it all. Once you do, I think you will agree that when MPT began to make its way from the classroom to the markets, it was highly probable that it would be welcomed as a way to demystify something that appeared to have no rhyme or reason.

The Market Then and Now

Our story, then, begins in the period prior to the Crash of 1929, before the investment community and vaudeville stars began to ask the questions that set the stage for the emergence of Modern Portfolio Theory. Books about the stock market during the Roaring Twenties or even earlier are available at your local library. Few investors read them, but if they did, they would encounter a strange world, one quite remote from the current investment landscape. The differences between "then" and "now" are so striking that one might well wonder if there is any continuity at all. Baseball fans will often say that the nineteenth-century version of the game was so different from modern baseball that the two are essentially different sports. The same might be said about investing in stocks. Let's review some of those differences, starting with the basic characteristics of the market at the time, and then move on to the key issue of how stocks and portfolios were understood and managed.

Individuals, Not Institutions

The "who" of the marketplace offers one of the most striking contrasts. The large institutional investors (pension funds, mutual fund companies, endowments, index and ETF managers), black-box-driven quantitative investors, and complex hedge-fund investors—the entities that currently dominate the stock market in terms of holdings, transactions, and news flow—were all absent in Groucho Marx's time. In contrast, the stock market of old was led not by those faceless "LLCs" and "LPs," but by individual investors—the well-known captains of industry and other wealthy individuals, as well as small-scale speculators. These were the swashbuckling adventurers like Jesse Livermore, a boom-to-bust-to-boom-to-suicide "investor" brought to life in Edwin Lefèvre's *Reminiscences of a Stock Operator*, first published in 1923. As voiced by Lefèvre, Livermore viewed "life itself from the cradle to the grave [as] a gamble."[3] His view of the investment community was even starker. According to his biographer, Livermore "considered Wall Street to be 'a giant whorehouse,' where [brokers] were 'madams,' the customers' men, 'pimps,' and stocks 'whores' the customers threw their money away on."[4] As unseemly as this account might appear today, Livermore's enterprise attracted like-minded risk takers. Edward Johnson II, the founder of Fidelity, became interested in investment after reading about Livermore. He recalled, "I'll never forget the thrill. Here was a picture of a world in which it was every man for himself. No favors asked or given."[5] In Johnson's mind, Livermore was like the sixteenth-century English adventurer (some would say "pirate") Sir Francis Drake watching from his ship's deck "during a cannonade. Glorious."[6]

Of course, most people, then as now, have no desire to invest as a pirate, as colorful as that might sound. And prior to the 1920s, the vast majority of individuals who had funds to invest stayed as far away from the stock market as possible, preferring assets like real estate or bonds that were perceived to be much safer. The latter were "investments," while stocks had the reputation as being purely "speculative." This is not to say, of course, that the rate of participation in the stock market did not increase in this period. It did, and rapidly so during the Roaring Twenties. Calculating the precise level of participation is difficult due to lack of reliable and well-defined statistics. Nonetheless, it's probably safe to say that as of 1917, no more than half a million Americans (0.5% of the total population and 2.5% of the total households) owned *any type* of security.[7] In the 1920s, ownership grew sharply as commerce expanded briskly and the United States supplanted the European powers as the world's leading economy in the aftermath of World War I. By 1922, some 4 million persons are estimated to have owned shares or bonds in American corporations. United States Steel was held by 150,000 distinct shareholders; the Pennsylvania Railroad had a similarly broad ownership.[8] By 1929, after a nearly decade-long, nationwide stock market party, the number of investors was much greater, perhaps 8 million, representing over a quarter of all households. According to the historian Julia Ott, Main Street could no longer resist the temptations of Wall Street.[9]

This isn't to say, naturally, that there were no institutions designed to gather money from numerous individuals to invest collectively. To be sure, there were pooled investment structures—predecessors to today's mutual funds and hedge funds—but prior to the 1920s, they were few and far between beyond the insurance companies and banks that invested their premiums and deposits collectively in bonds. The origins of investment-oriented pooling of assets can be traced as far back as eighteenth- and early-nineteenth-century Europe.[10] It was there that financiers first figured out that you could attract a lot of smallish investors to the market by explaining to them the benefits of combining their money in a "fund." The idea limped along in Europe and finally made its way to the United States at the end of the nineteenth century, where it slowly grew in popularity. But by 1929, reflecting the new popular enthusiasm for stocks, there were over 700 funds available, many of them having been created in the previous few years just as the U.S. stock market took off. Most were originally structured as trusts run by brokerages or banks and with a set amount of capital. They looked more like what we would call today closed-end funds or unit investment trusts. By the late 1920s, many of them had also become the convenient dumping ground for securities that were otherwise unsalable. Also by that time, many of the largest funds, such as the Goldman Sachs Trading Corporation and the United Founders Corporation, had the look of pyramid schemes, owning stakes in other trusts and having increasingly elaborate cross-ownership structures. Nevertheless, they were still relatively small players on the broader stage.

Syndicates and Pools

Though institutional stock market participants, as we know them today, were rare before the 1929 Crash, individual "players" could and often would band together as a syndicate or pool, buying and selling their shares in unison to manipulate the price of a stock. These speculators knew that they could "beat the market" if they "made the market." So they got together in temporary alliances to exploit a momentary opportunity, as the following example from 1896 shows:

A street rumor has it that the Kaffir mining party under the leadership of Barney Bernato has formed a syndicate to speculate in American securities, and bought on Thursday over 30,000 shares of Louisville & Nashville, St. Paul, and other stocks to be sent to London by today's steamer. . . . It appears somewhat surprising that Europeans under existing political conditions in this country should have been so suddenly impressed with the desireableness of our securities as to form a kind of blind pool for their purchase.[11]

Oh, to be on today's steamer to London with thousands of shares of railroad stock in the safebox! And by the way, Jeeves, where is my top hat?

A few years later, a temporary market sell-off was attributed to the activities of these "cliques":

Sugar [the American Sugar Company] . . . has been almost entirely under the guidance of cliques as usual. Tuesday this

*stock sold as high as 129½, but when this high level was reached,
a pronounced tendency to sell long stock was noticeable, which
has caused many to believe that the pool that has been operating
in it has begun to liquidate.*[12]

The consequences of these manipulations were clear to many
market observers. During a rise in the market in October
1910, a newsletter writer observed:

*Speculative pools have been working persistently to advance their
specialties. . . . Fortunately, thus far the public does not seem
to have been drawn into the speculative operations to any great
extent. That element in Wall Street operations which is designated as "The Public," and which is usually painted by a preju-
diced observer as a lamb ready for the slaughter, is proverbially
short memoried, but it is to its credit that at this time it is giving
less attention to the specialties which the speculative cliques are
playing . . . than to the more standard issues, including the better
class of industrial preferred shares, which pay their dividends
through thick and thin, and which are, therefore, much safer than
the average common stock issues, even though lacking in the latter's most striking possibilities from a speculative point of view.*[13]

Though the market of a century ago looked a lot different
than it does now, perhaps certain elements of investor behavior remain the same?

The most famous syndicate story of them all is that of RCA.
Radio Corporation of America—or simply "Radio" as it was
then called—was perhaps the country's first tech stock. It had
a fancy, magical product that everyone seemed to want, and it
was run by a star CEO, David Sarnoff. Yet Michael Meehan,
a former theater ticket salesman turned stock trader, friend
of Sarnoff's, and the New York Stock Exchange (NYSE)

"expert" on RCA, felt the stock was selling too cheaply. So he decided to form a syndicate to pump—and soon after dump— the stock. This sort of thing was standard operating procedure on Wall Street at the time, so Meehan had no trouble rounding up investors for his stock-manipulating pool. Among them we find some famous moneymen of the day—Percy Rockefeller, Walter Chrysler, William Durant—and the *wives* of the very people who managed the syndicate—Mrs. Meehan, for example, took a million-dollar position. Not to be left out, Sarnoff apparently had his wife make a sizable investment.

Over one week in March 1928, Meehan's pool bought and sold 1.4 million shares of Radio, making it look very hot indeed. The manipulators were aided in their endeavor by a column in the *New York Daily News* praising RCA. Whether they planted the story or not is unknown. In any case, the stock jumped 50% in short order. At that point Meehan and all his confederates sold their positions and made out like bandits.[14] Perhaps "bandits" is too strong, for they had done nothing illegal. Rather, Meehan et al. had briefly brought order to an otherwise chaotic market and profited handsomely. They had a "system" and were, therefore, very much ahead of their time. (Groucho Marx's experience with Radio would come the following year.)

Brokerages and Exchanges

The average reader has at least some notion of the current brokerage community, in which financial advisors make investment recommendations to clients and traders behind the scenes bring together buyers and sellers. It is hard not to miss their ads on TV, the Internet, and what's left of the print media. Big brands now dominate. They include the so-called "wire houses" such as Merrill Lynch, UBS, Morgan Stanley, etc., as well as strong national networks like Raymond James and "discount" trading platforms such as Schwab and TD Ameritrade. They have offices with real-live people in them, but they also allow you to both track and manage your portfolio online. Most of them are publicly traded themselves or are part of larger, publicly traded financial services firms. A century ago, however, the brokerage landscape was entirely different. There were no big corporate players. Rather, there were numerous small brokerages—over 1,000 of them in 1900—that were essentially unregulated private partnerships. They were personal operations, serving family, friends, and the local business community. The larger brokerages might have multiple offices and even a sales staff, but they were the exceptions.

In the investment media of the age, the brokerages invariably advertised their conservatism, the specific type of trades they liked to conduct, and the inventory of stocks and bonds they had on hand. A mid-1910 issue of a popular investment newsletter included a half-page advertisement from A. H. Bickmore & Co. of 30 Pine Street, New York, which encouraged purchase (through it, of course) of the preferred and common stock of National Light, Heat and Power Company as "A STOCK THAT PAYS."[15] Another member of the NYSE, S. H. P. Pell & Co., advertised that it was a specialist in the securities of General Motors, U.S. Motor, DuPont Powder, and International Nickel, as well as a dealer in unlisted and inactive securities.[16] The flyer for Bodell & Company of Providence, Rhode Island, read:

To Purchasers of Textile Stocks

At the present time we own and offer a limited number of shares in one of the best mills in Rhode Island which has been in successful operation for a number of years. The Company has no bonds, notes or preferred stock so that the entire earnings above

*expenses belong to the common stock holders. The Company
earns 15% and at the present time pays 8% dividends (4% May
15th and 4% November 15%) on its capital stock. It is expected
that later larger dividends will be paid either in cash or stock.
The books of the Company are regularly audited by a representative firm of certified public accountants. Its looms have operated
20 hours a day for 5 years and orders are booked for months in
advance. A majority of the stock is owned by the board of directors of the company which includes some of Rhode Island's foremost manufacturers. To those interested in this class of security
we will be pleased to send further information.*[17]

All but a handful of the brokerage names from that time are
distant memories. Most did not survive the periodic downturns. And most of those that did make it to 1929 did not
survive the Crash. And if they somehow made it through the
resulting Great Depression, they did not survive wave after
wave of consolidation in the postwar period. Still, echoes of
the past resonate to the present day. A small advertisement
in 1910 for Kidder, Peabody & Co., 115 Devonshire Street,
Boston, and 56 Wall in New York, announced that the company offered Investment Securities, Foreign Exchange, and
Letters of Credit and served as agents and attorneys for Baring
Bros. in London.[18] Kidder only succumbed to consolidation in
1994 when it was purchased by PaineWebber from its corporate parent at the time, General Electric. (Baring lasted only
one year longer, failing in 1995 due to losses caused by a
rogue trader.)

Brokerages also played more of a social function a century ago than they do today. At that time, the only way to
find out how your stocks were doing before the share price
appeared in the morning paper was to go down to your local
broker's office and check the ticker tape yourself. It's true

that you can visit a stockbroker's office today, and you ought to go at least once a year or so to review your portfolio. But that annual and likely short visit is not a social occasion. In contrast, investors visited their brokers' offices frequently in the 1920s. And not only did they come, but they stayed because the offices were interesting places to spend time. Brokerages often had customer waiting rooms where one could see share prices posted on large boards, await the latest news, and spread rumors and opinions with other investors *cum* speculators. The higher-end brokerages offered plush leather chairs and other amenities. Lower-end ones might have just benches. According to the son of celebrity speculator Groucho Marx,

Every morning, after he [Groucho] had eaten breakfast and read the newspapers, he would get in his car and drive down to New-man Brothers & Worms, his Wall Street representatives who had a branch brokerage office on Great Neck's main street. There he would solemnly study the ticker tapes and watch the boy marking the latest quotation on the huge board. He would sit in the office by the hour, watching his stocks go up and up, and gloating over his good fortune. He was not alone. . . . He'd meet all his friends and neighbors and the local tradesman in the place, and they would exchange tips and discuss the latest financial trends, as if they really knew what they were talking about.[19]

Brokerage offices were a place to go, to spend time, to see, and to be seen. There were 10,000 ticker tape machines clattering away in the 1920s. Some of them were in corporate offices, newsrooms, radio stations, and prominent hotels. Most, however, were in small brokerages scattered all over the country. You could even visit a brokerage office on passenger ships crossing the Atlantic.

Prior to the government intervention starting in the 1930s, these entities were essentially completely unregulated. They came and went. The *Commercial & Financial Chronicle* nicely captured the demise of one in 1896:

An event this week which, according to the earliest reports, appeared to threaten wide consequences and very disturbing results was the announcement of the failure of the Moore Brothers of Chicago. The news was accompanied by the closing of the Chicago Stock Exchange, with the statement that the liabilities of the firm would reach $20,000,000 and that the affair would seriously involve many Eastern as well as Chicago banks. . . . It seems that the reason for the suspension was the inability to carry through engagements with reference to the stocks of two industrials, the Diamond Match and the New York Biscuit Company, which have been speculated in largely at the Chicago Exchange and prices put up to at least double their real value.[20]

There would be no bailout for Moore Brothers of Chicago, or for the thousands of other small brokerages that catered to individual investors in the late nineteenth and early twentieth century. They were hardly "too big to fail." Indeed, they were often too small to succeed, and so when they failed, only those directly affected would have noticed.

For the purchase of stock, brokerages would generally extend credit and allow their clients to buy on margin, putting up only a small percentage, sometimes just 10%, with the brokerage fronting the rest. In a rising market, it looked like a tempting proposition. As a result, by the late 1920s, it was fair to say that many Americans didn't "own" stocks; they "rented" them. But if the share prices went against the investor, he (or much more rarely, she) would quickly get a margin call. Unless he ponied up the extra cash, the shares would be sold, and the investor would be wiped out, as many found out to their chagrin late in 1929. Not surprisingly given the inherent riskiness of buying on margin, many market participants shared the belief that the market was manipulated—by the captains, by the pools, by the brokerages, by somebody.

Furthering the conviction that stock ownership was a game, there existed alongside the genuine stock brokerage industry a parallel universe of purely, explicitly speculative betting parlors on stocks. These were the "bucket shops." In these storefront enterprises, "investors" could wager on the price of a share without having to purchase or sell the underlying security. Instead, the punter would bet with the house on the future price of the security. One might think of bucket shops as the first derivatives markets. The legitimate brokerages disliked them, perhaps because their very existence suggested that investing and gambling were not that very different. The bucket shops of old, of course, no longer exist. But their spirit lives on. An elderly acquaintance of mine told me that until recently he and his buddies would gather at their local watering hole and place bets on the NYSE's advance-decline number released shortly after the market's close at 4 p.m. every day.

The situation with stock exchanges was similar to that of brokerages. Today, there are, broadly speaking, two exchanges for stocks in the United States: the New York Stock Exchange and the Nasdaq electronic exchange. A century ago, however, numerous physical exchanges dotted the landscape in every large and in many medium-sized cities in the United States. New York City led the way with the NYSE, but even within New York, there were other markets, such as the "curb" exchange for lesser companies that were not or could not be listed on the NYSE.[21] The curb traders moved indoors in 1921 and became known as the American Stock Exchange in

1953. Other exchanges were oriented toward specific industries. For instance, the Consolidated Stock Exchange in New
York focused originally on petroleum and mining stocks.
Outside of New York, the major exchanges would primarily
list local companies as well as a selection of national corporations. In particular, Philadelphia, Boston, and Chicago
had quite large trading floors. Other exchanges were regional
in nature: Cincinnati, San Francisco, Baltimore, Detroit,
Cleveland, Pittsburgh, etc. They are all gone, but many of the
buildings—usually grand late-nineteenth-century "bourses"
inspired by the lavish style of Belle Epoque France—remain
as food courts, offices, and retail space.

Indexes and Quantification

It is reasonably hard to find a financially literate person in the
United States who does not know what, in general terms, the
Dow Jones Industrial Average, the S&P 500 Index, and the
Nasdaq Composite are. They are, of course, the major U.S.
market indexes, and they have become a standard part of the
daily news diet, just like the weather and the sports scores.
We read about them in the papers, hear about them on the
radio during the hourly news update, get updates on them
from cable TV news, and monitor them through the Internet.
You can have them streamed to your smartphone by the minute. According to common (though completely erroneous)
wisdom, they tell you not only how the national economy is
doing, but also how you are doing financially.

A century ago, none of this was so. An investor could judge
the value (and therefore the health) of a company—approximately, of course—by its stock price and its dividend. There
was, however, no way to judge the value (and therefore the
health) of the stock market on a day-to-day basis because the
aforementioned indexes did not exist. When investors talked

about stock market performance in the late nineteenth century, they said it was "strong," or "weak," or "narrow," or "broad." On a good day, there was a noted "trend upward" or an "advance in values." In its July 1909 issue, *Moody's Magazine* observed that "in the closing days of June a substantial revival took place in the activity of stocks, but no real advance is yet in evidence."[22] That's nice, but what does it mean? In contrast, in the summer of 1910, a different market newsletter led off with a discussion of the "severe slump in the stock market . . . [and] the heavy liquidation of securities at steadily declining prices" due to weakness in railroad issues following a tariff reduction ordered by the Interstate Commerce Commission.[23] As with the advance, so with the decline; no generalized quantification was offered or even really possible. A few years later, John Moody (of the eponymous journal) was again commenting on the market's movements in the most simplistic term. About a market rally that sputtered out, Moody wrote that "the upward movement in security prices, which was so widely advertised a month ago, has now rather abruptly ended, and while stocks do not go down much, neither do they go up."[24]

As the market for publicly traded equities grew, investors and commentators realized that they needed a way to measure the overall market's disposition in more specific terms. Enter the stock market index. At the end of the nineteenth century, an investment newsletter from the brokerage Clapp & Co. used a simple average of 12 active railroad stocks and a separate one of 20 other railroad stocks to provide weekly price averages.[25] Other brokerages had similar conventions, but there doesn't appear to have been an effort to sell that information or to analyze the market on the basis of it. The crude indexes appeared in the brokerage newsletters, and that was about it.

The indexes that really took off came not from the broker-ages but from publishers.[26] One of them, Charles Dow, intro-duced his simple price index (as opposed to a "total return" index, which includes dividend payments) of 12 industrial companies (the Dow Jones Industrial Average) in 1896 by taking their share prices, adding them together, and divid-ing by 12. The same year, he created a similar index of 20 railroad issues, which became the Dow Jones Transportation Average.[27] His indexes were—by our standards at least—thoroughly faulty. But they did provide a number, a quantita-tive way to answer the question, "How is the market doing?" Investors loved them. The industrials list was expanded to 20 stocks in December 1914 when the stock market reopened after a three-month closure resulting from the outbreak of World War I. It was expanded to its current level of 30 stocks a decade later in 1928. The Standard Statistics Bureau created its own index in 1923 using the market prices of 233 U.S. companies, a very large endeavor at the time. The index was computed weekly, and notably it was the first major index to be weighted by market capitalization—larger companies had a bigger weight in what had previously been exclusively equal-weighted efforts. Three years later, Standard Statistics introduced a slimmer version, with just 90 companies, but one that was computed daily to meet the need for immediate information that became apparent as the 1920s wore on and share prices marched upward.

Today we discuss the Dow and the S&P Indexes, but we could just as easily be discussing others. The Gibson Averages, provided by Thomas Gibson's Advisory Services—a competi-tor to Dow—were calculated daily and were based on NYSE prices for 23 railroads and 18 industrials. They could be encountered in the investment media from the 1900s through the 1930s.[28] Market watcher and economic forecaster Roger

Babson regularly published several indexes in the early decades of the twentieth century, a composite of 40 stocks: 20 railroads and 20 industrials.[29] At around the same time, the *New York Times* was using its own generic average of 25 "typical" railroad issues and a similar simple average of 25 industrials to describe the activity of the market.[30] Although crude and imprecise, these measurement tools offered investors and commentators some quantitative means of assessing the markets and their holdings.

In this early period of quantifying the market, you could do more or less whatever you wanted. Just hang your shingle out and offer your numerical wares. Almost nothing of that period remains, with the exception of the Dow and Standard & Poor's. (Moody's survives as a bond rating company.) In 1938, the Cowles Commission at the University of Chicago made available average monthly returns for NYSE stocks from 1871 onward. Given the technology of the day, that was no small feat, and it permitted the burgeoning professional and academic community to start poring over those data sets. But the major indexes that we know today (other than the Dow and the S&P 500) were the products of the 1970s through the 1990s, boom years for quantification of all types: the Nasdaq Composite in 1971, the Wilshire indexes starting in 1974, the Russell measures beginning in 1984, and so forth. The appearance of these indexes and broader databases of share and company information is an important part of our story because they essentially laid the groundwork for the emergence of an investing "system." MPT involves quantification of human behavior. It's very hard to do that without some form of overarching data out of which the quantitative formulas can be created and then backtested. That itself is noteworthy. That a database of prices leads to a theory of investment based on—you guessed it—prices should not come as a surprise. But more on that later.

It goes without saying that in the absence of specific indexes, and in the absence of a framework for analyzing stocks, there were no formally characterized "growth" stocks, no "value" stock indexes, no "mid-cap" benchmarks, no "large-cap" equities. No one had created these formal classifications. Indeed, the 10 (now 11) formal Global Industry Classification Standard (GICS) sectors (tech, discretionary, staples, etc.) that investors casually discuss today were only introduced in 1999. Prior to that time, most casual market participants spoke in terms of the four overall groupings within the stock market: industrials, transports, utilities, and financials. [31] Those in turn date just from 1976. For the 20 years from the S&P 500 Index's creation in 1957 to that time, the main groupings had been just three: industrials, utilities, and rails. The precursor to the S&P 500 Index, the 90-stock version computed daily from 1926, had the same three basic groups and consisted of 50 industrials, 20 railroads, and 20 utilities. A century ago, the NYSE market was broadly divided into just two categories: railroads and industrials, with the latter being a catchall for just about any manufacturer or service company that wasn't a railroad. At that time, banks and insurance companies traded on the curb exchange, not the NYSE. They would later come "inside" and eventually join the main indexes in the 1970s.[32]

Prior to the creation of these labeling conventions, there were just stocks, clumped together in the few natural aggregations that appeared obvious to market participants. Labels did exist, however, but they were much more subjective. In the mid-nineteenth century, for instance, "fancy" stocks were those that had little if any business behind them and were well situated for manipulation by traders and brokers. In effect, there was little chance of a real business being hurt. During the canal-building period in the decades before the Civil War, one such stock, Morris Canal, was "cornered." According to a mid-century account,

Most of the operators in the Board and on the street believed it to be ruling above its value, and sold it short. On this a shrewd clique bought up all the loose stock, and locked it in a trunk. The shorts discovered as their contracts matured, that there was no Stock to be had, except of the cornering clique, and they demanded an exorbitant price. . . . The bears accused the corners of conspiracy, and denounced the corner as a piece of roguery. The bulls retorted by inquiring why their antagonists had sold that which they did not possess and apparently could not produce.[33]

Today "fancy" stocks might be called shell companies and are generally to be found in small and micro-cap territory and well away from the regulated exchanges. Even in this earlier era, stocks without dividends or without some sort of business behind them were not for the faint of heart. People knew that they were very risky. Stocks with strong dividend records and wider ownership were viewed differently, even if there were fewer terms than today to describe them. By the 1920s, one does see stocks being considered as "growth," befitting the age, and placed in juxtaposition to plain "income" stocks, but that was about as far as categorizations went.

Disclosure

Pointing out that there wasn't too much useful information about the stock market in the nineteenth and early twentieth centuries may well be starting at the wrong end of the horse. There was almost nothing. Prior to the 1890s, investors saw share prices and the occasional dividend declaration, and that was about it. For all the capital that the railroads raised in the nineteenth century, investors got precious little information about where that money went. There was no central regulatory authority, no accepted standards of disclosure. Corporations might, or might not, release a summary of results. In 1825, the New York Stock Exchange requested one of its most recent issuers, the New York Gas Light Company, to shed some light (pardon the pun) on its operations "so the public might be informed through us of the existing state of things in relation to the company."[34] The request apparently went unanswered. Forty years later, little had changed. Imagine if a company today responded as the Delaware, Lackawanna, & Western Rail Road Company famously did in 1866 to a request for information from the NYSE, the railroad replying that management will make "no reports and publish no statements and have done nothing of the sort for the last five years."[35] Companies could go many years without issuing an annual report of their operations. One reason they might have been able to get away with extended silence was that demand for U.S. securities from abroad, specifically England, remained robust through much of the nineteenth century. English investors understood America to be the veritable land of opportunity and were less inclined to ask lots of questions.

Before the 1930s, the only mandated source of financial reporting for companies appears to have been the listing agreement with an exchange. The NYSE expected—though it is not certain that it actually received—periodic reporting for all new companies trading on that exchange after 1916. As of 1920, companies wishing to be listed on the NYSE were required to "publish at least once in each year . . . a statement of its physical and financial condition, an income account covering the previous fiscal year, and a balance sheet showing assets and liabilities at the end of the year."[36] As of 1926, one-third of NYSE companies reported annually and another third either semiannually or quarterly. The remaining third had no specified reporting frequency.[37]

Even when companies did provide a glimpse at operations, there was no single standard of reporting. It would take decades after the mandating of periodic reporting before generally accepted accounting principles (GAAP) were put in place. Given the options that exist for treating depreciation (a really big issue for capital-intensive railroads involved in the nineteenth-century build-out), inventory accounting such as LIFO versus FIFO (an equally important matter for the manufacturing and distributing businesses coming into being at the same time), and revenue recognition (another key question for the service companies that appeared in the mid-twentieth century), early reporting was a hodgepodge of information, much of which might not be comparable to the reports of other companies. The sense that analysis of companies was a pointless exercise was exacerbated by the rapid consolidation of many industries late in the nineteenth century into monopolistic trusts. Despite the Sherman Anti-Trust Act of 1890, many industries remained highly "organized" into the twentieth century. It was indeed fertile ground to think that the game was rigged.

By the early twentieth century, however, the flow of information to investors began to improve materially. The creation of the Interstate Commerce Commission in 1887 and a specific reform introduced by it in 1906 required railroads—the dominant stocks of the day—to report operating statistics on a regular basis. These were then made available to investors. The situation was much the same for banks, which made regular reports of deposits, loans, credits, and specie (precious metals). It wasn't much, but it was something. Among the publicly listed industrials, however, information was scarcer. As an exception, United States Steel provided monthly amounts of unfilled orders and quarterly reports of earnings, but apparently it did so voluntarily because it had become one of the most visible and widely held stocks in the country.[38] For prospective investors in the other up-and-coming industrials, the information landscape was barren. Market watcher Thomas Gibson noted with dismay in 1919 that

the owner or prospective buyer of industrial securities faces one serious impediment which conservative men would never countenance nor endure in any line of business except the stock market. This impediment arises from the impossibility of keeping track of the progress of an industrial corporation's business and profits. Practically all large corporations . . . decline to issue full and frequent reports as to their condition and earnings. . . . [The investor] is a partner in a business about which he can secure nothing but infrequent and insufficient after-event knowledge.[39]

Having the books audited by third-party accountants was also a rarity. United States Steel again led the way in 1903 when it had Price Waterhouse & Company bless its results for the previous year.[40] The practice began to catch on in subsequent decades as the imposition of corporate taxation led to greater standardization of reporting and disclosure.

The stock market Crash of 1929 changed everything. In response to it, the federal government created regulatory authorities that began to impose some order on the "open town" that the stock market had become in the 1920s. The 1933 Securities Act (in regard to issuers) and the 1934 Securities Exchange Act (on the exchanges and creating the

SEC) established much of the framework for disclosure and reporting that is now in place. As a result, the amount of quality information coming from companies to current and prospective investors rose significantly. The Investment Company Act of 1940 covered the pooled vehicles (what we now know as mutual funds) and the companies that manage and distribute them. There was also an additional Investment Advisers Act of 1940 to regulate the activities of individual financial advisors. But even after the new system was implemented in the decade following the 1929 Crash, full and uniform reporting was still the exception rather than the rule. A review of reporting conducted in 1935 determined that "even . . . those companies whose issues are listed on the New York Stock Exchange do not disclose enough information to render their balance sheets and income statements intelligible to the average, well-informed investor."[41] Part of this might have been the absence, after the shell shock of the Crash, of a sufficient pool of readers of those statements, but the fact remains that there still wasn't a lot of information available for investors to consider. Indeed, it wasn't until 1970 that quarterly reporting appeared, and statements of cashflows became standard only in the 1980s. That is, for decades after 1929, there was still a good deal more darkness than light in financial reporting.

Investment Information (or Lack Thereof)

Though it is perhaps a curse in disguise, today's investors are blessed with a vast amount of commentary on the stock market. Should you choose to, you can explore an almost unlimited amount of "analysis" of your favorite stock and read at least some third-party views on the most obscure publicly traded companies. The security analysts employed by the brokerages fill the e-mail inboxes of institutional and individual investors with a daily torrent of commentary and suggestions on what to do *today*. Turn on the television or go on the Internet, and you can have round-the-clock exposure to the doings of the market and its participants. Numerous "old" publications such as *Barron's*, *Forbes*, and *Fortune* are still well distributed and well read. The *Wall Street Journal* and the *Financial Times* fill out the media landscape. Your local bookstore (if you still have one) is filled with "how-to" treatments of investments that include at least a modicum of analysis. And if you are academically inclined, there are dozens of finance journals to help you pass the time. The investment industry is now composed of a veritable army of heavily armed soldiers wielding MBA degrees and Chartered Financial Analyst (CFA®) certificates. Prior to the Crash, however, none of this infrastructure of analysis existed. The amount of analytical information about stocks, not to mention intelligent commentary, was minimal.

Newsletters

Most of the information and analysis that did exist came from a publishing perspective, with a heavy emphasis on journalism and data gathering rather than analysis. The early newsletters did little more than list the prices for leading issues—Clapp & Co. provided quotes for 65–70 stocks each week in the 1890s—and give a subjective account of the news of the market. There was no analysis, quantitative or otherwise. In regard to industrials, a Clapp missive of July 28, 1893, noted:

Gas and Electric monopolized the bears' attention, much to the disadvantage of stockholders. Selling now is more dangerous. Sugar rallied better than some on the breaks, but had to give

*way. Lead was simply heavy. Cotton Oil dull and slumpy, with
no investment demand. Tobacco, Rubber, and a lot of other
fancies, appear to be forgotten in the desire to sell stocks that
enjoy some kind of a market.*[42]

"Lead was simply heavy" is about as poetic as Wall Street
gets, and it is not very useful.

By the early twentieth century, investment-oriented newsletters and magazines had become far more substantial and
analytical. Titled *United States Investor*, the *Financial World*,
McNeel's Financial Service, *Moody's Magazine*, among many
others, as well as the market "letters" of numerous brokerages
(such as the aforementioned Clapp & Co.), these publications
would discuss the overall tenor of the markets and individual
companies, make recommendations, and respond to specific queries. In advertising its services in 1913, the *United
States Investor* made clear the challenges for individuals who
wanted to investigate investments. The newsletter had been
established in 1891, and its stated aim was threefold:

1. *To take its readers behind the returns. Most financial
   magazines are content to hurl a mass of statistics at their
   subscribers, and leave the subscribers to interpret these
   statistics. We aim to tell what these statistics mean . . .*
2. *To warn them away from poor investments. Our columns
   were the first to point out the weak features of the great crop
   of new industrial preferred stocks put out in recent months.*
3. *Through our Inquiry Department to answer every question
   that arises in any subscriber's mind about any security he is
   thinking of buying.*

A three-month subscription was just $1.25. Its peer, the
Financial World, had been founded in 1902 and claimed

70,000 subscribers at $4 per year as of 1913.[43] Thomas
Gibson headed one of the larger financial publishing ventures of the time. In the early 1900s, his *Thomas Gibson's
Market Letters* were delivered daily every afternoon, with
weekly letters covering general matters and with special letters as warranted. Subscription to the service also entitled
investors to the "privilege of a reasonable number of inquiries
by mail or telegraph." Subscribers were to rest "assured that
every question affecting future values and prices of securities will be thoroughly covered." Thomas Gibson advertised
that his Advisory Service was "based upon a careful study
of precedent and basic and technical conditions affecting the
market as a whole and an examination of the relative merits
and prospects of individual securities."[44]

The newsletters were generally optimistic about stock
investment. How could they not be? In the introduction to a
collection of its weekly letters from 1893, Clapp & Co. wrote:

*Corporation laws are defective but are gradually improving.
Rights of the public to definite knowledge are not fully recognized, but there is growing demand for details. Protection against
fraud, through illegal purchases by collusive boards of directors, over-capitalization, and forestalling profits by bond and
mortgage is not yet what it should be; on the whole, things are
improving. Sooner or later the laws will be amended or changed
so as to bring about more favorable conditions for the investor.[45]*

For subscribers to these services, the rewards to be had by
following their advice were supposedly substantial. In 1922,
Roger Babson offered his newsletter subscribers an average
of 40% return "since the beginning of the present period
of accumulation" with average investment periods of 10
months. "If you would like a similar return on your money

without the risk, worry or loss of time involved in ordinary speculation, tear out the Memo—now—and hand it to your secretary when you dictate the morning's mail."[46] In his advertisements, Babson claimed that "the accumulation and use of [Babson] statistics should in all cases be an insurance against any financial loss, and should in many cases be the means of the subscriber accumulating great wealth."[47]

The newsletter industry continued to flourish into the 1920s and up to the Crash. By 1927, the *Financial World* was weekly, had 32 pages per issue, cost $10 per year, and declared that it was "dedicated to legitimate and conservative investment." The January 1927 issue ran articles on automobile manufacturing and freight railroad rates, a feature on Bloomingdale Brothers—only recently listed on the NYSE— and write-ups of Chrysler and the sugar company Central Aguirre.[48] With around 100 pages per issue in the 1920s, the *Magazine of Wall Street* (1907–1936) was quite substantial. Its issues in the 1920s read much like a current *Fortune* or *Forbes*, without the top 10 lists. *Fortune* itself was founded by Henry Luce in 1930 in response to the Crash; *Forbes* had been started in 1917 by two partners, one from the Hearst organization and the other from the *Magazine of Wall Street.*

For retail investors, it's not clear how helpful the newsletters or the magazine recommendations were. The 1930s' market observer Alfred Cowles explained why these services were still in demand even though the advice wasn't very good: "They [subscribers] want to believe that somebody really knows. A world in which nobody really knows can be frightening."[49] The same basic logic applies to the appeal of MPT. The math is comforting to those who want to believe that every human endeavor is well ordered and can be mastered. Not surprisingly, almost all the newsletter writers were consistently bullish throughout the 1920s, with the exception of Roger Babson, who correctly forecast the stock market crash but was roundly pilloried for his views, until he was proved correct.

Investment Manuals

The profession of "securities analyst," as we know it today— divided into "sell side" and "buy side"—is a relatively recent development. Prior to the postwar period, individuals looking at stocks and subjecting them to what we would call today fundamental analysis were few and far between; they worked with very limited information and were dismissed on Wall Street as "statisticians" or "part-time librarians."[50] Those statisticians had gotten a start during the railroad boom after the Civil War. Businessman, attorney, and publisher Henry Varnum Poor and his son Henry William Poor gathered all the information they could about the nation's burgeoning railroads and published it in 1868 as Poor's *Manual of the Railroads of the United States.* That turned into an annual publication exercise about railroads and then other companies. This was not analysis, just the gathering of data in thick volumes. John Moody produced similar volumes starting early in the 1900s, as did Floyd Mundy, a member of the Chicago Stock Exchange who for many years issued his annual collection, *The Earning Power of Railroads.* By then, publishers were offering compendia not just on railroads, but also on the other basic groupings of companies with publicly traded debt and equity, the industrials, and the utilities.[51]

Some of the original Poor and Moody volumes may still be available at your local library, likely in the remote storage facility. Covered in dust and with cracked spines, they are worth a review for a glimpse into the economy of the time. The 1913 edition of *Poor's Manual of Industrials* (Volume 4) came in at a hefty 2,268 pages and included essentially whatever information it had gathered for thousands of different companies, sometimes only names (of directors) and addresses and a brief description of the company's business and its outstanding securities. In other instances, it offered a very simplified list of assets and liabilities reported by the company, a list of interest payments to debt, and/or a record of dividend payments to preferred equity and common equity. Early in the volume, one learns that the Alaska Packers Association, a salmon fishing and packing operator in Alaska and Canada, owned 15 canneries and 86 vessels and packed 1.2 million cases of salmon in 1912. It had paid-in capital of $5.75 million in stock and had bonds outstanding of $978,000. Dividends paid the previous year amounted to $345,048. Amounts are all listed in aggregate. There are no per share figures. Total assets as of 1912 were $9.389 million. In recent years, the capital stock had been paying a 6% dividend, issued quarterly.

Among companies still existing today, we note the entry for the Pittsburgh Plate Glass Co., now known as PPG Industries, Inc., which had been incorporated in 1883. As of 1913, it owned 8 factories and had 22 warehouses and salesrooms around the country. The listing includes 8 years of sales, profits (not defined), preferred dividends, common dividends, depreciation (not defined), and the surplus for those 8 years. A simplified balance sheet for seven years lists "Investments," "Treasury Stock," "Glass & Paints," "Materials and Working Account," "Cash," "Bills and Accounts Receivable," and "Balance of Capital Subscriptions." The liabilities listed include "Capital Stock," "Bills and Accounts Payable," "Insurance Fund," "Sinking Fund," and "Surplus." The directors of the company are listed, as are the dates of payments of the various dividends. The preferred equity had a nominal yield of 12%, while common paid 6%.

The listing for Procter & Gamble Co. includes a brief history of the firm and a description of its capital stock: $12 million in common stock with a par value of $100 per share and $2.25 million in 8% preferreds. Both common and preferred are noted as being listed on the Cincinnati Stock Exchange. The recent dividend history is also included. Of the eight listed directors, three were Procters or Gambles. Of the officers, the president and vice president were a Procter and a Gamble, respectively, even though the original company had been founded 75 years earlier in 1837.[52] Procters continued to run the company until 1930, nearly a century after its founding.

However useful, these heavy volumes were cumbersome and could become easily outdated in a fast-paced business environment. Indeed, in 1919, the Moody's and Poor's manual business merged. Early in the twentieth century, Luther Lee Black went in a different direction with his publishing effort: the Standard Statistics Bureau. Rather than copy the annual tome approach, he published company information on smaller index cards that could be more readily updated. (The Babson "system" of statistics was also card-based.) In 1941, Standard Statistics and Poor's Publishing merged to form the company we know today as Standard & Poor's, or S&P.

Studies of the Market

Beyond the data-less newsletters and the data-packed but unanalytical hardbacks, investors were pretty much on their own, which is probably one reason the field was dominated by speculation and intrigue. Academic research on the markets was essentially nonexistent. Although Joseph Wharton founded a business school at the University of Pennsylvania in 1881, it was another two decades before other major educational institutions followed suit: the University of Chicago in 1898, the University of California–Berkeley in 1898, Dartmouth in 1900, and Harvard University in 1904. The academic "science" of finance didn't really exist at that time. Professor Solomon Huebner began teaching what he considered the first class on the capital markets at Wharton in 1904.[53] Irving Fisher's seminal *The Nature of Capital and Income* came out only in 1906. While it firmly established the basic understanding that all assets derive their value from the income that they generate, his analysis was general, not applied directly toward the stock market. The next big works in investing wouldn't appear until the 1930s. The academic journals focusing on finance, which were key to the elaboration and transmission of MPT, were founded after the 1929 Crash and in response to it and the Great Depression.

There is one exception, a colorful story that you will find in every significant account of investment theory history. It is about an obscure French mathematician, Louis Bachelier, who laid out the basic elements of the efficient market hypothesis (EMH)—an important viewpoint that emerged side by side with MPT—working independently in France in the 1890s. His efforts were rediscovered in the 1950s, and he was promptly recognized as the intellectual father of the EMH. His work is behind your index fund, and to a lesser extent your ETFs. As a practical matter, however, Bachelier belongs to the period of the 1950s and later when his work was acknowledged and disseminated.

That's not to say that there weren't books about investing. By the 1920s, there were plenty of how-to manuals for investors wishing to try their hand at buying and selling stocks. On an annual basis, Thomas Gibson reprinted his newsletters in a bound volume, suggesting that they had a shelf life longer than a week. Along with his newsletters and articles in *Moody's Magazine*, Gibson also generated lots of additional book-length advice. His works included *The Pitfalls of Speculation* (1906) and *The Cycles of Speculation* (1907), both published originally by Moody. Within a few years, he had set up his own publishing house and put out *The Elements of Speculation* (1913), *Simple Principles of Investment* (1919, an exception—it was published by Doubleday), *The Facts About Speculation* (1923), *Basic Principles of Speculation* (1926), and *Profit & Loss in Investment and Speculation* (1931). Does a theme emerge here? In his early works, Gibson advocates a thoughtful, disciplined, research-oriented approach to trading stocks, arguing that the successful speculator needs (1) a knowledge of values, (2) a knowledge of general conditions, (3) a knowledge of the machinery of speculation, and (4) "something" besides.[54] Like Frank Bennett (the force behind *United States Investor*), Gibson believed that a reasoned and reasonable speculation can be done by the diligent everyman, an everyman who has been unjustly chased away from speculation by the very individuals who got rich doing it, saying that it is too difficult for them. Gibson offered his advice as a way to level the playing field. For him, "speculation is an inherent part of human nature, and . . . a majority of human beings are bound to indulge in it in spite of everything." There was, he said, no reason individuals couldn't and shouldn't be "intelligent" about it. "It is fully realized that a work which defends stock speculation in any degree, will meet with much criticism. Nevertheless, people will speculate and if you are one of those who will—do it right."[55]

Gibson fit into the general Progressivist tone of the time, believing that the investing public was becoming increasingly educated and oriented toward serious economic discussion. Against that backdrop, and with his advice, he believed the emerging investing class could make money trading stocks. That message clearly resonated with the increasing numbers of individuals who had the resources and the inclination to invest in the market. Those investing masses got an academic seal of approval from Harvard economics professor Thomas Carver, who thought that broad ownership of corporate securities would be good for the country and the companies themselves, as well as the investors. In the early 1920s he advocated what came to be called the New Proprietorship. The historian Julia Ott recently chronicled his effort: "Carver and his adherents envisioned that mass distribution of corporate stock would redeem American democracy by enabling salaried or waged citizens to regain a classical republican sense of political stake-holding, along with the economic autonomy that only property ownership could convey."[56] General Motors executive John J. Raskob put it much more simply. In what became a famous article in the *Ladies Home Journal* that appeared in August 1929, Raskob argued that "everybody ought to be rich." He wanted many more people to join the party and outlined a margin-buying-based plan that would allow millions more Americans to own stock. In his thinking, the ordinary workingman should have "the same chance that the rich banker has of profiting by the rise of values of the common stocks of America's most successful companies."[57] Fortunately for the ordinary workingman, Raskob did not have a chance to implement his plan prior to the 1929 Crash.

Analysis Prior to MPT

The pre-Crash works of Gibson and others, while fascinating to read, are not particularly analytical. Most of the space is allocated to what might drive share near-term price changes, including what economy-wide (the term "macroeconomic" did not exist yet), local economic (same with the term "microeconomic"), or company-specific factors might result in gains or loses. Candidates included the price of "call money" (near-term loans), the price of commodities, overall demand, the activity of cliques or syndicates, regulatory matters, bank failures, acquisitions, etc. Keep in mind, however, that the study of economics as we know it today was in its infancy. We take for granted now the heavy macroeconomic and microeconomic textbooks that burden dormitory bookshelves, but until the postwar period, they just didn't exist. The works of Adam Smith, David Ricardo, and Karl Marx, among many others, tended to focus on the specific issues of their times. One of the earliest attempts to bring the various threads together, Alfred Marshall's *Principles of Economics*, was published in 1890. But as far as understanding how to approach the challenge of investment, it was pretty much white space until Irving Fisher's *The Nature of Capital and Income* from 1906.[58] (We turn to him later in this chapter.) And even then, very few brokers and investors were reading Alfred Marshall, Irving Fisher, or anyone else of their ilk.

Analysis at the company level was basic: explaining to investors the difference between revenue and income, the relevance of accounts receivable, the importance of how depreciation is calculated, etc. In regard to railroads, John Moody's analysis (in *The Art of Wall Street Investing*) was conducted in the broadest, most simple terms. It consisted of a review of a company's physical plant (its "roads," equipment, and other assets), its earnings power (revenue, profits), and its financial condition (debt load and balance sheet strength). That sounds reasonable, but Moody's approach, like that of almost all the others at the time, is essentially devoid of any mention of how those analyses should actually be conducted, as well as any valuation exercise. In short, prior to the 1930s, there were few numbers and few specific analytical guidelines. The stock market bubble of the 1920s certainly generated lots of commentary, but it produced little systematic reasoning or consideration as to why stocks should be at their very high levels, and it provided even less about the underlying businesses. Instead, as in the late 1990s, the rising market was presented as an opportunity to enjoy the ride and not think about it too much.

Stocks Versus Bonds and the Purpose of Both

The absence of substantive analysis was not just a matter of the information infrastructure not being in place. It was far more fundamental. Confusion was rampant. Indeed, the little analytical material about stocks that was available up to the Crash in 1929 seemed to fumble around figuring out exactly what stocks were and how they could be used beyond near-term speculation, which everyone seemed to understand quite clearly. In the 1890s, for instance, the newsletter of the brokerage Clapp & Co. advertised the firm's services: "Correspondence invited regarding Investment or Speculation."[59] The fact that so much stock was owned on margin contributed to the view of stocks as purely speculative.

More serious efforts grappled with the relative merits of bonds versus stocks. Then as now, debt was highest on the capital ladder, with a fixed coupon and a promise to pay unless the company went bankrupt. Next was preferred stock, a form of hybrid investment that emerged during the mid-nineteenth century for the numerous "busted" railroads of the day that were still in need of capital but couldn't raise any more equity unless it came with a promise of payment. Preferred stock was "equity"—an ownership stake in the business—but had a fixed, or "preferred," coupon that put it above regular common equity. The price of preferred moved around a bit, but its dividend had precedence over dividend payments to common equity holders. Preferred issues were much more common at the time than they are today. At the turn of the century, most of the actively traded railroads and industrials—88 out of 134 counted on the NYSE in 1906— had both preferred and common equity in circulation.[60] Nearly 30 years later, when Benjamin Graham was parsing the market, preferreds were nearly as popular. In 1932, there were 440 listed preferreds to 800 common stocks on the NYSE.[61] Finally, common stocks—the lowest main rung on the capital ladder—offered and attracted investors with the prospect of a high and rising coupon, reflecting the underlying prosperity and growth of the company in question. But the dividend of a common stock was not guaranteed. It could go up or down or not be paid at all.

The cash yield of the various types of securities reflected their position on the capital ladder and the perceived risk taken by the investor. For instance, the bond of a particular railroad might have a coupon translating to 5% of the purchase price, while the preferred might offer a 6.5% cash return, and the common equity might trade with a yield of 8%. This range of yields is notable: investors in the debt and equity of companies were offered a spectrum of payment streams. All business investments, except the most speculative or start-up, came with income streams, period.

That is no longer the case. Modern investment practice now draws a much clearer distinction between asset types. While bonds are still largely viewed as a source of income that is "safe" (and with relatively little movement in the price),[62] equities have come to be treated as an entirely different animal. They are there to generate capital gains: to buy low, sell high, and repeat frequently, without regard to a current or future income stream. They are about the price of the asset (the share price), not the utility of the asset (reflected

in its distributable cashflows). In its most common application, MPT for all intents and purposes has stripped stocks of
their dividends, effectively leaving investment in them largely
if not entirely about the market price. This is the conclusion of Miller and Modigliani in 1961; more on them later.
Ironically, MPT enshrines in theory what had become common practice in the late 1920s and the late 1960s, and would
be again in the late 1990s, in regard to the trading nature of
stocks. The notion that there might be a real company or a
cash stream associated with an equity investment—the dividend—is secondary, at best, for many stock investors, and it
barely matters at all in Modern Portfolio Theory.

In the earlier period, however, both dividend-paying stocks
and coupon-paying bonds (and preferred) were issued with a
similar goal—the original purpose of the "capital markets"—
to raise capital for the expanding railroads and the similarly
burgeoning manufacturing enterprises of the nineteenth and
early twentieth centuries. Laying all that track and constructing all those factories was expensive, and the stock market
was part of the financial engine contributing to the emergence
of the United States as an economic powerhouse. A 1922 textbook introduction to the stock market placed it in that positive light: "The modern corporation [financed with publicly
traded stocks and bonds] has made it possible to combine
the small savings of the millions into huge sums for the creation of mammoth enterprises, capable of performing services
entirely beyond the reach of an individual."[63]

Here too it is useful to contrast the nature of capital raising
then and now. In regard to using the market to bring together
funds to invest in businesses, a lot has changed. The public
markets today aren't really about raising capital anymore;
that function has reverted to the private markets. Instead,
they are much more about moving existing capital around.

This is unfair to these few companies nowadays that actually raise capital in the public markets to fund operations. Real estate investment trusts (REITs) and utilities are good examples. If you see them issuing debt or equity, it is probably because they need it or want it to invest in their operations. But the initial public offering (IPO) of a technology company's stock is rarely about raising new capital to invest in the business; it is usually a mechanism to allow early-stage investors to cash out some or all of their chips. It is probably the case, however, that those early-stage investors are willing to front their capital precisely because they know that they will be able to exit the investment in a few short years. So one could argue that having the stock market in the background does contribute somewhat to the actual raising of capital for emerging businesses. Still, among the S&P 500 Index companies, raising additional funds is a rarity unless the companies are in trouble, such as the banks in 2009 and energy companies in 2015 and 2016. Many S&P 500 Index companies have not sold significant new shares to the public in decades, though they regularly issue smaller amounts of new shares to employees. So a century ago, companies raised capital, with the additional benefit of that capital repricing on a daily basis and providing "liquidity"—the ability to get in or out easily—subject to periodic market bubbles and busts. That function is now reversed. The stock market exists presently mostly for the daily repricing of assets and only occasionally for getting new funds for investment.

Stocks Are Risky

Although both types of assets—debt and equity—could be and were used to raise capital in the pre-Crash period, it wasn't at all clear which was a "better" investment, beyond the common knowledge that bonds were for long-term investment and stocks were for near-term speculation. That view changed somewhat in the direction of stocks in the mid-1920s when Edgar Lawrence Smith argued that stocks did no worse than bonds over long time periods and were worthy of consideration by serious investors.[64] That view was welcomed by the growing number of U.S. investors willing to consider owning stocks as the Roaring Twenties progressed.

But the stock alternative was still seen as risky, and not just due to fly-by-night brokerages and bucket shops. Capital raising itself had very much of a Wild West flavor to it in the decades prior to the Crash. The terms of art were "water" and "watered" stock, presumably referring to the dilutive function of H_2O.[65] The late nineteenth century saw lots of watered stock—where way too much capital was raised from investors versus the current or prospective actual physical assets of the business. Now we are used to service and intellectual property businesses that can raise billions of dollars from investors without having physical assets beyond a foosball table and a deluxe coffee machine, but during our manufacturing and heavy industry heyday, the amount of capital a company had or could raise largely corresponded to the physical assets it had or proposed to have shortly. How could it be otherwise? When the amount of money raised went well beyond that level, an individual's ownership stake was said to have been watered down. We have less fictitious capital raising today, though during the Internet bubble, the inflated stock issued to pay for inflated assets might have met the water standard.

In addition to watered stock, pure stock scams were frequent in an environment not only without regulation but also without any commonly accepted rules or guidelines about what company investments should look like. John Moody tells the charming story of a flotation for the "guaranteed egg company." Promoters offered 7% guaranteed preferred stock at par for a stake in an egg-producing and selling business. These particular hens were supposed to lay eggs at a furious pace that would allow the company to make handsome distributions. The hens and a 20-acre farm were the only assets of the company. Moody observed:

Absurd as this whole proposition was, there were enough investing idiots walking around loose in New York City to "nibble" at this bait to the extent of over $80,000 in cash. And it was stated on good authority that most of these subscriptions came from New York city people who had never seen a chicken farm in their lives, and probably didn't know any more about the chicken and hen laying business than the chickens themselves knew about the preferred stock they were assumed to be guaranteeing the dividends on.

After the money was raised, the promoters disappeared with it. Moody tells another story—more classical in nature—of a scheme to generate gold from seawater which apparently raised a million dollars before the promoter decamped for Europe.[66] Perhaps not surprisingly, mining and minerals appeared to generate a disproportionate amount of stock scams. Many of these promotions were offered directly to the public rather than through brokerages or through special-purpose brokerages that disappeared at the same time as the promoters.

As a reflection of the lesser status of stocks, fiduciaries and trust officers (individuals charged with managing the assets of others such as those handling the affairs of the archetypical "widows and orphans") were in many places forbidden by state law to own stocks and in many instances were not inclined to do so. Indeed, the early legal interpretations of the Prudent Man framework for fiduciaries, dating from 1830, largely precluded the world of wild and woolly stocks, even those with large and stable dividends. A more important ruling was *King v. Talbot* in which the New York Court of Appeals in 1869 got specific about what trustees investing on behalf of others could or could not hold. And common stocks usually ended up outside the fence, being by definition "imprudent." Over the next few decades, state legislatures drew up similar lists of permissible holdings. Common stocks were rarely present on lists that were dominated by high-quality bonds and government securities. "Equity participations were almost universally excluded. Common stocks were emphatically 'taboo.' The trustee who purchased or retained unauthorized securities became in substance a [personal] guarantor against depreciation."[67] The sharp movement up of stocks in the 1920s and then the sudden reversal after 1929 didn't do much to rehabilitate the reputation of stocks among trustees or judges. An investment manual written in 1931 made clear that "common stocks, as such, are not superior to bonds as long-term investments, because primarily they are not investments at all. They are speculations."[68]

Stock Valuation: It's All About the Dividend

Investment analysis prior to the 1930s had little if anything to say about the valuation of individual stocks. And what was said almost always involved the presence or absence and perceived trajectory of a company's dividend. That's a sensible approach, and without the help of the academics, at least some investors of the time understood that a publicly traded business was no different from any other business venture and should be considered in light of the distributable cash-flows that it could generate. A high yield from a safe income stream was better than a low yield. A dividend that had the potential to increase bested one that was at risk of a cut. This approach was consistent with the (unacknowledged) linkage of value to income that was enshrined in print in Fisher's *Nature of Capital and Income* from 1906. Fisher appears to "have been the first to propose that *any* capital project should be evaluated in terms of its present value."[69] Stocks, that is, should be treated no differently than any other business venture.

But in the absence of a specific analytical framework to measure the present value of a stock's income stream, most of the commentary at the time was more general, about the perceived quality of a security. Here, there was a clear rank order: railroad preferred, railroad common, industrial preferred, industrial common, and very much finally, non-dividend stocks. Quality was linked to the presence, amount, and strength of a company's dividend. Stock valuation work, if it existed at all, was very simple and consisted of listing the dividend yield or earnings yields (net income divided by market value) of leading equities. For instance, the 1910 issues of the *United States Investor* refer to "the Two Standards of Comparison: of Present Investment Yield on Basis of Current Dividends and Prevailing Market Price, and on Basis of Present Earnings on Prevailing Market Values." The tone suggests the absence of other measures of valuation. Each issue of the newsletter included a list—the best of the top-yielding (dividend and earnings) railroads and industrials. The tables read as a form of a recommended list. A sample from July of that year showed dividend yields of the leading industrials running from a high of 14.85% for American Malt Corp preferred to 2.85% for Consolidated Gas. The average was 6.45%. Thirty of the fifty recommended were preferred stocks. On earnings yield, the common of U.S. Rubber headed the list, trading at four times net income, while Utah Copper was the worst of the best list with an earnings yield of 3.45%. (We would express those figures today as trailing P/Es of 4 and 30, respectively.)[70] In the question-and-answer section of the same issue, a subscriber asked why American Malt was on the recommended list when it had a 5% yield at par and a market yield of 15%.[71] The editors explained the history of the company and how the current management was working to right the ship: "We have no hesitation in stating that the present management of the company is not only conservative, but honest and able."[72] Perhaps, but honest and able were as hard to confirm a century ago as they are today.

The key issue for these investors, as opposed to pure price speculators, was the future of the dividend. One of the prominent market commentators of the period, Franklin Escher, offered his preferred four metrics on how to value a stock:

1. What is the character of the business? Is it stable, mature, discretionary, etc.? Does it have room for growth that would allow for a higher dividend?
2. How many bonds stand between the equity holders and their dividends?
3. What are the company's earnings over the past five years? For Escher and other analysts at the time, earnings were defined as revenues minus all operating expenses as well as interest charges and preferred dividends. That is, how much was left to pay the dividend on the common? Where there was some uncertainty, it was usually around how realistic were the depreciation charges.
4. And finally, what is the dividend record? According to Escher: "By many shrewd appraisers of security values, the [dividend record] is given more weight than almost anything else. Just as actions speak louder than words, so dividends actually paid speak more forcibly for the value of a stock than earnings statements or anything else."[73]

Escher offered no numbers, no formulas, no ranges, no quantitative framework, just a basic assertion that successful businesses make high and rising profit distributions to their owners.

Four years later, Escher echoed his earlier sentiments, which James Carville would have rendered nearly a century later as "it's the dividend, stupid!" It is worth quoting at length:

What is this particular stock or this particular group of stocks likely to do? Is its present yield in line with what stocks of its class ought to yield at the present time? What are the chances of its dividend being maintained at the present rate? . . . To be attractive, at least from the standpoint of the man who invests for profit as well as for income, it seems to us, a stock ought not only be reasonably sure of the maintenance of its dividend, but ought to yield well up around 8 per cent. That may seem an arbitrary figure and to some perhaps a little high, but it is a matter of fact that any number of good stocks can be bought to yield that much, and that unless a stock does yield that much it is hard to see where there is any particular ground for expecting an increase in its market price. A few very old and seasoned securities— Pennsylvania, for instance—may continue to sell at a price to yield nearer 6 per cent than 8, and, because of their distribution among investors, may seem fairly attractive from the standpoint of an investment made for pure income, but these are hardly, at least so it seems to us, the kind of thing that a man wanting to invest his money to the best possible advantage ought to buy. As against a stock like Pennsylvania, which for the reasons mentioned above sells at a price to yield considerably less than can be safely obtained in a good many other directions, it would seem to be the part of wisdom rather to buy stocks of the class of Union Pacific, which because the yield is so high have a chance of

increasing in price to a point where the yield is more in keeping
with what, even under present circumstances, may be regarded as
a fair return.

In contrast, continues the author, in regard to Bethlehem "B,"
trading with a 12.5% yield, there is "a very serious doubt
as to whether, after the war, any such rate of dividend can
be maintained." And "Steel Common, to take another case,
would not possibly go on selling around 90 were it not evident that the present 17-per-cent-per-annum dividend rate is
bound to come down in the not distant future."[74]

The role of the dividend in determining value was casually and broadly accepted. In 1922, the journal *Industrial
Management* sought subscriptions from readers of *Forbes* with
an advertisement featuring the headline "The Art of Earning
Dividends Is Inseparable from the Art of Management."[75] The
Magazine of Wall Street described in 1923 that U.S. Realty
& Improvement two years earlier had been selling around
$40 per share despite an asset value of $118 per share and
annual earnings of $5–$10 per share. At that time, the journal told investors that they could reasonably expect "a share
of the company's profits within a reasonable period. . . . Last
November, or under two years from the time when the above
conclusion was stated in these columns, the directors placed
the stock on a $6 annual basis. U.S. Realty is now selling
around 87, having naturally advanced in anticipation of the
dividend."[76] The key word is "naturally." What else would
drive a major fundamental change in share price if not the
change in the dividend? "Is Pullman's Dividend Safe?" or
"Can Linseed Resume Dividends?" were typical and unsur-
prising headlines from the 1920s investment literature.[77]
Despite not understanding the new financial climate of the

late 1920s, Groucho Marx was on to something when he asked why Radio did not pay a dividend.

Notwithstanding the generally shared assumptions about dividends (and Fisher's text of 1906), I have not encountered prior to the 1930s a single detailed, comprehensive effort in the financial media of how to value a stock's income stream. That is, how should an investor forecast dividends and determine the appropriate rate of risk to apply to those future income streams? For that matter, there's no evidence of a detailed application of the other theoretical ways of valuing ongoing enterprises—the cost to replace the physical assets, or prices based on transactions for similar businesses. Even other stock market valuation measures such as a price-to-sales ratio are absent. Is it perhaps an issue of sources? I have reviewed a wide range of books, magazines, newspapers, and historical accounts and found essentially no reference to any substantial valuation effort beyond the simple measures discussed above. Is it possible that someone or even many people were doing a primitive discounted cashflow analysis, or an asset replacement cost, or a relative forward earnings valuation? Of course, it is possible, and in a "ruleless" world, it could have behooved such an investor to keep those methods under his straw boater or her cloche hat. But it seems awfully unlikely that such approaches were widely used without knowledge of it leaking out into the broader marketplace.

Now to be fair, there was some measure of general business analysis in the investment literature of the time. It involved assessment of economic conditions, such as discussions of demand (no numbers), or output (a few numbers), or prices (some numbers), or profitability (back to no numbers). The situation did improve somewhat in the early twentieth century when more economic and company-specific data became available. But to the modern reader—arguably awash in too much information—the analysis is still very impressionistic, data poor, and big picture. The exceptions generally involved those companies that issued frequent operational updates or were more forthcoming in their annual reports. The latter become more frequent as a result of the institution of taxes on corporate income in 1909 (on the eve of the institution of personal income taxes in 1913) and more demanding listing requirements with the exchanges. By that time, major companies such as Union Pacific, Southern Pacific, and oft-mentioned United States Steel Corp were issuing annual reports with reasonably detailed income statements and balance sheets.

Portfolios, Diversification, Risk, Discount Rates, and Expected Returns

As we'll discuss in greater detail in the chapters to follow, systematic diversification and the quantification of risk and return are the hallmarks of Modern Portfolio Theory. These two foundation stones are hailed as vast improvements over what went before. That claim is impossible to dispute. Prior to Markowitz, diversification, if it existed at all as a concept, was anecdotal at best, requiring no further explanation than perhaps a reference to Antonio in the *Merchant of Venice*.[78] Or in less Shakespearian terms, as one investment guide from 1913 put it: "The wisdom of distributing one's funds over a variety of securities is so obvious to the trained man in investment affairs that it is practically an axiom."[79] In England, the investment pioneer Henry Lowenfeld favored geographical diversification in his *Investment: An Exact Science* from 1909, and he created an exchange where investors could access government bonds from all over the world. The earliest Dutch and English mutual funds employed this basic geographical approach.[80] For Edgar Lawrence Smith in the 1920s, there was nothing to discuss: "The only principle of sound investment that has been applied to the selection of stocks [in his study of their performance vis-à-vis bonds] is that of diversification. Without diversification, the purchase of common stocks cannot be considered."[81] Even within the realm of pure price speculation, some diversification was considered wise. Pioneer Fund founder and long-time manager Phil Carret urged punters in 1930 to "never hold fewer than ten different securities covering five different fields."[82] By the standards of the day, that would have counted as a material risk control measure. But even in these accounts, the benefits of diversification were not spelled out, and they were certainly not quantified.

In the same period, there were plenty of heavy hitters in the anti-diversification camp. One frequently encountered Andrew Carnegie's supposed advice to "put your eggs in one basket and watch that basket." In that tug-of-war, the Scotsman appeared to have great sway among the investing and speculating public. The culture of the day was about making good trades or smart individual investments. It was rarely if ever about managing a portfolio of securities. Is it possible that individuals prior to 1952 were managing their portfolios in a modern manner to minimize volatility in shares prices for any given expected return—as MPT would suggest they do? Perhaps, and if so, investors would have had good reason to keep their methods to themselves. But without a shred of evidence of such practices in the historical record, it seems unlikely that anything similar to *portfolio management* as we understand it today existed or was practiced.

The quantification of risk, and even consistent definitions of risk, is similarly lacking in the investment record prior to the Crash. Beyond the intuitive notions that the investor in stocks could lose money, there is not much more to be found

in the written materials. The notion of risk per se, of risk as
we define it today—of risk as inflation, as a discount rate, as
a factor in a formula, as the calculated and reasoned concern
that something might not happen when and how we expect it
to—simply didn't exist in the stock market culture of the day.
Here the basic distinction between bonds—where the chance
of default and principal loss is small—and stocks—where the
risk of principal loss (and gain) is ever present—came into
play . . . in favor of the bonds, of course. The term "risk" is
itself rarely used in writings about investment of the day, and
where it is, it is casual. As a writer for the *Magazine of Wall
Street* averred in 1923: "The average investor would do much
better to concentrate on the idea of fixing in advance of his
purchase what degree of risk he is willing to assume in consideration of a given possibility of profit."[83] The idea that risk
and return are in some sort of relationship is understood—
but is largely undefined and entirely unquantified.

To wit, the word "discount" with the meaning that it has
today—that "a bird in the hand is worth two in the bush"—is
infrequently encountered prior to the 1930s. A 1922 over-
view of the market by Wharton professor Solomon Huebner
speaks of "the discounting function of exchange markets"
and asserts that "stock exchanges have come to be recognized more and more as agencies for the collective expression
of human judgment concerning the present and prospective
value of securities." Huebner continues, "Without an exception every business depression or boom in this country has
been discounted by our security markets from six months
to two years before the dull times or prosperity became a
reality."[84] In Huebner's specific example of discounting that
follows, note the centrality of the dividend. Because the market participants, he wrote,

*always have in mind the future, rather than the present, their
initiative in making purchases and sales will tend to discount the
effect of coming events on any given security. It is for this reason
that the price of a stock often bears no definite relation to the
present earnings of the corporation or to the dividend paid. A
non-dividend-paying stock may seem to command an apparently
unwarranted price, yet upon the declaration of a dividend, the
price will usually fail to advance much and may actually decline.
Similarly, a dividend-paying stock may apparently sell much too
low, yet upon a cut in the dividend, the stock will usually fail to
decline appreciably and may actually advance.*[85]

That is, the market has already priced in, or discounted, these
developments. The term is now common, and the discount
rate is key to just about all formulas that involve risk and
return, no matter how defined.

Finally, prior to the Crash, an expected rate of return—
another key input for subsequent MPT-based formulas—is
rarely if ever mentioned. In regard to bonds, it is considered
nothing more or less than the coupon. A 5% bond is expected
to yield 5%—$5 for each $100 invested—annually. For investors who buy at issuance at par and hold their bonds to matu-
rity, that simple math is unchanged to this day. For equities,
the expected return was generally treated as the dividend
amount flavored with a degree of uncertainty—perhaps more,
perhaps less, depending on the direction of the coupon and
the share price itself. But there were no explicit discussions
and certainly no quantitative treatment of an expected long-
term return from a stock. Why would there be? For many
investors—read "speculators"—stocks were "borrowed" and
traded for a few points of gain (or loss). There was no long-
term return, and the near-term return was self-evident. You

either made or lost money. An expected long-term rate of return just wasn't necessary.

Early Variants of Modern Finance, Efficient Markets, and Behavioral Finance

Despite the chaotic nature of the pre-Crash investment culture, certain threads in current investment culture may well have existed, if under different terms. Indeed, in the spirit of "There is nothing new under the sun . . . What has been will be again," the historian of finance William Goetzmann has found snippets of what we consider key finance concepts going as far back as Sumer and the earliest periods of recorded human settlement.[86] The evidence is fragmentary, but he suggests that contracts, the time value of money, insurance, derivatives, and so forth existed in some form or another for several thousand years. The math would have been simpler, but the ideas were similar to what we might recognize today as modern finance.

The same is true, to some extent, in the decades prior to the 1929 Crash. Years before the notion of "efficient" markets emerged in the 1960s, the market as a purportedly correct arbiter of prices was a view regularly espoused by numerous observers. In 1912, G. C. Selden held forth that the market represented all possibilities and probabilities, even remote ones.[87] At about the same time, the NYSE was trying to burnish its admittedly bad public image. In one of its publications, it wrote that "the combined judgment of thousands of experts" would result in a "scientific" price for its securities and that those thousands of experts constituted a "natural regulator of securities prices."[88] Ten years later, in the early 1920s, an analysis of the stock market from another well-known market watcher asserted that "the market represents everything everybody knows, hopes, believes, anticipates, with all the knowledge sifted down . . . to 'the bloodless verdict of the market place.'"[89] That is a succinct statement of the efficient market view, without the layers of academic mumbo jumbo.

In the past few decades, behavioral finance—the study of how humans actually behave in economic matters—has emerged as an important corrective to the notion of mechanical, rational man that underpins most modern social sciences and certainly MPT. We make mistakes; we have biases; our views and goals change over time; our judgment is not as cool, calm, and objective as we imagine it to be. This too is not particularly new. Indirect precursors to what we might identify as behavioral economics can be seen as far back as the eighteenth century.[90] And in the decades prior to the 1929 Crash, plenty of commentators noted that psychology played a critical role in the markets and that speculation was as much about the mind of the speculator as about the market. Jesse Livermore's colorful accounting of his activities can be read as a rich and deep tract on how humans really behave when faced with conditions of uncertainty—the key analytical framework for analyzing investment choices (and most other big choices in life). Others were aware of the difference between how we should behave and how we actually make decisions: "It is a fact well recognized among practical traders and investors that all the smaller movements of prices and many of the larger swings are the result of a condition of the public mind."[91]

Though not nearly as elegant as the modern work of Daniel Kahneman and Amos Tversky, discussed in Chapter 4, G. C. Selden's *Psychology of the Market* from 1912 makes it clear that many market participants—not just Livermore—understood that the outcome of an investment depends at least as much on the thinking of other investors as it does on the merits of the company in question. Selden asserted that "the movements of prices on the exchanges are dependent to a very large degree on the mental attitude of the investing and trading public." Long-term changes might be fundamental, but short-term ones were psychological. Post–Kahneman and Tversky, we wouldn't really recognize Selden's work as serious behavioral analysis, but it is explicit in introducing a psychological component to understanding the market. And Selden makes the same basic points that we know today: that too many investors succumb to excessive confidence and optimism when share prices are high and they are ahead, and they adopt excessive caution and bearishness when prices have fallen and they are in the red. The professional trader "comes habitually to expect that nearly every one else will be wrong, but is, as a rule, confident that his own analysis of the situation will prove correct." Selden also observes, as modern social scientists have confirmed, that investors simply assume that current trends will continue indefinitely: "It is a sort of automatic assumption of the human mind that present conditions will continue, and our whole scheme of life is necessarily based to a great degree on this assumption." One century later, that is still the state of the art. Selden continues that the typical investor lets his judgment be swayed by his hopes. A panic

represents a decline greater than is warranted by conditions, usually because of an excited state of the public mind. . . . The boom is in many ways the reverse of the panic. Just as fear keeps growing and spreading until the final crash, so confidence and enthusiasm keep reproducing each other on a wider and wider scale until the result is a sort of hilarity on the part of thousands of men, many of them comparatively young and inexperienced, who have "made big money" during the long advance of prices.[92]

Written in 1912, this is close to a pitch-perfect description of the Internet bubble and its bursting.

Reading the Tape

In the absence of what we would consider modern, fundamental analysis, efforts to discern patterns or trends in the price charts that would lead to profitable trades—called technical analysis—were alive and well. According to the *Magazine of Wall Street* from 1912:

The Most Important Factor in Trading or Investing is a Knowledge of The Trend. It is better to know which way the general market is likely to swing than to know earnings, dividends, or fundamentals. The tape gives very definite indications as to the immediate future. Our Trend Letter, written from the tape, contains this information.[93]

A decade later, the *Magazine of Wall Street*'s editor, Richard Wyckoff, makes his claim for studying the tape: "It is a technical position of the market which finally determines whether to buy or sell, regardless of intrinsic values."[94] Indeed, the *Wall Street Journal*'s editor, Charles Dow, asserted a ticker-reading theory of the stock market. Dow had shared his views in a series of pieces in the *Wall Street Journal* in 1901 and 1902, the year he died. Twenty years later, the *Journal*'s subsequent editor, William Peter Hamilton, published his view of what came to be known as the Dow theory and his assessment that it did explain, with some revision, the previous twenty years of stock price movements.[95] Hamilton used the two existing Dow averages—the Industrials and Transports—as barometers of business activity that then forecasted stock market outcomes. It was really a form of trend analysis for the overall market, less so for individual securities. At times, Hamilton appeared to contradict himself by asserting his own version of the efficient market hypothesis: "the sum and tendency of the transactions in the Stock Exchange represent the sum of all

Wall Street's knowledge of the past, immediate and remote, applied to discounting the future."[96] By today's standards, the Dow theory's trend analysis and a belief in efficient markets could not both be true, but in Hamilton's time, it would not have been seen as a big contradiction. Technical analysis was (and is) pure price speculation, but ironically, it comported with the only cogent analytical framework of the day—that of economic and market cycles.

The (Gold) Cycle

To the extent that there was some sort of broader analytical framework about the stock market prior to the emergence of MPT, it was almost always associated with the cyclical economic activity that dominated the U.S. economy in the nineteenth and early twentieth centuries. The stock market directly reflected that cyclicality in that much more of the economy and many more stocks than today, as a percentage of the overall market, were involved in cyclical industries such as minerals and materials extraction, manufacturing, and transportation. The United States had experienced major economic dips and associated contractions of the stock market in 1837, 1857, 1873 (the original Great Depression), 1893, and 1907. And this cyclicality was much more extreme than how we think of economic growth and decline now. In these cycles, banks closed, depositors lost everything, railroads stopped operating entirely, and businesses closed abruptly. This was not the gradual reorganization of Chapter 11 protection that we have become accustomed to, but often immediate closure and liquidation.

The downturns were remarkably regular—every 20 years or so—and economists and market observers of the time were struck by this lawlike periodicity. Some subdivided more finely and saw momentous events every 5 or 10 years.

And as if on cue, there was the Crash of 1929, followed by a new Great Depression. Despite the apparent pattern, very few people tended to see the peaks and valleys ahead of time; they just knew that there would be ups and downs. In this context, serious stock market analysis necessarily reflected this framework of economic cyclicality. Even Gibson's very optimistic publications in regard to speculation are strongly rooted in the economic reality of the day: business and investment activity were highly cyclical. Successful investors had to take that into account. Charles Dow's theory, as asserted by Hamilton, "was based upon his profound belief in the recurrence of financial crises, at periodic intervals . . . of a little more than 10 years."[97] Roger Babson had gotten into the economic forecasting business after the 1907 takedown—he had previously been a bond salesman—and was convinced that the industry, and therefore the stock, cycle was driven by an inevitable series of phases—prosperity, decline, depression, and recovery—that could be tracked through the statistics, however paltry, that were available at the time.[98] In the late 1920s, Babson was almost alone in predicting a sharp market correction. He had the good timing to repeat his warning in September 1929.

A key issue in the analysis of the business cycle and its impact on stocks was one that is quite remote now for most investors: gold. We've been off the gold standard for many decades, so it is easy to forget how closely economic activity and asset values were tied to the supply of the yellow metal in any given country. Simply put, the amount of gold on hand played a big role in determining the money supply, and that in turn influenced credit creation and asset values. A rise in gold balances was the default explanation for an increase in securities prices that otherwise would be inexplicable. More gold meant more money; more money meant higher asset prices.

That is something akin to the stock market's strong rise in 2013 and 2014 as the Federal Reserve continued to print money without a corresponding rise in economic activity.

Even Edgar Lawrence Smith was laboring in the shadow of cyclicality as he investigated his "bonds versus stocks" investment question. That is because the answer turned on the purchasing power of the dollar, which was itself linked to the supply of gold. Bonds had looked good when the dollar was strengthening from the 1860s to the turn of the century during the first Great Depression. Stocks looked much better when the cycle turned and inflation began reducing the dollar's purchasing power. Smith's conclusion was that even during the period of dollar strengthening, stocks still bested bonds in terms of the constancy of income and the safety of principal, two notions central to investment considerations of the time, particularly for trustees.[99]

A Functional Chaos?

Was the pre-Crash stock market as chaotic as I've depicted it to be? It is unfair and inaccurate to assert complete dysfunction. After all, capital was raised, track laid, factories built, and a rickety, highly cyclical, but effective means of capital formation and deployment was established and grew along with the country in the nineteenth and early twentieth centuries. It was, in fact, the heyday of American economic growth, despite (or perhaps due to?) the lack of a clearly delineated system of investment. However wild and woolly, it generally worked to the basic satisfaction of most of those individuals who participated in it. More importantly, it survived its greatest test—the stock market Crash of 1929 and the Great Depression—that called into question the basic free-market organization of our society. Remember that in Europe, those questions were being answered quite differently by the 1930s, with the creation of centrally planned economies in the Soviet Union and Nazi Germany.

And the pre-MPT period saw more than just a few moments of keen understanding, even if not backed up by voluminous data and expressed in extended algebraic formulas. Gibson's version of intelligent speculation sounds a lot like today's approved definition of high-quality value investing:

A man may buy the securities of an established enterprise on the same basis as he would buy a partnership in any line of business, exercising the same care and thought in one case as in the other. He may examine the history and financial status of the concern, form a decision as to its future prospects, and decide to become a partner in the business through the purchase of stocks, or a secured creditor through the purchase of bonds. This class of buyers consists mostly of thoughtful men, and their chief concern is to "buy cheap," confident that if prices are below values, the hiation must inevitably be reconciled in the fullness of time.[100]

That very sober approach to investing would easily pass muster today. Similarly, John Moody's advice rings true: "As a rule, the best time to invest is when others are unloading. In money matters, it is never safe to follow 'the crowd.' Nor is it safe . . . to purchase a security on the 'boom.'"[101] That sounds a lot like Warren Buffett's "Be fearful when others are greedy and greedy when others are fearful" comment from 2008, except that it came many decades earlier.

Moreover, amid the various crosscurrents—the cycles, the pools, the buying on margin—there emerges a pretty basic understanding of the difference between investment (bonds, high-quality, dividend-paying common or preferred stock) and speculation (activity on margin, fancy stock, pool activities, watered stock). There was no attempt to make the speculation anything other than what it was. And in regard to the investment side of the equation, there was an absolutely sensible focus on dividends. Even without the math as to why—that is, pre–John Burr Williams, discussed in the next chapter—the value of dividends was widely understood. Thomas Gibson once again stands out: "The buyer of non-dividend-paying stocks is a speculator pure and simple, whether he pays for his securities outright or carries them on margin."[102] We will return to consider that assertion, after a long detour through MPT. Even the oft-disenchanted John Moody—the seemingly polar opposite to the ever-optimistic Thomas Gibson—had an understanding of good long-term investment that would be well received today:

The investor buys securities to keep . . . does not give much thought to the temporary condition of the market, and it does not matter much to him what the temporary course of prices may be. . . . The investor buys to secure an income; that is to say, he places his money in what he thinks or is led to believe is an absolutely secure piece of property, and he has no other purpose in view than that of receiving a current return upon it in the shape of interest or dividends. Such is the pure investor, while the pure speculator is one who pays no attention to dividends and interest as an income, but is actuated entirely with the idea of profit on principal.[103]

Moody also passed the basic test on diversification at a time when Carnegie's notion of concentration generally held sway. He charged that while Carnegie's principle may be

sound enough for the expert or specialist who is in a situation to at all times see and watch the basket, [it] is not applicable to the average ordinary investor. The average investor simply cannot "watch the basket" in the way implied by Mr. Carnegie, and therefore it is a safe principle for him under all ordinary circumstances, to limit his chances of loss to the greatest possible extent through a wide and judicious distribution of his capital.[104]

Despite these moments of clarity and wisdom about the human condition, the frequent keen insights into the challenges of decision making under conditions of certainty, and the unquestionable reality of a dominant economic power coming into being, there was still no articulated, comprehensive explanation of the investment process prior to MPT. Few if any human activities require a blessing from the academics or other writers to be widely accepted, but for such activities to rise to the level of a paradigm that is broadly adopted, understood, and discussed by its participants, some sort of intellectual template is required. And prior to the Crash of 1929, that was missing. In the next chapter, we shift from a largely static description of the pre-Crash investment climate to a narrative of how MPT was born out of this chaos and how it grew into today's orthodoxy.

2

The Founding Fathers Come Together

Making Sense of Chaos

The prior chapter offered a snapshot of the chaotic investment climate prior to 1929. Yes, there were some advancements in what might be considered investment thought, but there was no clear sequence of events leading to the emergence and acceptance of a broad-based investment paradigm. While 1952 is hailed as the Big Bang for Modern Portfolio Theory, it is probably more accurate to say that the Crash of 1929 led to that bang nearly a quarter century later. Pre-Crash investors might have gotten used to periodic market corrections, but the economic cycle's turn in 1929 was different, in magnitude and consequence, from what had gone before, and it led to much more systematic thinking about public market investments. By the mid- and late 1930s, academics and market professionals were in high gear, producing major analyses of what had happened and what a better way forward might be. Three works stand out: Benjamin Graham and David Dodd's *Security Analysis* from 1934 tried to bring analytical rigor and discipline to the profession of investing where little had existed before. Two years later,

The General Theory of Employment, Interest and Money by English economist John Maynard Keynes was published. Mostly addressing what we now call macroeconomics, *The General Theory* offered a chapter on the capital markets, "The State of Long-Term Expectation," that succinctly captured the critical challenge—forecasting the future under conditions of uncertainty—of investing in businesses through the casino-like portal of the stock market. Finally, in 1938, John Burr Williams published his disciplined, narrow account, *The Theory of Investment Value*, of how to value securities based on discounted cashflows.

Taken together, the works could be viewed as an exercise in cleaning up after a tornado had swept through town. They bulldoze through the debris of the Crash, the rampant speculation, and the widespread casual attitude to investing, and they lay out certain ground rules for understanding financial instruments. Graham and Williams, in particular, were determined to offer those guidelines and generate that benefit. Williams made the claim grandly:

That investment analysis until now has been altogether unequal to the demands put upon it should be clear from the tremendous fluctuations in stock prices that have occurred in recent years. . . . Proper canons of evaluation, generally accepted as authoritative, should have helped to check these price swings somewhat, and thereby reduce in some degree the violence of the business cycle, to the benefit of all the world.[1]

While not necessarily agreeing with one another or fitting together in a comprehensive fashion, the three works do stand as a primitive road map for investors: Graham and Dodd as a practical guide to analyzing and comparing individual securities, Williams as a theory of how to value the cashflows of a security, and Keynes for placing the challenge of stock market investment against the big-picture backdrop of general economic activity.

Numerous other post-Crash analyses were published in the 1930s, but in terms of influencing subsequent generations and still being referenced 80 years later, these three stand out. This chapter reviews how these works laid the groundwork for the emergence of MPT, not only in terms of their specific contributions, but also how they established a way of talking about investing, creating a professional narrative of investment analysis, investor expectations, what is "value," etc. Though the stock market was already hundreds of years old in its English and Dutch variants, the 1930s represented its intellectual coming out. It had become large enough and significant enough, and after the Crash, disturbing enough, to warrant serious intellectual attention from thoughtful market participants and academics.

Benjamin Graham Writes It All Down

The "let's-clear-the-debris" function is most evident in Graham and Dodd's work, *Security Analysis*, published in 1934 soon after the very bottom of the stock market in 1932. Graham viewed the immediately preceding period (1927–1933) as exceptional, not the norm, and therefore not a reason to permanently discredit investing in stocks and bonds. Graham himself had been involved in the market since graduating from Columbia College two decades earlier. By the time of the crash, he was 35 years old and a successful investor as well as occasional commentator. He had started teaching at Columbia in 1928. While he took his share of losses during the Crash, Graham managed to salvage enough capital to remain in business and stayed on Wall Street for decades thereafter. Still, Graham could not completely dismiss or forget what had happened. At times, that darkness comes through, and circa 1934 he is still licking his wounds, viewing only a minority of stocks as investment-worthy, with the rest falling into the speculation category. "Today," he admitted, "the doctrine of common stocks as long-term investments seems discredited." Later in *Security Analysis* he specifically lambasts Edgar Lawrence Smith for his role in creating the speculative bubble of the late 1920s.[2] (Several years later, Williams will make the same accusation.[3])

The original *Security Analysis* runs for 725 pages, and its first half was focused on fixed income analysis. My goal here is to highlight how it set the stage for the emergence of MPT in the postwar period, but it is hard to do without pausing and giving Graham credit for the professionalization of the overall investment industry, specifically its analytical element. As a practical matter, the publication of *Security Analysis* is when the process begins. Reading the 1934 edition now, one is struck by how comprehensive it is. For hundreds of pages, it explains what financial investments are, down to the smallest details and for all sorts of variants. Terms are painstakingly defined; colorful examples are given; stories are told. The analysis is both quantitative and qualitative. Graham spends much of his time in the first edition—the content changed significantly during the subsequent decades—contrasting what should be sound, sober investment practice to what had gone on in the speculative period a few years earlier. Some of what Graham listed and stated was not fundamentally new. But in *Security Analysis* it was presented in one place, as part of a coherent, analytical narrative. No one, not Huebner, nor Gibson, nor Moody, nor Escher, nor Bennett, had assessed securities in as thorough a manner—income sheet, balance sheet, implied cashflows—as he did. Graham was the first and deserves full credit.

Graham's impact was not limited to his publishing. He was also a driving force in getting a group of oft-dismissed "statisticians" who had been meeting informally to come together in 1937 as an organization, the New York Society of Security Analysts. That organization began publication of the *Financial Analysts Journal* (*FAJ*) in 1945; it still hits my desk regularly. In the very first issue of *FAJ*, Benjamin Graham echoed his sentiments in *Security Analysis* and supported professionalization of the industry through a credentialing system, but it would be several decades before that became a reality in the form of the CFA Charter, for all intents and purposes the investment management profession's union card.

Curiously, given all the complexity that would follow in investment analysis, Graham's original normative work—when he gets to it—is quite straightforward. When considering the purchase of an individual stock, Graham urges a detailed review of the financial statements of the company. What we now call "Graham & Dodd fundamental analysis" starts 350 pages into *Security Analysis* and consists of poring over the income statement and the balance sheet with a fine-tooth comb. Cashflow statements did not exist at the time, but cashflows could be analyzed through review of the depreciation and capital equipment accounts, current assets and liabilities, and the like. This is at a time when accounting standards, not to mention accepted norms on how to analyze the accounting, still varied widely. But Graham provides plenty of examples to make his points. Most are of malfeasance to avoid, for which Graham could choose from a long list given the events of the previous decade, but he does punctuate the litany of charges with counterexamples of good managerial oversight. The key things to look at, according to Graham, are the dividend rate and its record, the income statement to understand the company's earnings power, and the balance sheet to understand the value of its tangible assets.

After that review, the analyst or prospective investor should come up with a multiyear (10 if possible, but not less than 5) average of earnings for the company under consideration, and then apply a "quality co-efficient"—what we would call a P/E multiple—of approximately 10 to capitalize those earnings and determine an appropriate price, or "intrinsic value." The multiple can be a little higher if the company has a realistic chance of growing its profits in a sustainable fashion, but Graham seems to cast doubt on the persistence of rising earnings. The practical goal of the investor then becomes to pay below 10 times the earnings amount when market conditions make it possible to do so, and to sell securities trading well above this amount.[4]

Graham is now justly famous as the father of intrinsic value investing, but I wonder if many of its adherents would recognize it in its original formulation. Intrinsic value today is treated as a golden number waiting to be discovered. Graham is much more subtle and less dogmatic:

We must recognize . . . that intrinsic value is an elusive concept. In general terms, it is understood to be that value which is justified by the facts, e.g., the assets, earnings, dividends, definite prospects, as distinct, let us say, from market quotations established by artificial manipulation or distorted by psychological excesses. But it is a great mistake to imagine that intrinsic value is as definite and as determinable as is the market price. . . . The essential point is that security analysis does not seek to determine exactly what is the intrinsic value of a given security. It needs only to establish either that the value is adequate . . . or else that the value is considerably higher or considerably lower than the market price. For such purposes an indefinite and approximate measure of the intrinsic value may be sufficient. To use a homely simile, it is quite possible to decide by inspection that a woman is old enough to vote without knowing her age, or that a man is heavier than he should be without knowing his exact weight.[5]

Not to diminish Graham's contribution, but that's pretty much it for the father of value investing, at least in its first, 1934, version. A good portion of its "value" undoubtedly is in the approach's simplicity, underpinned by its rigorous analytical framework of the underlying business and expressed with great clarity.

Graham also notes several other specialist investment approaches, such as looking at companies that are selling below their net asset value or liquidation value. His basic advice in most instances, however, is to look closely at the earnings record and capability and multiply by 10. As a practical matter, he considers "seasoned" issues with considerable "margins of safety" in the earnings calculation to be the base material for investments. The remaining issues, or high-quality companies trading at 16 times or higher, would be considered speculative.[6] But even those falling short of investment status can be analyzed, and a rational if speculative investment decision can be made about them.

Graham's analytical focus was on earnings, but he made it quite clear that companies should pay out most if not all of their earnings, other than a modest reserve, as dividends. He chides investors for letting corporate managements hold on to the profits rather than distribute them, lamenting the "despotic powers given the directorate over the dividend policy."[7] Little has changed in this regard in 80 years, but the directorate's despotism is now manifested in a preference for share repurchase programs over dividend payments.[8]

Graham's work is just as interesting for what it does not include. He pretty much eschews the types of grand theories and absolutes that became fashionable after the war and that still dominate academic finance. Graham makes no net present value claim, though applying a P/E of 10 to an earnings figure is mathematically equivalent to an NPV (net present value) calculation using a 10% discount rate on a flat income stream. For Graham, however, the 10 multiplier is just a reasonable means of estimating intrinsic value. In contrast to coming up with a precise number within a rigid valuation framework, Graham's focus is more on the principle of asset ownership. Get that right, he believes, and the value proposition will take care of itself. Indeed, for the person so closely associated with the notion of intrinsic value, Graham's observation that "security analysis cannot presume to lay down general rules as to the 'proper value' of any given common stock" might come as a shock.[9]

On what would become the key issues of MPT—diversification, expected returns, and discount rates—Graham assumed the first, dismissed the second, and said very little about the third. Diversification heads his "canon of common-stock investment" in which "investment is conceived as a *group* operation, in which diversification of risk is depended upon to yield a favorable average result." Elsewhere he employs insurance metaphors to explain the logic of diversification:

The principles of common-stock investment may be closely likened to the operations of insurance companies. . . . Any individual risk may result in a loss far exceeding the premium received, but the average result is depended upon to yield a business profit. . . . [An] insurance company [relies] upon diversification to average out the effects of unforeseeable future developments upon individual commitments.[10]

Graham was openly dismissive of specific long-term forecasts. "Some matters of vital significance, e.g., the determination of the future prospects of an enterprise, have received little space, because little of definite value can be said on the subject." Although Graham lists an effort to determine "the future outlook" as part of his overall "canon of common-stock investment," he does not elaborate in any detail. In regard to quantifying risk, he is similarly reluctant, writing that "security prices and yields are not determined by any mathematical calculation of the expected risk, but they depend rather on the popularity of the issue," which he goes on to define with many nonquantitative factors. He continues that "the relation between different kinds of investments and the risk of loss is entirely too indefinite and too variable with changing conditions, to permit of sound mathematical formulation."[11] That subtle, humble, and profoundly nonmechanical view of risk did not survive the development of Modern Portfolio Theory. The question remains, however, whether the postwar formulas are indeed sound or not.

John Maynard Keynes Addresses the Human Condition

English economist and civil servant John Maynard Keynes did not set out to solve the mystery of the stock market.[12] In the aftermath of the 1929 Crash and the Great Depression, he was hunting bigger game: what could be done to resurrect the Western economic system, specifically to increase the level of employment in the Depression-plagued economies. Attending to this big-picture challenge, Keynes paused only briefly on the stock market. (In his personal life, however, he was an avid speculator, perhaps the only personal attribute he shared with Groucho Marx.) In the twelfth chapter of *The General Theory*,[13] Keynes directly addresses the issue of decision making under conditions of uncertainty, a challenge we all face in small or large measure throughout our lives: which school to attend, which person to marry, whether to take one job or another, etc. Investing is just such a challenge. Where do you put your capital, and what will the outcome be? Versus the rest of his work on the functioning of modern industrial economies, Keynes's treatment in Chapter 12 is a subjective digression. But as he admits, it is a necessary one because expectations of returns from investment form a critical component of overall investment activity, which in turn plays a big role in determining employment levels.

As posed by Keynes, the questions are, What are the long-term expectations for return on investment, and how are those expectations formulated? In Keynes's assessment, "the state of long-term expectation" is highly subjective, shifting, and largely psychological, and it relies itself on the "state of confidence" of investors. And in its turn, that state of confidence is abnormally affected or distorted by several characteristics present in the stock market. For instance,

Day-to-day fluctuations in the profits of existing investments, which are obviously of an ephemeral and non-significant character, tend to have an altogether excessive, and even an absurd influence on the market. It is said, for example, that the shares of American companies which manufacture ice tend to sell at a higher price in summer when their profits are seasonally high than in winter when no one wants ice. The recurrence of a bank-holiday may raise the market valuation of the British railway system by several million pounds.[14]

Another problem is that the stock market discourages investors from focusing on fair value, but instead encourages them to strive for what they believe others will think fair value is. In this environment, investment shifts from reasonable if flawed long-term forecasts of business performance to "a battle of wits to anticipate the basis of conventional valuation a few months hence." Rather than choose the best investment, too many market participants are persuaded to choose what other people think will be the best investment, and do so in the midst of numerous others engaged in the exact same exercise. "We have reached the third degree where we devote our intelligences to anticipating what average opinion expects the average opinion to be. And there are some, I believe, who practice the fourth, fifth and higher degrees."[15]

But the market characteristic that really bothers Keynes is the daily repricing—what he calls the "fetish of liquidity"—of long-term assets:

Of the maxims of orthodox finance, none, surely, is more anti-social than the fetish of liquidity, the doctrine that it is a positive virtue on the part of investment institutions to concentrate their resources upon the holding of "liquid" securities. It forgets that there is no such thing as liquidity of investment for the community as a whole. [By which he means, everyone can't be a seller at the same time.] The social object of skilled investment should be to defeat the dark forces of time and ignorance which envelop our future. The actual, private object of the most skilled investment today is "to beat the gun," as the Americans so well express it, to outwit the crowd, and to pass the bad, or depreciating, half-crown to the other fellow.[16]

This daily repricing of generally stable businesses takes most individuals who enter the process claiming to be calm, cool, and collected investors with long-term investment horizons and turns all too many of them, almost by necessity, into near-term speculators with almost no regard for the underlying fundamentals of the business under consideration. That seems like a harsh judgment, but if you were writing in the mid-1930s, with the ruins of the European economy surrounding you, the conclusion doesn't seem particularly dark at all. (Today's penchant for day trading and the emergence of high-frequency traders suggests that the problem persists.) Keynes's postwar heirs would make a strong effort to correct that situation, by creating elegant, mathematically derived long-term return expectations. But even though Keynes clearly sides with the effort to cast economic activity in mathematical terms that can be reasonably forecast, he still attributes the ultimate decision to invest to near-term "animal spirits" rather than an "outcome of a weighted average of quantitative benefits multiplied by quantitative probabilities."[17]

Williams Works Out the Math

Last but not least among the authors of our 1930s trilogy, John Burr Williams provides almost a textbook narrative on the need to bring order to the chaos of the investment world at that time. Trained as a mathematician and chemist—two very rule-oriented disciplines—Williams found himself working at a brokerage as a stock analyst, but without the tools to fulfill the basic job description of valuing securities. Many years later, he recalled thinking that "how to estimate the fair value was a puzzle indeed."[18] So Williams returned to graduate school at Harvard to come up with the formulas that would help him determine what price to pay for a security. Though Fisher had made clear 30 years earlier that the present value of an asset was a function of future income streams, he had not worked out the math of net present value calculations. Williams set out on the task of filling in the details.[19] The context of this work, however, was quite different. It was the 1930s, in the aftermath of the Crash and amid a severe economic contraction. Like Graham and Keynes, Williams was motivated to figure out what had gone wrong and how a healthier investment culture could be created.

Not lacking in self-confidence, Williams makes several assumptions that frame the math that follows. The first, which we have already referenced, is that the "the investment value of a stock [is] the present worth of all the dividends to be paid upon it."[20] Given that this is the case, the task of the investor then becomes to calculate that investment value and then to purchase the security at or below that price.

If a man buys a security below *its investment value, he need never lose, even if its price should fall at once, because he can still hold for income and get a return above normal on his cost price; but if he buys it above its investment value his only hope of avoiding a loss is to sell to someone else who must in turn take the loss in the form of insufficient income.*[21]

Second, Williams necessarily accepts rational actor theory (before it was regularly called that). Williams justified his methodology by saying that determination of investment value through discounted dividends "is in harmony with the time-honored method of economic theory, which always begins its investigations by asking, 'What would men do if they were perfectly rational and self-seeking?'"[22] This is not really true—this "time-honored" method would receive much fuller dissemination in the postwar period. Although the roots of an explicit rational actor theory can be traced back to Adam Smith's famous quip in the *The Wealth of Nations* that "it is not from the benevolence of the butcher, the brewer, or the baker that we expect our dinner, but from their regard to their own interest," rational actor theory as an elaborated assertion of how people are supposed to behave in investment matters is a development of the twentieth century.

Operating in the 1930s, Williams was more or less making the rules up as he went along, blazing a trail parallel to that of *Homo economicus*, but in this case in regard to investments.[23] So, combining the two precepts of present value and rational behavior, a good investor "would never pay more than the present worth of the expected future dividends. . . . Such a price is what we have already defined as the investment value of a security."[24] It sounds simple now—maximize present value in a rational manner—but at the time, expressing that approach in a cool, methodical manner represented a step change in investment thought.

Having answered the big questions, Williams proceeds to lay out those formulas necessary to determine investment value. His method involves a series of algebraic equations to assign a present value to the future cash flows under various dividend scenarios: flat, rising steadily, rising irregularly, declining, or some other pattern, as well as the impact of additional equity issuance, rights, preferred, etc. The treatment is exhaustive, but for the hundreds of formulas, the key terms come down to just a few. The dividend is one of them. You would think that this would be straightforward, but Williams is writing in the mid-1930s when the country was still in the grip of the Great Depression and the dividends of many corporations had been cut or eliminated. As a result, Williams spends a fair amount of time forecasting dividends once the economy recovered to mid-1920s levels, what he considers a more normal economic environment.

The second major factor is the growth of the dividend. In what probably comes as a surprise to most current-day investors, Williams and many other commentators of the time, including Graham in 1934, generally assume flat dividends. That the distribution might rise is treated as a nice possibility, but it is not necessarily assumed. And even if it is to increase, the gain may not have much additional present value because, if the growth is inflation related, it would be offset by a similar rise in the discount factor. That is, in Williams, there is not much room for long-term "real" (above the rate of inflation) growth in individual investment income streams. Where there is real growth in the dividend forecast, it is for a finite period, say 5 or 10 years. At that point, a flat dividend is then assumed. In contrast to that assumption of little to no real growth, investors today have gotten used to over 30 years of declining interest rates and low inflation, so much so that growth is generally perceived to be mostly real and something that can be sustained in perpetuity. But prior to this "great moderation" in price rises, inflation—and at times genuine deflation—was a serious consideration in all economic calculations, and it is worth keeping in mind how unusual the last three decades have been. (Creating new businesses or taking share from existing businesses is another and important way that companies today can generate real growth, and, to be fair, this type of expansion has been a material part of the low-inflation gains of the past few decades.)

The third factor is the discount rate, which Williams generally refers to as the rate of interest. In the critique of Modern Portfolio Theory that is to follow, the discount rate is critical. Understanding how the first full explication of discounted cashflows treats this all-important "haircut" provides the necessary context for understanding what would follow in the postwar period. Modern readers and investors are now accustomed to a simple formulaic approach to the discount rate ever since an expected rate of return—mathematically the same as the discount rate for a given "correct" asset price[25]—was solved in the mid-1960s. In contrast, the inexplicit approach to a discount rate prior to the emergence of MPT can be discomforting, as it should be. Despite the working out of that formula in the 1960s, there is still no certainty in defining and forecasting the risks that we encounter during the course of our lives. We may take comfort in having a formula generate an answer for us, but the mere existence of a formula does not make it right, and the formula-free period before was in some ways intellectually more honest.

For all his forthrightness and assertions of precision, Williams is frustratingly oblique about the discount rate. First, he distinguishes between a general market interest rate and a personal one. That some investors might demand a 10% return and another 2% "as minimum wages of abstinence"[26]—what they demand in return for giving up a certain amount of capital today to get something tomorrow—will lead to varying investment values for the same business to different individuals. This notion rings true psychologically, but it has been pretty much banished from MPT, where the rules allow for little customization. Moreover, Williams states that individuals should use their personal rate of interest when making investment decisions. Yet he has not a word about how the personal rate might differ from the general rate. That latter rate, he says, should be used by analysts looking at the market as a whole.[27]

Leaving the personal discount rate aside, Williams proceeds to work out the market's general discount rate. Here too he is arbitrary, but simply accepts as standard a model based on a so-called risk-free rate: "The customary way to find the value of a risky security has always been to add a 'premium for risk' to the pure interest rate, and then use the sum as the interest rate for discounting future receipts."[28] For Williams, the pure interest rate is the cost of borrowing for the highest-quality government and private securities. This structure of defining a risk-free rate and then adding some amount extra for the investment under consideration survives to this day. It is fundamentally a relative notion—what if the risk-free rate is abnormally low or high?

Williams essentially leaves the equity risk premium undefined. Instead, he arbitrarily asserts that for "good stocks, horizontal trend" (re: flat dividend) a 5.75% discount rate had been used in the past, a 4.75% rate was being used in the period of low rates in the mid-1930s, and a 5.75% rate would be the appropriate rate in the future.[29] For an argument that is as tightly argued as Williams's, this is a loose formulation. In his case studies, Williams employs existing prices to back out the equity risk premium. For instance, he suggests using a discount rate of 4.75% for GM based on its June 1937 dividend of $2.90 per share versus a 10-year Treasury rate at the time of 3%. In his forecast, the dividend remains at this level. By our standards, that's a low equity risk premium (1.75%), but Williams views his calculation as being high, and deservedly so, because "industrial enterprises . . . have the habit of going to seed eventually, with only the best being able to survive for two or three generations."[30] He thinks rates will rise, so proposes using the 5.75% rate for later years. He then very simply suggests that the right discount rate for GM should be the average of the two—5.25%.[31] The same back-of-the-envelope math is applied later to United States Steel where he again suggests 5.25% for the enterprise, 5% for the higher-rated senior securities, and 5.5% for the lower-ranked common equity. In the case of the country's leading steel manufacturer, he allows for a decline in the equity risk premium over a period of several decades due to "the reappraisal of the risk factor as the company gradually proved its worth."[32]

Williams admits the difficulty of making long-term forecasts, joining Graham and Keynes in recognizing the uncertainty factor. But Williams dismisses it somewhat blithely, suggesting that the current price of a security essentially has long-term forecasts embedded in it. His work simply makes those forecasts more explicit.[33] Williams appears generally content to use the risk measures implied in the markets at the time, with some modest adjustments given his view that rates would be moving up. For a person determined to introduce mathematical rigor to the investment process, this is a circular and flabby offering, but it highlights the challenge faced by all of us all of the time—making decisions under conditions of uncertainty: "A careful estimate of the probabilities is all that the investor has to go on; beyond that he has to take his chances with uncertainty, just as does the field marshal in going into battle, or the young man in choosing a career."[34]

Although Williams falls short of banishing uncertainty, his work is clearly an improvement over what went before in that he frames the challenge of forecasting and discounting dividends, even if he cannot solve for it definitively. And he certainly believes that having an intellectual framework, albeit one that is incomplete, is superior to the environment that created the 1920s excesses and the subsequent Crash:

Had there been any general agreement among analysts themselves concerning the proper criteria of value, such enormous fluctuations should not have occurred, because the long-run prospects for dividends have not in fact changed as much as prices have. . . . Is not one cause of the past volatility of stocks the lack of a sound theory of Investment Value? Since this volatility of stocks helps in turn to make the business cycle itself more severe, may not advances in Investment Analysis prove a real help in reducing the damage done by the cycle?[35]

In that assertion, Williams foreshadows an important claim that would emerge to the fore in the postwar period: that with a proper theory of investment, risk itself might be materially reduced, if not entirely removed.

Finally, like Graham before him, Williams assumes that diversification can minimize the potential for loss. He states it and then moves on: "Strictly speaking, however, there is no risk in buying the [security] in question if its price is right. Given adequate diversification, gains on such purchases will offset losses, and return at the pure interest rate will be obtained. Thus the *net risk* turns out to be nil."[36]

Similarities and Differences

Taken together, Graham, Keynes, and Williams offered not a plan, but a plan for a plan. They were in clear agreement on the difference between speculation and investment and the analytical effort required for the latter.[37] And they were equally clear in calling for a businesslike approach to the stock market. Williams quotes Alfred Marshall in observing that "everything of importance which is now known to economists has long been acted upon by able business men, though they may not have been able to express their knowledge clearly."[38] Graham makes a similar point, observing that businesspeople, upon entering the stock market, cast aside that very analytical approach that made them successful in the first place. In the final chapter, we return to this notion, that an investment portfolio should at its heart be treated as any other business venture. If you want a good analysis of your stock portfolio, take it to a successful businessperson. Sum up the amount of capital deployed, the net (after fees) income stream derived from that capital, and the volatility of that income stream, and see if it passes the sniff test. I fear most orthodox MPT portfolios would not.

But the differences between the three are equally significant. Today Keynes is read and often critiqued.[39] Graham and Dodd's work is read and usually worshiped. Williams is respected but just cited. There's a reason for that. *The Theory of Investment Value* is filled with enough math to chase away many a non-quant. The math is not exceptionally complex—basic and extended algebraic formulas—but there is an awful lot of it for the tastes of most businesspeople and investors. The text is enlivened somewhat between the formulas by more than a few jabs at the Roosevelt administration and organized labor. Those comments aside, Williams's worldview is rigid and mechanical, without the subtlety of a Keynes or the applicability and wit of a Graham and Dodd.[40] For all his practical investment experience, Williams offers just theory, not practice. Putting his formulas into action would be difficult to do without the everyday experiences of Graham and Dodd or the forest-level insights of Keynes.

The spurt of intellectual productivity in the mid-1930s was not sustained. From then on until the appearance of Markowitz in the 1950s, there was not much development in the art or science of investing, which was not surprising given the events of the intervening period. Circa 1952, when Markowitz published his first article, investing in stocks was pretty much the same as it had been in the calmer moments of the prewar period. The focus was on individual stocks, and the analysis—such as it was—was mostly subjective and centered on the dividend or the look of the price chart.

The Evolution of Benjamin Graham

To the extent that there was any analytical progress, it came from none other than Benjamin Graham. The third edition of *Security Analysis* came out in 1951. As Graham wrote in the preface, this version was not so much revised as rewritten. Gone were the extended digressions on the failures of the

1920s and the early 1930s. The stock analysis section was given greater prominence by being moved from the second half of the book to the first, switching places with the analysis of bonds. More importantly, the valuation of common stocks was materially fleshed out. The formula for intrinsic value was not much changed—"that value which is justified by the facts—e.g., assets, earnings, dividends, definite prospects" and calculated by multiplying "indicated average future earning power" by a "capitalization factor."[41] And Graham continued to emphasize that value investing among the available options is his preferred modus operandi: "We incline strongly to the belief that this last criterion—a price far less than value to a private owner—will constitute a sound touchstone for the discovery of true investment opportunities in common stocks."[42]

But there were some notable shifts in emphasis. Graham circa 1951 has recovered intellectually from the 1929 Crash and is looking forward into the postwar period. As a result, he takes a much more positive view of common stocks, writing that "a longer perspective permits us to view the roaring new-era stock market as a unique phenomenon. It still carries valuable lessons and warnings, but it need not control our basic attitude toward stock investment. The time is indeed 'twenty years after,' and like Dumas' musketeers, we can all take a mature view of those tumultuous events."[43] To that end, he is far more willing than he had previously been to look into the future and forecast company earnings and dividends and to imagine growth in both. In Graham 1951 one can also see signs of an increasing "present value" sensibility that was not noted in Graham 1934 and is hard not to attribute to the work of John Burr Williams. It is reflected in observations such as "The present investment value of a common stock essentially depends upon the future income to be expected from it."[44]

In regard to the key elements of what would become Modern Portfolio Theory, however, Graham 1951 is still on the sidelines. For his capitalization rate (P/E ratio), he still eschews an explanation other than to write that "the multiplier takes into account a large number of valuation elements, such as the expected stability of earnings, the expected growth factor, the expected dividend policy—all of which may be comprehended in the 'quality' of the company—and perhaps the assets behind the shares."[45] Over time, however, that multiplier has crept up, and he observes that a multiple of 15 has become standard for much of the quality end of the market. He prefers a range but is frank about how approximate the whole exercise is: "For reasons difficult to defend in detail, we favor a range from 8 to 18, with a midpoint of 13. (The figure of 15 for the Dow Jones group reflects its higher-than-average over-all quality.) The choice of the specific multiplier will be made by the analyst without benefit of definite formula."[46] It is worth noting that had Graham offered that type of open-ended, subjective answer today, he would have had a hard time passing the CFA® exam.

Graham 1951 remains a steady proponent of diversification:

Diversification is almost a necessary adjunct of the margin-of-safety [buying below intrinsic value] idea. A single issue for less than it is fairly worth may still "go sour"' for some special reason and produce a loss. A group of twenty or more such issues will average out the individual favorable and unfavorable developments. Thus if the margin of safety is soundly calculated it should have full opportunity to create profits in the aggregate result.[47]

Notice, please, that Graham appears to see reasonable diversification at the "twenty or more" level, not the many hundreds or even a 1,000 or more holdings that diversification has come to mean today. The number of holdings necessary to be successfully diversified has become a central issue within Modern Portfolio Theory. Please keep in mind Graham's view when we address the topic in Chapter 4.

Heading into a period that would be overwhelmingly based on—if not overwhelmed by—quantitative analysis and the assumption that weighted probabilities are always and everywhere superior to subjective judgments, Graham remains steadfast in emphasizing qualitative factors. Yes, do the math, but do not be blinded by it. Experience, wisdom, and judgment play a major role in Graham's investment process. In recent decades, the pendulum has swung far in the direction of taking individual judgment out of the investment equation. Has it swung too far?

Somewhat ironically, Graham's most direct statements in regard to portfolios and risk came not in his thick book for professionals, *Security Analysis*, but in a thinner work for individual investors, *The Intelligent Investor: A Book of Practical Counsel*, which first appeared in 1949. (Like *Security Analysis*, it would go through many editions in the decades after it was initially published.) In it, Graham lays out two basic approaches for investors, one for the defensively minded in which he suggests a combination of secure, fixed income assets—at that time he preferred U.S. savings bonds—and a portfolio of 10 to 50 high-quality common stocks to safeguard the income stream against inflation. The bonds would represent 25% to 75% of the portfolio depending on the individual. In his aggressive portfolio, for the "enterprising," the formula was much the same, just more in the way of common stocks with greater return potential. In his mind, the aggressive portfolio could roughly double the return of the "safe" portfolio without taking much additional risk.

That's the rub. Are not risk and return correlated? Is that not the whole point of Modern Portfolio Theory? Graham acknowledges that "it is an old and sound principle that those who cannot afford to take risks should be content with a low return on their invested funds,"[48] but he moves beyond that notion to suggest a different correlation, not that of risk and return, but of effort and return. Little effort leads to little return; more effort to more return. "The minimum return goes to our passive investor who wants both safety and freedom from concern."[49] His defensive investors include the usual widows, but also most nonprofessional investors:

The majority of security owners should elect the defensive classification. They do not have the time, or the determination, or the mental equipment to embark upon investing as a quasi business. They should therefore be satisfied with the reasonably good return obtainable from a defensive portfolio, and they should stoutly resist the current temptation to increase this return by deviating into other paths.[50]

In contrast, for Graham and others of his ilk, "The maximum return would be realized by the alert and enterprising investor who exercises maximum intelligence and skill. In many cases, there may be less real risk associated with buying a 'bargain issue' offering the chance of a large profit than with a conventional bond purchase yielding under 3 per cent."[51]

Having made this distinction about effort, Graham proceeds to offer his nontraditional definition of risk:

The idea of risk is often extended to apply to a possible decline in the price of a security, even though the decline may be of a cyclical and temporary nature and even though the holder is unlikely to be forced to sell at such times. . . . But we believe that what is here involved is not a true risk in the useful sense of the terms. . . . The risk attached to an ordinary commercial business is measured by the chance of its losing money, not by what would happen if the owner were forced to sell.[52]

Thank you yet again, Benjamin Graham. Post-Markowitz, risk is defined as mostly price movement—versus expected return—and how asset prices move together. That's the "rule" and has been for 50 years. It determines how your portfolio is run and measured. But here, from none other than Benjamin Graham, is an entirely different definition of risk, one that more or less ignores daily price movements in favor of the underlying business and long-term trends. "Many common stocks do involve [genuine] risks of such deterioration. But it is our thesis that a properly executed group investment in common stocks does not carry any substantial risk of this sort and that therefore it should not be termed 'risky' merely because of the element of price fluctuation."[53] *In effect, prices may move around, but that is not necessarily risk.* To be sure, Graham's definition of risk is somewhat different than the one I will propose later in this work. My point, however, is that the monopoly on definitions that has been in place for the past half century need not be accepted and remain unchallenged. Alternatives were available in the past, and should be again in the future.

In the aftermath of the Crash and the Great Depression, Benjamin Graham, John Maynard Keynes, and John Burr Williams started a meaningful conversation about investing which Harry Markowitz encountered as he entered graduate school in the postwar period. Williams and Keynes, in particular, had given the academics something to assess, criticize, and develop further. And that is precisely what they did.

3

The March of Progress—
The Emergence of MPT

*One thing badly needed by investors—and a quality
they rarely seem to have—is a sense of financial
history.*

—Benjamin Graham, *The Intelligent Investor*, xxvi

The story of how MPT emerged in the postwar period has been told and told well. But the context that explains its adoption and entrenchment has not, and that is the purpose of this chapter. The first part has already been identified: MPT emerged from the analytical near vacuum that characterized the prewar period, especially the decades prior to the Crash of 1929 and the Great Depression. After this "ruleless" period, a basic system of guidelines had, not surprisingly, a good chance of being welcomed. Graham, Keynes, and Williams had laid down a foundation in the 1930s, but little progress was made to turn those first steps into a systematic theory of portfolio investment. The second major contextual factor was the quantification of human behavior sweeping through the social sciences at the same time as the effort to figure out the capital markets. That is taken up in greater detail at the start of this chapter. The third factor was the economic development and prosperity that characterized the postwar decades and provided the raw material—the wealth—upon which the investment industry grew. Together these conditions created the environment in which MPT could emerge, take hold, and become accepted wisdom. Usually this story is told as an example of *the march of progress* or of *truths discovered.* It is part of the broader narrative of the postwar intellectual triumphs that included discovering a vaccine for polio and putting a man on the moon, among others. It reflected the widespread expectation of permanently eradicating a wide variety of societal ills.

In the narrower endeavor of finance, MPT is treated as a great *final* achievement: it was as if time had stopped after the discovery of *the* definitive answer on how to tame risk, banish investment uncertainty, and dramatically reduce the ups and downs of the business cycle. While this chapter focuses on how MPT came to be viewed as the solution to our core investment challenges, my purpose is not just to review the history, but to suggest that MPT arose in a specific historical context, which most certainly served the needs of the time. A half century later, however, it has become equally clear that it is far from the universal and timeless solution that most market participants accept it to be.

The Quantification of Human Behavior

The appearance of a thoroughly quantitative approach to investments occurred almost exactly on cue. If anything, investment was late to the party, not surprising given that finance itself was just coming into its own as an organized discipline. But in other areas of the human experience, the wave of quantification was already well advanced by the time Harry Markowitz put some numbers around the investment process in the 1950s and William Sharpe simplified the formulas in the 1960s. The intellectual roots of quantification were much older. Indeed, systems of taxation emerged necessarily with the appearance of organized, hierarchical societies thousands of years ago. The kings (pharaohs, emperors, etc.) and their tax collectors needed to know if their subjects were meeting their obligations. The very first written human artifacts of which we know—cuneiform tablets—were essentially tax ledgers. The emergence of the census followed in the same manner: keeping track of people to be taxed. You have certainly heard that the Romans ordered a census of Judea around 2,000 years ago. You may know that 1,000 years ago, the English king, William the Conqueror, threatened by invasion from Denmark, ordered a detailed survey of his kingdom so that he knew what resources—including tax payments—would be available for his defense of the realm. The result was the Domesday Book.

The quantification of human affairs was limited to census taking and taxation until around 1600. It was at this point that more sophisticated calculations began to enter the picture. A variety of Westerners who had learned of more advanced mathematics invented by the Greeks, Arabs, and Chinese did something these innovators had not: they applied that math to human affairs, or more specifically, they applied math to the task of making money. Gambling was one way to make money, and math could help there by creating an understanding of the probabilities of expected returns. In 1654, Blaise Pascal and Pierre de Fermat—two gods of modern math—had a brief correspondence about card playing, the result of which was the foundation of modern statistics, especially in regard to "expected value." A few years later, the scientist and astronomer Christian Huygens contributed his *On Reasoning in Games of Chance.* Insurance was another way to make (or lose) money, and math could play a role there as well. In 1663, the Englishman John Graunt published *Natural and Political Observations upon the Bills of Mortality,* greatly advancing the math behind the insurance industry. Three decades later Edmund Halley—of Halley's comet fame—founded modern actuarial science by using data from Breslau in Germany, of all places, to value life annuities correctly. In 1725, Abraham de Moivre published *Annuities on Lives,* much to the relief of life insurers everywhere.

In this remarkable period, roughly 1650 to 1725, the initial quantification of certain human affairs came together in a loose and baggy sort of way.[1] All that followed for the next 150 years was refinement, propelled by the Enlightenment project to know, understand, and master our universe. That broader project represented a dramatic shift from a worldview of cowering individuals always on a knife's edge, to individuals with the notion—perhaps only an illusion—that they understood the world around them, and then to go a step further, that they might actually be in control of their fate. That lofty goal was hatched by the salon intellectuals of the eighteenth century and became widespread in the nineteenth century. The key was observation, quantification, and the discovery of underlying mechanical or physical "laws." Almost all the great scientific discoveries of that period—germ theory, the periodic table, electromagnetism, etc.—were the result of this math-heavy method. The era's incredible faith in numbers is reflected in the famous statement by English physicist Lord Kelvin in 1883: "I often say that when you can measure what you are speaking about, and express it in numbers, you know something about it; but when you cannot measure it, when you cannot express it in numbers, your knowledge is of a meagre and unsatisfactory kind."[2] The new gold standard was simple: If your approach was not quantitative, then it wasn't science. If it wasn't science, then it wasn't going to matter.

By the late nineteenth century, the natural sciences were well on their way to being fully categorized, explained, and reduced to mathematical formulas. Much work remained in physics, where the underlying, fundamental forces were still being discovered, but the path was clear. Now the focus turned to society itself. Although tax collection, insurance, and gambling had already been effectively mathematized, little else in the study of human affairs was until the second half of the nineteenth century. For these emerging areas of inquiry, however, the course was obvious: embrace quantitative methods as quickly and thoroughly as possible.

The term "social sciences" was not broadly used until the twentieth century, but by its very name, the concept suggested that human activity could be understood with the same precision as chemistry, geology, and mathematics. This new scientific approach to human affairs emerged in the nineteenth century and was aggressively applied in the early twentieth century with the goal of understanding and mastering society in the same decisive manner that the natural world had been conquered by science in the previous century. In the academy, for instance, politics and narrative political history became political science, by which the application of rules—sometimes quantitative rules—became the norm for understanding political activity.

Not surprisingly, this call to quantify was particularly strong in economics. Prior to this period, most economics was what might be considered theoretical or narrative. Of course, Smith, Ricardo, Malthus, and Marx used statistics. But they were more interested in the way human nature shaped economies than the way economies framed human nature. The new, quantitative economics put the role of human nature aside by simply assuming a "utility-maximizing" rationality (*Homo economicus*) and proceeding to the empirical, quantitative analysis. Macroeconomics, microeconomics, and econometrics were all built on pure Newtonian science: observe, quantify, and reduce to equations. Mathematical modeling with a heavy dose of probability and statistics became mandatory for serious economics. Although the process had made some headway in the late nineteenth century, Alfred Marshall's *Principles of Economics* of 1890 was still really in the old model. It reads now like a cheerful Victorian novel; all's well that ends well.[3] The great leap forward in quantification of human economic relations occurred as a result of the 1929 Crash and the Great Depression and the serious academic effort thrown at economics and data collection in the 1930s and thereafter. (For example, the journal *Econometrica*—the name says it all—was founded in 1933.) By the 1950s, the quants had prevailed. Their standard bearer was MIT professor Paul Samuelson, who offered the first comprehensive, post-Marshall textbook of macroeconomics, precisely rendered in mathematical equations. Samuelson took his mechanical cues from the emerging science of thermodynamics, which he then diligently applied to the economic "system."[4]

Quantification of our understanding of finance and stock markets would take a little longer, and for good reason: the capital markets were only just coming into their own early in the twentieth century. But these markets were not likely to remain qualitative and without rules for long. Moreover, the shock of the stock market Crash required some sort of explanation and remediation. This is the intellectual primordial soup from which MPT emerges. And the main players bought into it. The Cowles Commission, which was gathering data about the stock market at this time, adopted the motto, "Science Is Measurement."[5] Williams most certainly bought into it: he states outright in his preface that the first aim of his book is "to outline a new sub-science that shall be known as the Theory of Investment Value [as a branch] of the larger science of Economics."[6] Keynes wanted to buy into it but acknowledged the significance of nonquantitative factors—the animal spirits—that drive human decision making. Rationality may be an ideal worth moving toward, but looking at the capital markets, he didn't see too much of it. Benjamin Graham was somewhere in the middle, wanting the rigor and discipline of a quantitative analytical framework but not handing over the investment decision to the counting machines: "Mathematics is ordinarily considered as producing precise and dependable results; but in the stock market the more elaborate and abstruse the mathematics, the more uncertain and speculative are the conclusions we draw therefrom."[7] And that was penned in 1949, well before the quants had steamrollered the investment process into a series of unequivocal mathematical outcomes.

Don't misinterpret me: measurement is good, and the move to analyze human behavior in measured form was an enormous improvement in understanding over what went before it. But as is often the case with new methods, the expectations of how much benefit would be derived were too high. Practitioners believed that these new tools—as if by magic—could explain everything in the past and could predict the future without fail. And it's not just that humans are emotional and subject to various biases in a way that carbon atoms and rock formations and bacteria and triangle sides are not. It's also that quantification of the natural world is in most cases neutral in a political or normative sense. But in the social sciences, that is almost never the case. It is hard to imagine a less neutral setting than the analysis of economics, politics, etc. If it's about humans, it's political; and if it's political, attempts at a rigid quantification are going to be fraught with difficulties.

In regard to financial matters, the allure of quantification may have been even greater than in other social sciences because *money* was at stake. Cue the song from *Cabaret*: "It makes the world go 'round." Or for a more academic take,

The allure of a unifying, perfect mathematical formula with which to generate a fortune from financial markets is powerful. It is as irresistible to the quant nerds as the formula for turning dross into gold was to the alchemists. . . . In the frequently irrational financial markets, mathematic models offer the hope of cool reason and certitude, a sort of godlike wisdom.[8]

Observe how in the financial media many of the quantitative hedge-fund gurus are regarded as omnipotent, the supposed "smartest people in the room." They appear to know the secret words, the abracadabra formula to creating vast wealth. Yet I would argue that bringing the promise of certainty to the fundamentally human challenge of decision making—in this case, about money—under the typically prevailing conditions of profound uncertainty was a bridge too far, a promise too great, a grasp beyond the reach of the promoters of the quantitative arts. This is the crux of the matter. If you view it as I do, the critique of MPT flows naturally. If you are of a view that most or all human behavior can be easily and surely reduced to precise formulas, you will object to just about everything that follows. This distinction is not a matter of finance or mathematics at all; it is one of personal philosophy and worldview.

MPT—A Short History

It is impossible for anyone who is serious about investment and the history of investments in the U.S. stock market not to have a tremendous respect for the journalist and investment advisor Peter Bernstein. Over a multidecade career, he chronicled the development of investing and did so with great intelligence and enthusiasm. And he lived long enough to capture the evolution of a system he was clearly enamored with. His works should be read and reread by those in the investment industry if they wish to know whence they came. I wish he were still alive to offer a spirited rebuttal to this critique. (He passed away in 2009 at the age of 90.) I hope his intellectual heirs will do him proud in that function. What follows is a brief history of the creation and dissemination of Modern Portfolio Theory. It covers some of the same territory as Bernstein's *Capital Ideas: The Improbable Origins of Modern Wall Street* (1992) and a follow-up volume, *Capital Ideas Evolving* (2007). He told the story in long form. I will be moving along quickly. The facts, names, dates, and specific innovations will be the same (albeit summarized), but the interpretation will be quite different, in many instances the exact opposite of how Bernstein saw the developments he relayed and embraced.

Bernstein treated the emergence of the rules of MPT as little short of revelation, and he saw the graduate students and finance professors who came up with the formulas as the heroes who conquered Manhattan: "In their quiet way the academics eventually overcame the old guard and liberated the city of capital. Before they were done, they had transformed today's wealth of nations and the lives of all of us, as citizens, savers, and breadwinners." His text boils over with things that are "novel," "innovative," and "new." From

Bernstein's perch, modern capital markets theory had basically vanquished serious risk and all but stopped the up-and-down stock market cycle:

The innovations triggered by the revolution in finance and investing . . . helped investors deal with uncertainty. They provide benchmarks for determining whether expectations are realistic or fanciful and whether risks make sense or are foolish. . . . They have reformulated such familiar concepts as risk, return, diversification, insurance, and debt. Moreover, they have quantified these concepts and have suggested new ways of employing them and combining them for optimal results. Finally, they have added a measure of science to the art of corporate finance.[9]

Sixty years after the initial development of MPT and forty years after it made the leap from the lecture hall to your retirement account, most investors still treat the basic tenets of MPT as truisms consistent with Bernstein's characterizations. Even those individuals who work in the financial services industry, and who have at least some sense of the system's shortcomings, still accept the tenets of MPT as universal rules to live by.

Bernstein's journalism is not limited to MPT. In *Capital Ideas* and his other works, he presents and embraces numerous other financial innovations, but the main thrust of his narrative is the new and very specific understanding of risk and return that emerged with Markowitz and how it came to dominate the investment industry. My purpose here is twofold: to place those developments in the context of a particular time and place and to suggest that Bernstein conflates complexity with progress. These new tools did not represent a Fukuyama-esque "end" of financial history. They did not achieve time-stopping perfection, and most importantly they did not put an end to economic cyclicality and its manifestation in a volatile stock market. Note the continuation of major "corrections" of the market in the modern era: 1987, 2000–2001, and 2008–2009. Indeed, one can argue—as I will in the following chapter—that MPT has contributed mightily to those major downdrafts by creating the illusion that the periodic crises couldn't and shouldn't happen again given the widespread application of the new tools.

Markowitz (and Roy)

Bernstein's tale reminds me of Michelangelo's purported statement that every stone block has a statue inside waiting to be released. In our story, the sculptor of MPT hailed not from central Italy, but from Chicago. Born in 1927, Harry Markowitz was the only child of immigrant parents who owned a small grocery store. As he wrote in his Nobel Prize autobiography, "We lived in a nice apartment, always had enough to eat, and I had my own room. I never was aware of the Great Depression."[10] Revolutionaries and heroes come from a variety of backgrounds, but the young and by most accounts personally demure Markowitz seemed an unlikely candidate to change the course of history.

Nevertheless, the investment industry treats Markowitz in almost biblical terms, with the publication of his first article, in 1952, as year 1 of the modern era. As Bernstein recounts, the prophet of the new age was unheralded, a graduate student writing an article on an atypical topic in the only academic journal of the time dedicated to finance, very little of which concerned the stock market. The article would appear, as would a book seven years later, to almost no effect. Further refinements in the idea would occur in the middle of the following decade (the 1960s), also to almost no effect. Investors

were still safe from Modern Portfolio Theory, though the academics were increasingly siding with it.

But let's give credit where credit is due. Markowitz tackled
two related, very legitimate issues unresolved from the investment climate that he inherited. The first was how to define risk,
and the second was shifting the understanding of risk from the
individual investment level to that of the portfolio as a whole.
Markowitz's original idea—his major contribution to modern
finance—is that the answer to these two questions is one and
the same: risk *is* how the portfolio performs, not how the individual assets do. And the specific measurement of risk then
becomes not how much money is made or lost from an individual security, but how the overall portfolio of assets performs
versus expectations, as the separate components of it go up and
down. That is, what is the variance of the portfolio's overall
return versus the expected return? As Markowitz put it simply,
"The investor does (or should) consider expected return a desirable thing *and* variance of return an undesirable thing."[11]

Prior to Markowitz, some degree of diversification was
assumed, but only as a secondary factor in investment. As
Bernstein wrote, "The literature on investing up to 1952
had either ignored the interplay between risk and return or
had treated it in a most casual manner."[12] Unless you were a
Carnegie, you diversified to reduce risk, with the danger of
not doing so being basically undefined and certainly unquantified. There was no detailed reasoning about why diversification made sense and no way to measure its benefits. Indeed,
the opposite was true. If an individual had a series of investment options and was hoping to maximize his or her return
(and who doesn't want to get the most out of his or her investment dollar?), the tendency would be to put the assets in a less
diversified portfolio, perhaps even in a single venture that one
felt had the greatest prospects.

But diversification required more justification than Shakespeare's poetic turn of phrase from *The Merchant of Venice* or a rejection of Carnegie's "eggs-in-one-basket" bluster in order to be accepted by the newly ascendant "everything-must-be-quantified" crowd. It required mathematical precision, and that's what Markowitz provided. For Williams and to some extent the early Graham (he assumed reasonable diversification but aimed for maximum value), expected return was preeminent. After you have focused on achieving that, yes, a bit of diversification is the right thing to do to provide a degree of protection. Markowitz goes a long way to reversing that order. In his 1952 article, "Portfolio Selection," he raises diversification from an assumed and secondary status to the primary means of achieving what he considers to be the most desirable outcome for investors. And for Markowitz, that outcome is getting the maximum return for a given level of volatility or variance around the expected return. Or if the goal is defined from the other factor—an expected return— then the best outcome is to have the minimum amount of volatility (variance) on the way to that investment return target. Here for the first time was an analytical construct showing the relationship between risk and return, and demonstrating that to achieve greater return, you would likely have to endure greater risk, defined as variance around your expected outcome. If you were content to accept less return, you would benefit from having less overall movement in the portfolio. In this view of the world, risk and return were correlated, and there was an ideal combination of assets for any given toleration of risk or expectation of return.

If you plot those goals—expected return on one hand and expected variance of portfolio return on the other—you get a series of optimal portfolios that constitute a curved line, which Markowitz deemed to be the "efficient frontier." It was a great name for an intellectual construct, and it endures to this day, far more so than does the underlying math. Bernstein acknowledges that Markowitz's work really is just "homey" advice: nothing ventured, nothing gained, an anti-Carnegie "Don't put all your eggs in one basket." But it is done systematically and mathematically, and that was entirely new. Well, almost completely new. At just the same time, an Englishman, Arthur Roy, came up with a nearly identical analysis and formulation. The title of his work, "Safety First and the Holding of Assets," captured the point of the exercise—the focus on the portfolio and the elevation of diversification to a primary goal.[13]

More than 60 years later, a few points about this argument stand out. First, figuring out how assets move together was not a trivial exercise in 1952. Getting the right "covariances" for each asset versus each other asset was almost beyond the technology of the time. With the passage of the years, that challenge became less of a problem due to advances in computing capability. But even before processing capacity picked up materially, the obstacle was essentially overcome one decade later in the mid-1960s when William Sharpe and several others came up with a simplification that got rid of the need for massive security-to-security covariance tables.

Second, Markowitz offers no formula for expected return. You just come up with one for each possible investment and then plug that into the calculations. That flaw—flaw in the sense that it involves a lot of ultimately subjective forecasts and a lot of calculations—was also solved a decade later (again by Sharpe et al.) with another simple formula to predict expected outcomes.

Third, Markowitz's definition of risk as the variance around an expected return remains pretty much unchallenged. I want to focus on that. It's the keystone to our

Markowitzian investment world, but I would suggest that we step back and acknowledge that there are other ways to define risk. Benjamin Graham offered a qualitative one centered on effort, and he more or less rejected near-term price fluctuation—at the heart of Markowitz's definition—as risk at all. But even within the more quantitative realm, there are other ways to define risk. Seven years after publishing his article, Markowitz provided a fuller view of his quantified risk and return calculations in book form.[14] In it, he explicitly leaves the definition of "return" from an investment open to the investor. As a practical matter, it can be income, share price movement, low volatility, or some combination of all of the above.[15] Markowitz also acknowledges that risk can be imagined in many ways. He defines six of them, all based on the total return performance—income plus asset price movement—in the public marketplace: standard deviation, semivariance, expected value of loss, expected absolute deviation, probability of loss, and maximum loss. He then mathematically proceeds to show that the standard deviation (the square root of the variance) of returns is the most appropriate measure of risk.[16]

Let me now hint at the one that I will offer in the final chapter of this book. As a businessperson, I understand that the health of my real estate business—a moonlighting position to my day job as a financial asset manager—can be clearly seen and measured in the cashflows that it generates and that can be distributed to the company owners—my wife and myself. If the cashflows are going up and the gains are sustainable, that's good and my business is likely worth more rather than less, certainly from a discounted cashflow (Williams) perspective and very likely from the perspective of a thoughtful investor who might be interested in paying for a stake in the enterprise (Graham). The same is true on the way down. Either way, day in and day out, I'm running the business and am close to those cashflows that can be accessed and distributed to company owners. Now and again, someone comes along and offers me a sum for part or all of the business. (This is Benjamin Graham's famous "Mr. Market.") The person may be coming up with a price based on the cashflows—if he or she knows them—or on some other factor such as what other properties in the neighborhood have been selling for. Perhaps I accept the bid; perhaps I don't. An hour, a day, a week, a month, or a year later, the prospective buyers keep coming back and offering a variety of prices. Sometimes the offers are more than the previous ones, sometimes less. If you were that businessperson, how would you define risk? Would it be in terms of the rise and fall of the cashflows that your time, energy, and assets generated, and that are real and can be taken out of the business, or would it be the rise or fall of an external bid price for the asset from an outsider? In the stock market, everything is about that bid price. But is the daily repricing of assets—few of which change materially day to day as businesses—a very good way to define risk? I don't think so, and yet that is how risk is defined in Modern Portfolio Theory. The prices on the stock market should reflect the underlying conditions of the listed businesses, but as a practical matter they do not, except over very long measurement periods. In the near term, it's all about the prices of the moment, and often only the moment.

There's nothing wrong with an obsessive, minute-by-minute focus on share prices. It can be fun; it might be profitable. It's just not sober, long-term business ownership. Before Markowitz, all questions of investment versus speculation had been at the individual security level (Graham, Williams), not their interaction or at the overall portfolio level. This is the real handicap that MPT overcame, but it also was a

Trojan horse, carrying a focus on asset prices and a definition of risk that has, some 60 years later, shown itself full of undesirable outcomes, including having bad investments justified in places where they shouldn't be—think the tech stocks in retirement portfolios right before the tech bubble burst nearly two decades ago—all in the name of asset diversification and covariance minimization, the hallmarks of MPT. While it was not Markowitz's intent 60 years ago to build a system of intelligent speculation, his definition of risk has had the consequence many decades later of having too many investors focus on the fleeting and largely irrelevant, and as a result turning much of the investment community into gamblers who don't realize they are gambling at all.

Ultimately, cashflows determine value. Fisher, Williams, Graham and Dodd, even Markowitz—and *any person on the planet who has ever run or owned a business*—subscribe to this view. Why not define risk in terms of those cashflows, their stability, their growth rates? Investment in a business should be about the business, not a disembodied share price that can appear to have a life of its own. This is one of the ways that Graham discusses risk, as the business risk to the enterprise, not the superficial matter of the share price moving around. But we've gotten ahead of ourselves. That's a preview of Chapter 5, where I sketch out an investment approach based on the underlying cashflows of an asset and not the ever-changing share price. But for now, it may be helpful to keep the distinction between asset prices and asset utility (cashflows) as we work through the development of the existing system.

It is grossly unfair to lay the flaws of today's stock market at the feet of a young Harry Markowitz. He was not a practitioner; he was a curious, mathematically inclined intellectual trying to figure out a challenging optimization problem. Also, his system operated at the level of a theory, not a precise model. Like others working on theoretical problems, he took lots of shortcuts, as he should have, to make broader points. And Markowitz 1952 was being quite general. He didn't specify types of assets; he just referred to portfolios that had varying expected returns and internal covariances. And the earliest Markowitz didn't even bother to define "return." It was just a number that the investor was supposed to provide. Recall as well that Markowitz and his intellectual predecessors were still working in the long shadows of the 1920s–1930s boom-and-bust market to come up with a better "system." Those are all good reasons not to blame Markowitz for the U.S. stock market all too often looking like a casino rather than the world's premier business investment platform. But the main reason Markowitz's initial analysis is so reasonable is that, as we saw in the previous chapter, the investment universe circa 1952 was dramatically different from our own. Unlike today, all but a handful of equities had robust dividends, reflecting their underlying cashflows. Some had higher yields, some lower yields, but the overall yield of the stock market in 1952 was nearly 6% compared with around 2% for the past two decades. The payout ratio— the dividend payment as a percentage of profits—was about 2/3 then versus 1/3 today. Other than in the late 1920s, the late 1960s, and the late 1990s, stock prices have more or less generally reflected the trajectory of the dividend, just as in a real business. Although Benjamin Graham was allowing some prospective growth in dividends in his 1951 analysis— that is, the stocks were expected to go up in value in line with the dividend growth—the majority of return would still come from the dividend stream. On the fixed income side, bonds were held for their coupon, not for their price movement. High-yield bonds and emerging market bonds—where the return comes as much if not more from the price move-ment—would have occupied a tiny percentage of the market, if they were available at all to mainstream investors.

In effect, the return for traditional portfolios at the time when Markowitz outlined his approach would have been mostly the income return—the dividend from stocks; and the coupons from bonds—and for companies doing well, some growth in that dividend that would be recognized by the market with a higher share price over time. If that is the case—and not everyone would agree with my characterization of the earlier stock market as a primarily income- as opposed to price-driven market—Markowitz essentially *is* defining risk in terms of income streams. Indeed, his assertion that investors prefer return that is "dependable, stable, not subject to uncertainty"[17] fits in nicely with an investment approach based on income streams, and perhaps better than a theory trying to capture the more fickle return patterns based on daily asset repricing in the stock market. Markowitz 1952 and 1959 could not have made a major distinction between income-based and non-income-based returns at the time, because he wasn't an investor, wasn't assuming and probably could not conceive of a day when non- or low-income-paying securities could constitute serious investment portfolios and utterly dominate the U.S. market, and generally subscribed to the cash-focused view of Williams in regard to individual security valuation. It's easy to read Markowitz now and see MPT as a covariance minimization strategy for *price-based outcomes in the casino,* but that's projecting today's gambling-like environment back into the past. The problem is not what Markowitz (and Sharpe and the others) sketched out in the 1950s and 1960s as a solution to the problems and questions that had arisen over the previous 30 years; it's what it has become in practice over the subsequent decades.

Simplifying with Sharpe
(Lintner, Treynor, and Mossin)

Markowitz's system as originally articulated in 1952 was simply too complicated to be anything other than a theoretical notion. Just for the companies of the S&P 500 Index, which came into being in 1957, an analyst would need to calculate 124,750 covariances as well as 500 expected returns. Even in 1952, there were other stocks that could be owned, in addition to the large number of bonds with public quotations, so the actual calculations involving all readily available financial securities to create a Markowitz portfolio would have numbered in the millions. An intermediate simplification was achieved in 1958 by the economist James Tobin, who concluded that all investors would do best to own the exact same Markowitz portfolio of risky assets—what he dubbed the "dominant" portfolio—and then adjust the risk (and return) to their liking by holding a certain amount of cash. Investors who wanted even more risk (and return) could go the extra step and borrow money to buy more of the dominant portfolio: "You would choose the same portfolio of nonsafe assets regardless of how risk-averse you were. Even if you wanted to change the amount of risk in the portfolio, you'd do it by changing the amount of the safe assets, relative to the nonsafe assets, but not by changing the different proportions in which you held the nonsafe assets relative to each other."[18] This solution was simpler than the Markowitz method, but it was just as impractical from a calculation or real-world application perspective.

By 1959, when Markowitz published his book on portfolio construction, he did all the work necessary for analyzing a nine-stock portfolio and readily admitted that some simplification was needed. And as a possible avenue of investigation, he observed that most financial assets are correlated. That is, their returns tend to move in the same direction, maybe not by the same exact amount, a correlation of 1, but by some amount. When stock returns are positive, most stocks are up. When bond returns are negative, most bonds are down. Indeed, that correlation was a problem for the investor seeking to derive the benefits of diversification. "One hundred securities whose returns rise and fall in near unison afford little more protection than the uncertain return of a single security." Markowitz understood that to get the benefits of diversification, he would have to find a way to deal with the movements of individual stocks one to another. This led to Markowitz's intellectually backbreaking work of getting the covariances down to manageable levels. In the end, having designed a very complex system, Markowitz admitted that practical portfolio analysis required that "the relationships between securities be portrayed in a manner less cumbersome than individual covariances."[19] He made some initial moves in that direction by linking stock price changes to index movements but let it drop there.

Or to be more precise, in the early 1960s he encouraged a UCLA graduate student, William Sharpe, to take the correlation observation to the next level of analysis. Sharpe's basic insight was that the Markowitz framework could be made much more practical if, instead of determining how everything moves vis-à-vis everything else, security returns were measured against a single yardstick that appeared to be relevant to all of them: "The major characteristic of the diagonal model [Sharpe's original name for his early creation] is the assumption that the returns of various securities are related only through common relationship with some basic underlying factor." The most obvious underlying factor was the stock market itself, in the form of a broad market index.[20] Sharpe's next step ended up addressing the other practical challenge posed by the Markowitz system, and that was to generate a reasonable expected return figure for each investment making up the investable universe. Since risk and return were related, Sharpe reasoned, the expected return was simply a formula that took into account the newly defined risk: how sensitive a security was to movements in the broader index. We now call this "beta" (the Greek letter β), though in his initial work Sharpe referred to it as "B." Company-specific risks (called "nonsystematic" in the trade) would be offset through basic diversification. Holding just a few dozen different businesses takes care of that. All that is left is "systematic" or market risk. Markets go up; markets go down. There is not much way around that if you own publicly traded assets. Sharpe's beta quantified how much an individual security could generally be expected to move around with the broader market, using past evidence as a guide for the future. So a stock's expected return was simply more (or less, or the same) as the broader market's depending on its postulated degree of sensitivity to that broader market.

Sharpe's overall formula for expected return started with the risk-free rate of U.S. Treasuries, plus an "equity risk premium" that was adjusted for an individual security's sensitivity to the equity universe. The equity risk premium predates the arrival of the quants and was a straightforward concept of how much more the stock market generally returned than a "risk-free" investment in order to compensate investors for the obvious additional peril of being in the stock market. Over long measurement periods in the United States, that has been around 5% nominal. Out of the algebraic blender came a stunningly simple formula that incorporated all the key elements:

Expected return = risk-free rate + β (equity risk premium)

That's the basic version. In the original articles, the proof is delivered through an avalanche of more complicated algebraic equations.

Recall that an expected return and a discount rate for future cashflows are mathematically the same for a given, properly priced asset. So the world of finance now had several powerful new tools to quantify what investors had been doing more or less intuitively for decades if not centuries. Like the efficient frontier, this one also came with a great title, the "capital asset pricing model," frequently shortened to CAPM and pronounced "cap-em."[21] The formula was and is utterly elegant, an $E = mc^2$ for people in the money world. And it fit in nicely with the basic Markowitz framework that correlated risk and return. More risk (beta, variance, volatility, etc.) will generate more return over time, but at the cost of more near-term movement up and down around the overall market's return. With this tool, "efficient" portfolios could be calculated with relative ease, though the appropriate boundaries for the universe of risky assets remained an open question. Nevertheless, it seemed like a lot of progress had been made. The 1920s and 1930s boom-to-bust cycle had resulted, some 30 years later, in a logical, internally coherent understanding of risk and reward, and in a theoretical mechanism to structure investments that would give investors a good deal more say in how their investing experience would work out. Sharpe's system had the additional benefit of being a lot easier to use to calculate efficient portfolios than the Markowitz approach of individual covariance by covariance. Using the S&P 500 Index as a base—recall it had just come into being in 1957—one only needed a single expected return for the overall market and then the 500 expected sensitivities (betas) for the individual constituents. In the mid-1960s, that was still not a trivial exercise, but it was a lot easier than calculating 124,750 covariances for the same opportunity set under Markowitz's original formulation.

More than 50 years after its creation, the CAPM formula still dominates professional investment activity, despite frequent assertions to the contrary. So I think it is worthwhile to pause for a moment of reflection, not in the spirit of criticism, but in the spirit of observation. First, Markowitz, Sharpe, and the vast majority of other early contributors were academics, not practitioners. Markowitz's particular interest at the time was linear programming, and that avocation is reflected in his work history (employment at RAND in the 1950s), publications (numerous articles on operations research and programming as opposed to just finance or investment), and even awards (a prize from the Operations Research Society of America, to go along with his Nobel Prize in economics). As Markowitz wrote in his biographical submission to the Nobel Committee, his "focus has always been on the application of mathematical or computer techniques to practical problems, particularly problems of business decisions under uncertainty. Sometimes we applied existing techniques; other times we developed new techniques. Some of these techniques have been more 'successful' than others, success being measured here by acceptance in practice."[22]

William Sharpe had a similar background. He too passed through RAND. His first finance article was published in the journal *Management Science*. At the University of Washington, where Sharpe taught in the early 1960s, he was initially an associate professor of operations research. At RAND, Sharpe recalls "[playing] with ideas until we found one that could save the Air Force some money. We then did a study, and returned to playing around with other ideas. The good old days."[23] Both individuals got much more directly involved with investments in the years after their breakthrough publications, but at the time, they were mostly interested in academic endeavors, blackboard puzzles to be figured out. And their solutions showed it.

Working independently of Sharpe, Harvard academic John Lintner and the Norwegian Jan Mossin (completing his PhD at Carnegie Institute of Technology, now Carnegie Mellon University) came up with approximately the same conclusions as Sharpe, though their proofs and agendas varied somewhat. Lintner's article was published in 1965, a year after Sharpe's was, and Mossin's article appeared the following year in 1966.[24] Both had passed away by 1990 when the Nobel Prize was awarded to Markowitz and Sharpe. Had they lived, they might have shared in the award. Jack Treynor had a less traditional path. Working at the consulting firm Arthur D. Little in the late 1950s, Treynor sketched out some equations that essentially amount to CAPM. He wrote up his work in 1960, and it was passed around academic circles until it reached the desk of Franco Modigliani, an MIT professor who will make his own appearance in this account shortly. In 1962, Modigliani invited Treynor to spend a year at MIT to refine his work. He did so and presented two articles to the MIT faculty during his stay.[25] Those papers circulated but remained unpublished at the time. Treynor went on to serve as editor of the trade publication *Financial Analysts Journal*, and he authored or coauthored dozens of academic and professional articles about investment and portfolio management. Though he did not receive the Nobel Prize in 1990 with Markowitz and Sharpe, he is now generally acknowledged to have played a central role in the development of CAPM and its dissemination through the industry.[26]

These individuals, and the countless other academics playing supporting roles, took the blackboard shortcuts typical of the classroom to come up with their formulas. At the same time, those shortcuts made it all but impossible to implement the formulas in a practical fashion. Indeed, with the emergence of CAPM to create Markowitz portfolios, the hard work was really just beginning, because those assumptions—no taxes, equal information for all market participants, no trading costs, one-period measurement, rational investors with similar utility curves, shared definitions and expectations of risks and returns, etc.—just didn't exist in the real-world marketplace. And they still don't. That's another reason Modern Portfolio Theory hid behind the ivy for yet another decade: there was no easy way to implement it.

From my perspective, however, the main notable feature of this new approach to investing was its increasingly narrow focus on asset prices—and the movement away from Graham/ Williams for expected return calculations and toward the challenge of getting the covariances right, in the end by not doing individual covariances at all. That approach came at another cost, one hardly acknowledged in the literature at the time or now: *the companies themselves had disappeared.* The goods and services that they provided, the ownership stakes that equity represented, the cashflows, the rise or decline in sales, the expansion or contraction in profits, the steady dividends as a manifestation of a business's success—Markowitz et al. had removed all these factors from the investment equation. The basic commonsense business matters standing behind every stock price were all gone, lost in a stream of algebraic equations and programming moments related to the share prices and their relationship to one another. Does the disconnect between owner and asset matter? Do investors really care or need to know what Acme Widget Company does or makes? *Does stock ownership really confer business ownership?* During the Internet bubble of the 1990s, as you may well recall, the answer was clearly no. That did not end well. And even when investors are not operating in what is clearly a bubble environment like that of the late 1990s, when it is just a list of assets in a brokerage account that get revalued on a daily basis, it seems to me, when talking with our customers or reading the popular media, that the sense that these are stakes in businesses is almost completely absent. Far too few investors ask how the businesses are doing; they just want to know how the stock is doing. In the final chapter, I propose to resurrect the notion that it might be a good idea to know what you own and realize that you own it for a reason other than its contribution to "covariance minimization" or some other worn MPT virtue.

Bachelier, Samuelson, and the Statisticians

The mathematics of the CAPM very quickly led to the stunning conclusion that the best overall MPT portfolio—the most efficient—is the market portfolio itself of all risky assets. It is the portfolio that offers the best combination of expected return and variance of that return. If you wanted less than the market's risk and return, you would hold some cash. If you wanted more, you would borrow cash to invest in the market. This conclusion placed Markowitz, Tobin, and the CAPM crowd in a single neat package. It also dovetailed nicely with a largely parallel line of inquiry emerging at the same time that stock prices were unpredictable, and therefore the market itself was unbeatable. If so, then buying the market made sense from both perspectives.

MPT started with a basic theoretical problem—how to invest sensibly in the aftermath of some very nonsensible periods—and came up with a blackboard solution. In contrast, the "can't-forecast-stock-prices" crowd started with real-world data sets—decades of actual stock, bond, and commodity prices—and subjected them to painstaking analysis to see if there were any discernible patterns. For as long as there had been tracked markets, traders and commentators had observed or claimed to observe patterns in prices—trends— that could then be used to generate market-beating profits. Against a veritable financial army of individuals trying to make a living off trading these patterns (or recommending them to others), statisticians began to look at the data. Their conclusions were striking.

Where Peter Bernstein wrote the "go-to" narrative for Modern Portfolio Theory, the single best recent chronicle of the emergence of what has become known as the efficient market hypothesis (EMH) is Justin Fox's *The Myth of the Rational Market: The History of Risk, Reward, and Delusion on Wall Street*, published in 2009. The account below covers briefly what Fox relates in much greater detail. More notably, unlike Bernstein, Fox is not a cheerleader or a participant. Indeed, he brings a critical eye to the enterprise, coming to the conclusion that this paradigm, which emerged from and utterly conquered academia, is wrong. To this day, that remains a minority view in the academy, and that is where the story begins.

While the exercise of looking for patterns in prices is as old as commerce itself, the modern analysis begins roughly at the same time as the rest of our story. In the 1930s, a Stanford statistician, Holbrook Working, showed that while commodity prices may seem to exhibit patterns, the percentage change in the price—what really matters to the investor—appears to be random.[27] That suggested that on average investors in commodities would have a hard time beating the overall market. This startling assertion didn't have much of an impact at the time. It was too early. Isolated articles by academics in journals about statistics during the mid-1930s were not going to dissuade traders from their firmly held belief that the ticker tape conveyed meaningful information. Indeed, it was two decades later before the issue was taken up again in academic circles. In 1953, a prominent English statistician, Maurice Kendall, reached the same conclusion as Working had after looking at data for stocks and commodities in England and the United States. In his words, "The best estimate of the change in price between now and next week is that there is no change."[28] Kendall found "little serial correlation."[29] In plain speak: no patterns. Look all you want. You may see "triple tops," "channels," "pennants," and "head and shoulders" that suggest where individual share or general market prices might be heading in the next few days and weeks, but you would still be guessing, with an equal chance of getting it right or wrong.

More articles from academics on the topic began to appear, but the analysis that had the greatest impact came from the archives. In the 1950s, a prominent University of Chicago statistician, Jimmie Savage, discovered a 1914 book by Louis Bachelier, a French mathematician whose 1900 dissertation at the University of Paris was the first to systematically analyze speculation in asset prices. Bachelier concluded that differences in opinions about the present and future value of publicly traded assets are priced into the securities at any given moment and therefore that material price changes would be impossible to predict: "It seems that the market, the aggregate of speculators, at a given instant can believe in neither a market rise nor a market fall, since, for each quoted price, there are as many buyers as sellers. . . . The mathematical expectation of the speculator is zero." Savage passed on his find to Paul Samuelson at MIT, who was very much taken by Bachelier'swork and began advertising it among his own followers. Statistics as much as finance drove this analysis, as people who liked data sets pored over data sets to see if they could find any patterns that would suggest predictability. The answer, enshrined in a lot of academic publications by the mid-1960s, was no. No patterns. Long overlooked, Bachelier was finally given his due in a collection of articles that appeared in 1964 with the catchy title of *The Random Character of Stock Prices.*[30] In it, Bachelier's thesis is reprinted in full at the beginning, and the subsequent contributors more or less validate his conclusions made over a half century earlier. Bachelier had passed away in 1946 in relative academic obscurity, but he is now fully enshrined in the pantheon of modern finance greats. A leading chronicler of the finance profession, Mark Rubinstein wrote of Bachelier that "this Vincent van Gogh of financial economics received only average marks on this thesis. Ironically, we can see now that it is undoubtedly the finest thesis ever written in financial economics."[31]

Many of those who studied stock prices in the 1950s and 1960s appear to have been only mildly interested in investment per se. Indeed, the underlying context for these investigations was not financial or even economic. It was drawn from physics, specifically, the "random walk" theory that was based on observations of particle motion made in the early nineteenth century by an English botanist, Robert Brown. His description of the seemingly patternless movements of pollen molecules came to be known as "Brownian motion." It has since been applied to a wide variety of phenomena, including finance.[32] As Bachelier's work was making the rounds, a physicist by the name of M. F. M. Osborne at the Naval Research Laboratory in Washington, D.C., took up the topic. His research, entitled "Brownian Motion in the Stock Market," was read at the U.S. Naval Research Laboratory Solid State Seminar on February 28, 1958, and published in a U.S. Navy journal called *Operations Research*.[33] In it, Osborne observed that "the value of money can be regarded as an ensemble of decisions in statistical equilibrium with properties quite analogous to an ensemble of particles in statistical mechanics." And therefore it was similar to Brownian motion or the random walk.[34]

The Naval Research Lab in the 1950s was not exactly a hotbed of capital markets innovation, and Osborne's article necessarily had zero impact on investment practices, but it was representative of the pure research funded by the government and large corporations in the postwar period. These decades were the heyday of IBM's Watson Research Center, of Bell Labs, of the RAND Corporation (the title is based on its mission—Research AND Development), and, somewhat later, of Xerox's famed Palo Alto Research Center (PARC), among others. It was a golden age of fundamental research that might have a practical application, or might not. To the extent that these institutions were looking at the functioning of capital markets, there was little possibility that the results would be understood (or even read) by practitioners. For instance, a direct attack in 1959 from University of Chicago professor Harry Roberts on the stock market technicians— those who believed that they could see profitable patterns in price charts—was published in the *Journal of Finance*, which, as Fox observes, was read "almost exclusively" by academics, not practitioners.[35]

Nevertheless, over the next decade, the random walk theory zigzagged its way out of the academy, making significant headway beyond the data-set-loving, physics-inspired crowd. Leading the charge was Paul Samuelson, the popular and prolific MIT economist. By the late 1950s, his textbook on macroeconomics was already dominant in the classrooms and considered a bestseller. He had a regular column in

Newsweek and was that rare breed in this country, a public intellectual. The stock market was but one of the many topics he wrote on. While Bernstein is effusive in his praise of the academics who liberated Wall Street from its ignorance, the encomiums seem warranted in the case of Samuelson. He was a really smart guy who was genuinely interested in whether someone could make money in stocks and who now and again tried his hand at it. In that regard, Samuelson fell between his fellow economist Keynes—an avowed speculator—and the physicists and statisticians poring over the data but with little engagement of the market itself.

Samuelson shared his view of efficient markets in what is now considered a finance classic, "Proof That Properly Anticipated Prices Fluctuate Randomly."[36] Samuelson basically says the same thing that his predecessors did—stock prices reflect all current and past information and therefore cannot be consistently gamed, though he draws a distinction between market price unpredictability and the narrower and stricter Brownian notion of randomness, from which he keeps some distance. Despite that distinction, his conclusions are roughly the same:

The market quotation . . . already contains in itself all that can be known about the future and in that sense has discounted future contingencies as much as is humanely possible. . . . We would expect people in the market place, in pursuit of avid and intelligent self-interest, to take account of those elements of future events that in a probability sense may be discerned to be casting their shadows before them.

Samuelson is more practical in his assertions than the narrower statisticians, observing that some individuals might end up being on the right side of trades—even a lot of them—but that doing so for an extended period of time would be difficult and that, on average, the averages had to prevail. We know this as a "zero-sum" game. For every winner, there is a loser. Winners and losers do benefit from the overall upward trend of the market over time, so this minimum benefit—the equity risk premium—is for all long-term investors.

Bringing Market Efficiency to Wall Street and to Main Street

As popular as Samuelson was, he was still primarily an academic economist, and his statement on the subject of stock prices appearing in *Industrial Management Review* wasn't going to affect practitioners. It fell to a newly minted PhD, Eugene Fama, to charge from the academic trenches and make his way directly to Wall Street's front line. In 1964, Fama completed his dissertation at the University of Chicago—on the random walk of securities prices—and then proceeded to publish it early the following year in the *Journal of Business*. A simplified version of his argument as it applied to practical investing appeared the same year in the *Financial Analysts Journal*, the main trade journal for stock and bond analysts. His campaign continued in another trade magazine, *Institutional Investor*, at investor conferences, and in a variety of other academic and practitioner publications through the late 1960s and early 1970s.[37] In these forums, Fama challenges the chartists and technicians, basically affirming and furthering the research of Working, Kendall, and the others.

One particular aspect of Fama's early work was, in some ways, even more interesting. He questioned whether or not the random walk argument held when price change distributions were "normal," by which statisticians mean bunched smoothly around a central tendency (the average and median) and then petering out as one gets further from that mean, a condition that is widely assumed and observed in nature and human affairs. It is popularly known as the "bell curve." The alternative was that the data would not be normally distributed, instead having "fat tails" when extreme events occurred much more frequently than would otherwise be expected. This nonnormal view of the world was championed at the time by one of the great minds of the twentieth century, Benoît Mandelbrot. Mandelbrot's singularly creative intellect and remarkable life story are for another day. Suffice it here to note that in his dissertation as published in the *Journal of Business*, Fama seems as interested in the very worthy cause of championing Mandelbrot as he does in supporting the random walk view. Nevertheless, support the random walk he does, subjecting it to further empirical review and concluding that

independence of successive price changes is consistent with an "efficient" market, that is, a market where prices at every point in time represent best estimates of intrinsic values. This implies in turn that, when an intrinsic value changes, the actual price will adjust "instantaneously," where instantaneously means, among other things, that the actual price will initially overshoot the new intrinsic value as often as it will undershoot it.[38]

I quote this particular piece of Fama's original article because as far as I can tell, it is the first instance in print where an observer borrowed the term "efficient" from the Markowitz notion of superior portfolios and extended it to a random walk view of actual asset prices. And in the same sentence, Fama takes the refutation of the chartists to the next level and argues that security analysts with their focus on company business fundamentals and future prospects—a topic of no interest to the chartists—are playing the same zero-sum game. This moment was, in effect, the formal emergence of the efficient market hypothesis. Why does this matter? If you invest in index funds, or more recently broad ETFs, you are buying into the EMH, whether you realize it or not. Even if you don't invest in the broad market indexes, a lot of people and institutions now do. As a result, index funds and ETF products often set the tone and can dominate the volume of trades in parts of the stock market on many days. You might want to know what the thinking behind all that activity is.

Within a few years, Fama had refined the notion of an efficient market to include three separate variants of the hypothesis. The first, known as the "weak," was basically the original refutation of the chartists. There was no investable—meaning profitable—information in stock prices alone. Look all you want, imagine a trend or a pattern, but the data showed random changes, though within the market's broad long-term positive trend. The "semistrong" variant took the battle directly to the stock pros, convinced that they could pick winners based on more fundamental information such as public information about a company, when it would pay a dividend, announce a stock split, report earnings, etc. But the really galling variant—at the time and to this day—is the "strong" version of the EMH. It suggests that all current and prospective information—including the private forecasts of future business developments and earnings—is already priced into a stock.[39] The overall reasoning was more or less the same that Bachelier had presented decades earlier—if the share price didn't reflect that information, the astute trader would buy (sell) it up (down) to the price where it did. As long as markets were reasonably liquid, with enough buyers and sellers paying attention, this condition would be met. If so, the entire apparatus of "stock picking" on Wall Street was at once both necessary—to make sure that stock prices were "right"—and a waste of time—because no one could get ahead of or outside that process.

Actually testing the strong version of the EMH, however, was a different matter. In the 1920s, Alfred Cowles had collected the recommendations of investment newsletters and found them wanting, but that was done in a far-from-systematic fashion. For decades after Cowles, the "Does it really work?" question of brokers and financial advisors had not been posed in an empirically convincing fashion. In part, it was a data issue. Getting a reasonable data set of recommendations or portfolio performance would be difficult if not impossible for the period from the 1920s to the 1960s. There was no Morningstar for mutual funds, no archive of recommended lists for the individual brokerages, no ranking of composites (performance records) for individual financial advisors or the emerging class of institutional investors. The records of trust accounts were not readily accessible, and in any case, trust accounts labored under a different set of rules that would muddy the performance waters. Legitimate indexes of market performance were only coming into being at that time. In that data-poor context, investors were faced with cigar-chomping brokers and bow-tied portfolio managers telling them what to do, but with no practical way of knowing whether it worked or not.

With the random walk argument making the academic rounds in the mid-1960s, the question was asked anew: Does stock picking work? Data was still scarce, but there was enough of it—in the form of mutual funds, which had become increasingly popular in the postwar period—to allow some analysis to proceed. Another recent University of Chicago PhD, Michael Jensen, looked at the performance of 115 mutual funds from 1945 to 1964 to see if he could identify excess returns above and beyond what the capital asset pricing model of Sharpe et al. would have predicted. Jensen's key insight was that while the CAPM was designed to forecast future returns, it could also be applied backward in time to explain past performance. Jensen designated any return beyond what was expected with the Greek letter α (alpha). So when doing retrospective analysis, the CAPM formula became:

Realized return = risk-free rate + β (equity risk premium) + α

This additional risk-adjusted return became known as "Jensen's alpha," or more commonly just "alpha." The presence of positive alpha would suggest a predictive ability by the investor or portfolio manager that would disprove the random walk or efficient market hypothesis. An alpha of zero for a wide sample would suggest support for the "can't-beat-the-market" view. Negative alpha would suggest that third-party stock picking by a mutual fund or a financial advisor did more harm than good, usually due to the expenses associated with the effort.

Jensen concluded that those early fund managers from the postwar period—really the very earliest days of the modern asset management industry—were not able to generate positive alpha. The median residual return for the funds was essentially flat, a negative 0.4%, and when fund expenses were included in the calculation, the average alpha was a more material negative 1.1% of risk-adjusted annual return.[40] At the same time, he acknowledged the rudimentary nature of the data and that several of the inputs and constraints were biased against the funds, but his conclusion was still inescapable: beating the market by enough to cover one's costs and offer positive alpha to clients was difficult indeed. At about the same time, Sharpe came to a similar conclusion in his own study of postwar mutual fund returns.[41] Jensen's observation about poor mutual fund performance notwithstanding, his measurement tool of excess risk-adjusted returns—alpha—caught on in a big way, and it has become the ultimate goal of the asset management industry today. As a portfolio manager, I am regularly asked whether I generate alpha, and if so, how? Products promoting their alpha-hunting capabilities dominate the institutional marketplace. "Portable alpha" lets you take it with you. *Alphaville* is a popular investment blog, and "Delivering Alpha" is the name of an annual conference sponsored by CNBC and *Institutional Investor*.

Following hard on Fama's charge that the securities analysts "couldn't do it," Jensen's assertion that the fund managers "hadn't done it" was a direct challenge to the emerging mutual fund and asset management industry. Former securities analyst turned Princeton professor Burton Malkiel went public with the charge in his 1973 *Random Walk Down Wall Street*, a synthesis of the academic work but written for retail investors. It has since gone through 11 editions and sold over a million copies. The word was out: investors, particularly individual retail investors, should stick to broad-based, index-oriented products. The problem was that such products did not exist at the time. At the end of his original work from 1973, Malkiel suggested that investors needed "a no-load, minimum-management-fee mutual fund that simply buys the hundreds of stocks making up the broad stock-market averages and does no trading from security to security in an attempt to catch the winners."[42] Malkiel suggested that the NYSE should sponsor such a product and run it as a nonprofit on behalf of small investors. A few years later, in 1976, Jack Bogle, a graduate of Princeton and veteran of a respected Boston fund company, launched the first practical, low-cost, retail product—the Vanguard 500

Index Fund—that was based on the market efficiency argument. It was originally called "Bogle's folly" by a very skeptical investment community.[43] That fund currently has $383 billion in assets (as of November 2017). And the firm that Bogle founded, Vanguard, manages $4.5 trillion—yes, *trillion*—much of it in index-oriented products. Who is laughing now?

Corporations

One other piece of the intellectual puzzle that completed modern investment theory and practice as we know it remained to be put in place. And it had to do with corporations. They now mattered. As a result of industrialization in the nineteenth century, small, family-oriented businesses (think farmers, carpenters, storekeepers, etc.) had ceded the economic center stage to new, large, complex manufacturing operations, ones that could have thousands of employees spread over multiple locations. Corporations in name and in law had existed since the Middle Ages, but as behemoth commercial entities, they were a development of the nineteenth century. Yes, the East India Company had been big relative to England's economic activity in the seventeenth century, but it was an exception. The nineteenth century brought the first wave of really big companies—the railroad companies in England and the United States. Construction of those roads led to the emergence of the manufacturing enterprises central to broader industrialization. They had become very big by the late nineteenth century, then got even bigger at the turn of the century when a Standard Oil executive discovered that a trust structure could be used to buy out one's competitors. That company led the way by creating an organizational behemoth that completely dominated oil discovery, refining, and shipping. Standard Oil was joined by other large corporate trusts including American Tobacco, United States Steel, and numerous leading enterprises in lower-profile industries. The U.S. government stepped in with the Sherman Act in 1890, and a period of trust-busting commenced, but the era of really big business had arrived. The academics were slow to figure out what to make of these newfangled entities. The landmark analysis—similar to the work of Alfred Marshall in economics (1890) and Irving Fisher in finance (1906)—was *The Modern Corporation and Private Property*, written by Adolf Berle and Gardiner Means in 1932, in the aftermath of the stock market Crash.[44]

Prior to the modern corporation, in the age of small business, the proprietor worked the store, worked the fair, worked the anvil, etc. The owner was the operator, and the operator was the owner. Business remained small in scope and scale. In contrast, Berle and Means emphasized how the emergence of more complex corporations allowed businesses to raise the capital needed for the large-scale endeavors of the industrial age. But raising that capital came at what is now known as an "agency" cost. Disposition of the raised capital and direction of the business were no longer done directly by the investors—that would not be feasible—but were overseen by a group of directors who hired the managers who actually ran the business. The owner was no longer operator; the operator was no longer owner. The authors' view of this development was strikingly negative. As a result of defused share ownership of large companies, control of industry was concentrated in the hands of the very few who made up the directorate. In their account, America was entering a new period of industrial feudalism.

Enter Miller and Modigliani

And so started a cottage industry of academics looking at these new entities. In one such exercise, two academics at Carnegie Tech in the late 1950s, Merton Miller and Franco Modigliani, sat down to think about the optimal capital structure of corporations: How much debt versus how much equity should they have on the books? How much should companies borrow to finance their growth and operations as opposed to equity put in by founders and retained profits? It's an important question for all businesspeople—small and large—and for anyone who has taken the time to consider the implications for the family balance sheet of taking out a mortgage (debt) to buy a home. M&M, as they came to be known, concluded somewhat shockingly that when a variety of chalkboard conditions held, it didn't really matter how much debt versus equity a corporation had. (They did not opine on family balance sheets. . . .)

M&M's original work, dating from 1958, is considered a landmark in the history of corporate finance, but one outgrowth of their work, addressed in a follow-on paper in 1961, may be even more relevant for stock market investors today.[45] Following the logic of their capital structure argument, M&M determined that whether a company paid a dividend or did not pay a dividend shouldn't really make a difference to the value of the firm's shares. Prior to M&M, investors understood dividends as a tangible manifestation of a company's success. A company with a high and rising dividend commanded a premium in the marketplace. Companies without dividends were viewed as entirely speculative. Not anymore. According to M&M, investors could collect a higher share of current profits as a big dividend but would have to accept a lower percentage of the company's future value because the company would need to issue more shares to raise the capital necessary to continue growing the business. That would dilute the existing shareholders. In contrast, a lower current dividend would free up more capital for investment, increasing the future cashflows. Do the math, and the value is the same for the current shareholder. The dividend payout ratio is irrelevant. QED.

Subsequent academics took the logic another step forward and wondered why corporations paid dividends at all or why investors would want regular cash payments for their stakes. In 1976, Fischer Black called it "the dividend puzzle" and explained away the illogic of companies paying dividends as basically pandering to hordes of "irrational" investors.[46] In this blackboard world, cash payments to company owners were inferior to every other use of the profits. That they continued to exist at all was attributed to the subjective and potentially unwise preferences of investors that fell outside the bounds of the standard rational actor framework.[47] Now, to be fair, at the time that these academics were railing against profit-making companies making profit distributions, the tax rate on dividends was higher than that on capital gains. In that environment, and if there were no transaction costs, perfect investor certainty about future share prices, an extreme aversion to paying taxes of any kind, and a willingness to lose money (if the market went down) rather than pay taxes on a dividend payment—under those circumstances some investors in taxable accounts might question why corporations paid dividends or investors sought them out. Even with the tax differential largely removed in recent years, the bias against U.S. companies distributing profits—publicly traded companies paying dividends—continues to this day.[48]

M&M 50 Years Later

The so-called dividend irrelevancy theorem, and its variants, has had profound implications for investors. It paved the intellectual path to what has emerged a half-century later as a world of publicly traded companies that do not distribute profits, even if they have them—Berkshire-Hathaway and Google come to mind—or distribute only a modicum of excess cashflows after all maintenance and growth investments have been met—think Apple. To this day, many corporate executives and investors, reaching back to their business school days, will still make passing references to M&M to explain their company's low regard for dividend payments. Yes, how people understand these seemingly distant and arcane academic matters really does affect your retirement portfolio today! That's why it's worth going back and understanding the context in which M&M produced their academic breakthroughs. Like Markowitz and Sharpe, so too M&M brought postwar mathematical precision to the task of figuring out these new entities—the corporation. The problem is not their analysis. It remains mathematically correctly and historically useful when seen in its proper context. The issue is what has been done in their name in the stock market over a half-century later, when that context has changed dramatically. Our world is not their world. With all due respect to Merton Miller and Franco Modigliani, their seminal 1961 article in the *Journal of Business* has contributed mightily to the casino-like atmosphere of today's stock market, where ownership of a company's equity does not confer ownership of a business, but instead possession of a piece of paper with an ever-changing price attached to it.

Of course, the creation of a massive stock market casino was not their intention. M&M's main point at the time was

that the value of a company is dependent on "'real' considerations—. . . the earning power of the firm's assets and its
investment policy—and not by how the fruits of the earning
power are 'packaged' for distribution." That was a sensible
statement in 1961; it's a sensible statement now, but it does
highlight the investment part of the equation—the amount of
capital needed to be put back into the business in order for it
to continue growing. Here M&M make several assumptions
that need to be reviewed today very carefully. They assume
that companies have growth opportunities that require more
capital than their net profits in any given year or even retained
earnings from previous years. Therefore, in M&M's world,
external capital is *always* required for the company to take
advantage of those opportunities. Depending on the dividend payout ratio, the amount of additional external versus
internal capital required will vary, but in the standard case in
which external capital is to be raised, M&M's condition of
dividend irrelevancy would generally hold, at least in theory:
either pay a higher dividend and raise the needed extra capital externally—with dilution—or pay a lower dividend, use
more internal capital, and have less dilution. "Thus, we may
conclude that *given a firm's investment policy* [my empha-
sis], the dividend policy it chooses to follow will affect neither the current price of its shares nor the total return to its
shareholders."[49]

So far, so good. M&M are quite correct as far as a theoretical construct goes. Let us now fast-forward a half century
and see how this idea has played out in practice. Before we
can do that, however, we need to make one adjustment to the
theory, but one that does not change the math. During the
intervening 50 years, share repurchase programs have come
to supplant dividend payments. Share repurchase programs
represent a simple transaction whereby a company uses its

profits to reduce the number of shares outstanding by buying them from existing shareholders and in most cases canceling them. It's basically using company cash to buy out one's partners. As a practical matter, such programs were few and far between at the time of M&M. In today's world, however, S&P 500 Index companies spend more each year on the purchase of their own shares than they do on dividends to company owners. It has been that way for the better part of the past two decades. From the perspective of the formulas used by M&M, it would not be difficult to update the dividend irrelevancy theory to include share repurchase programs and to show that investors should be indifferent to whether a company uses its cash for dividends, share repurchase, or growth investments.

Now for the bad news. Current real-world investors need to keep in mind that when M&M offered up the dividend irrelevancy theorem, the U.S. corporate landscape was dominated by rapidly growing industrial and manufacturing businesses, with fixed, tangible assets (factories, railroads, etc.) that depreciated and needed to be replenished on a regular basis. Growth investments required more of the same—expensive physical plant and machinery. And the economy was expanding nicely in the postwar decades. Growth opportunities abounded. The lower-growth, manufacturing-light, service economy we're now accustomed to was not part of this calculation. Right now, GDP growth is barely half of what it was in the 1950s. More importantly, only a small percentage of the large corporations making up the S&P 500 Index now *regularly* finance their growth plans with external capital. Those would be the utilities and REITs and a smattering of other old-economy enterprises. For those companies, if they have extensive capital expenditure ambitions, a higher current dividend payout ratio may well mean having to raise more external, dilutive capital at regular intervals. That is precisely what utilities and REITs do. A lower payout ratio may well mean less issuance and less dilution. For these select companies, one could argue that M&M's work still holds, if you accept that notion that investors are indifferent between regularly receiving a cash payment in the mail and regularly going out into the stock market to conduct a transaction—a very big "if" with which we deal below.

But those types of companies represent a small minority of the broader stock market at the present time. Utilities are 3.2% of the S&P 500 Index; REITs are just 2.9%.[50] The rest of the S&P 500 Index companies generally do not raise new capital for growth projects. They generate their investment funds internally, and in recent years from cheap debt. The most famous manufacturing company and stock on the planet as I write—Apple, Inc.—spends about $13 billion annually on plant, property, and equipment. But it generates profits of around $40 billion to $50 billion and cash flow from operations of over $60 billion. There is no need for external financing here. Amazon and Google are the same—their capital expenditure and acquisition budgets take up only a small portion of the profits that they generate. A more traditional manufacturer of "hard" goods—such as Boeing—is in a roughly similar position. It generates profits of around $5 billion and cash flow from operations of $9 billion to $10 billion, while spending $2 billion to $3 billion in capital expenditures and acquisitions. For the S&P 500 Index companies in aggregate in 2015, they generated profits of $853 billion; taking into account depreciation and noncash charges, they had operating cash flow of $1.7 trillion. Of that amount, America's largest companies spent approximately $662 billion on capital expenditures, leaving them with just over $1 trillion after all current expenses and internal growth investments had been made. Of that trillion dollars of free cash flow (after capital expenditures), $412 billion was spent on dividends, $403 billion on acquisitions, and $559 billion on share repurchases. The excess was covered by some share issuance and by new debt of $372 billion.[51]

For M&M in 1961, however, financing growth through internal resources—the norm today—was an "extreme" case.[52] And in that extreme case, M&M do acknowledge that "*dividend policy* is indistinguishable from investment policy; and [therefore] there is an optimal investment policy."[53] In effect, M&M admit that for internally financed companies, investment (dividend) policy does determine value—current and future. If a company pays out more dividends and leaves less for good growth projects, it will be worth less to the investor. And in the postwar years when growth was abundant and required significant capital outlays, using current profits for dividends rather than investments may well have amounted to forgoing those opportunities. But now the tables have turned. What was 50 years ago an exceptional situation is currently the norm, and M&M's base case—external capital raising for public companies—is less frequently encountered. Dividend policy is no longer separate from investment policy for most large, publicly traded companies. Dividend policy does matter.

The same holds in regard to share repurchase programs. For M&M's base case, where capital is raised externally to fund abundant growth projects, a share repurchase program would be for all intents and purposes inconceivable. Retiring shares is the opposite of issuing them. Now to be fair, companies in rapid-growth mode that actually need external capital don't usually engage in substantial share repurchase programs. But for M&M's extreme case—now the most common scenario—where external capital is not needed to fund growth, share buybacks would look like a dividend payment, both competing with growth investments. Once again, investment policy would determine which side gets the cash. In that case as well, dividend (investment, share buyback) policy matters.

M&M in Practice

It is not just that the amount of external capital needed by leading U.S. corporations has changed in the past 50 years. A half century of investment experience highlights other critical weaknesses in how M&M is applied. While the math of share repurchases might be neutral from a shareholder perspective on a classroom blackboard, the reality is quite different: they are terribly timed. Companies buy their shares when the price is high and ease off when the share price is low.[54] It is one thing to buy out your partners at a price that is fair to both you and them. It is quite another to overpay for your partners to exit and then have to raise capital from new partners in a dilutive fashion when times get tough. Yet that is precisely what has happened in recent decades. Investors should not be indifferent to losing money because an academic theory holds up poorly in the real world.

Perhaps even more disturbing is that M&M essentially assume that corporate executives have nearly perfect foresight and equally strong execution skills. That is a common trait of most postwar investment theory—it really does take an optimistic stance in regard to human nature. Academic theorists assume that managers, when considering the choice between investing in growth projects and paying out more of the current profits as a dividend, routinely have the ability to identify ventures that will generate excess returns (above what would be the market's overall rate of return and/or their own cost of capital) and can consistently implement those plans and realize those returns. That assumption is not only optimistic; it is also pretty much required for any classroom treatment of investment theory. But anyone who has ever actually run or even participated in a business realizes that it isn't as simple as that. Managers cannot tell at the time when they make a capital investment whether it will be a success or not. And companies that repeatedly make bad capital allocation decisions soon disappear from the measurement set. The profile of the remaining group of examples is improved through this survivorship bias.

M&M condescendingly dismiss the countervailing notion—a bird in the hand is worth more than two in the bush—because in modern investment theory, *a bird in the hand is worth precisely two (discounted) birds in the bush.* In theory, yes; in practice, probably not. After living through numerous business investment bubbles—the 1990s was a period of systematic, marketwide, money-losing overspend, and you don't have to reach nearly so far back to identify bad investments or wasteful acquisitions from your favorite company—we side more with the traditional notion that acknowledges the challenge of realizing many of those pie-in-the-sky growth plans versus the certainty of a cash payment. Growth is good. Investment is good. Assuming that all growth investments will work out perfectly is foolish.

Similarly, M&M's view that investors are "indifferent as to whether a given increment to their wealth takes the form of cash payments or an increase in the market value of their holdings of shares"[55] is another part of their proposition that looks good on the blackboard but just doesn't work out well in practice. There is a profound philosophical, almost existential, difference between making a cash payment to a company owner and having to go out into the marketplace, price an asset based on other people's bids, and conduct a transaction yourself if you want to realize that value. That's very different from receiving a dividend check in the mail; yet it is a hallmark of modern investment theory. It also requires a great deal of optimism. The ability to sell shares at a profit is required for investors to be indifferent to share price gains versus a dividend payment. And over long measurement periods, share prices in the U.S. stock market have risen in line with the growth of profits. That has meant that investors can feel reasonably comfortable about seeing their wealth generation take the form of a rising share price, not just a quarterly dividend payment. But that's not the case every day, not for every company and not for every investor. As we'll see in the next chapter, MPT is most often based on point-to-point analysis. It doesn't really capture the downdrafts. What if you need your income on that dark day (week, month, or year) when the stock market is down sharply? Are you inclined to sell a much-depreciated stock of a perfectly good company to pay your monthly bills? Are you indifferent at that time to receiving a recurring dividend payment versus having to sell an asset in a hostile marketplace? Probably not. During the Internet bubble meltdown, when the non-dividend-paying tech companies were disappearing, Kimberly-Clark—a company as remote from the shenanigans of Wall Street as possible—fell from a high of $67 in 2001 to a low of $41 in early 2003, a more than one-third drop. That's painful, *but the cash flows of the company were largely unaffected.* And the dividend was paid, on time and in full. Indeed, the increase in the company's dividend in March 2003 was notably large: a 13% jump from $0.30 to $0.34 per share per quarter. During the financial crisis six years later, the KMB shares again fell by one-third, from $68 to $42. *And once again, Kimberly-Clark's dividend continued its steady, multidecade ascent.*

In March 2009, the same month the market bottomed, KMB increased its quarterly distribution from $0.58 to $0.60. *In both cases, the share price of this steady-Eddie company quickly recovered from the drawdown caused by riskier assets.* Countless other examples outside the tech sector (in 2000–2002) and the financial sector (in 2008–2009) can be presented. Given what happened in those years, it is hard to argue with a straight face that investors are or should be indifferent to a share price gain versus a cash payment. And without that indifference, of course, the dividend irrelevancy argument falls apart.

Only in a late, follow-on section in their 1961 article—the mopping-up area—do M&M acknowledge a scenario in which investors might have a clear preference for either a capital gain or a dividend. If that were the case, the irrelevance argument is weakened, but M&M bring it back from the brink by observing that in "perfect" markets, a mix of companies with a variety of payout policies more or less matches up with a range of investor preferences. Hence the payout ratio does not matter. Higher-payout companies will be found by investors who want that, and lower-payout companies will be chosen by the others. A modernized M&M would include a third group of investors who sought out share repurchasers.

M&M considered their dividend irrelevancy theorem to be one of the things that is "obvious once you think about it." And in M&M's world, that may have been the case. But we do not live in that world of completely rational, identical investors and perfect capital markets. (Fama had yet to popularize the term "efficient markets.") Fifty years later, the shortcomings of this approach are "obvious once you think about them." I've already noted that perhaps it should not come as a surprise that academics working with databases of share prices came up with investment theories based on share prices. If Markowitz or Sharpe or Tobin or M&M had been businesspeople, perhaps . . .

Lack of Dissemination: The 1960s as the 1920s Redux

For all the exciting work being done in the ivory tower in the 1950s and 1960s, little of it made its way into practice at the time. Although the groundwork for a new intellectual system had been laid, it was not disseminated, and it did not move from the point of production to the point of consumption for another 15 or so years. Why the delay? Although an intellectual vacuum in the investment profession still existed through the 1960s, a catalyst to fill it was required. Indeed, the immediate need for a proper system of investing had become less pressing. The Crash of 1929 and the Great Depression were fading from memory. Asset prices (stocks, homes) were making steady gains in the postwar decades, and the country was benefiting from a prolonged period of general economic prosperity. Brokers and individual investors bought stocks because they were going up. The "ruleless" model seemed, once again, to be working just fine.

Indeed, at the popular level, the postwar investment culture was strikingly like that of the 1920s, perhaps without the explicit euphoria of 1929. For example, *Standard & Poor's Selecting Stocks to Buy for Profit* from 1956 is a mishmash of ideas about investing (with 77 recommended examples). Buy growth industries, buy low-priced stocks, buy high-priced stocks (so-called blue chips),[56] buy companies with insider ownership, buy companies with low labor costs, buy companies with big research programs, etc. The compilers provided two-page tear sheets on companies referenced in the thematic recommendations. Those tear sheets look like the pages out of a Poor's manual from 50 years earlier or the old index card format of the Standard Statistics Bureau. Recall that the two companies had merged in 1941 to form S&P, but little in the presentation of information had changed over a half century. It was just "practical, down to earth . . . recommendations, with no space allotted for the purely academic."[57]

Growth Is Good!

While the euphoria of the late 1920s was mostly speculation, with little rhyme or reason to it, the burst of stock market exuberance that emerged in the 1960s had a modestly more coherent theme: growth. And the emergence of a "growth" stock culture in the 1960s was the first sign of the style investing that we are familiar with today: growth, value, core, small, mid, large, alternative, etc. In this initial period, however, the investment culture was simpler. It was divided into "growth" and everything else. The investment literature of the time was all about finding the keys to growth, to timing your investment in IBM and finding the next IBM before it got too big. For these and the other "story" stocks of the 1960s, the conversation was all about innovation, expansion, and endless prospects—Avon, for instance, had an "unblemished" outlook. "Lovely, in fact."[58] Nary a word was said about the company's cashflows, what it might be "worth," or what it might cost to take a stake in said company in relation to what one would receive in return. Does that sound familiar?

Similarly, Philip A. Fisher's *Common Stocks and Uncommon Profits*[59] from the same period reads a great deal like Thomas Gibson's enthusiastic urgings from the 1920s. According to Fisher, the investment climate was even better than in the prior period, in part because the research commitment and innovation of U.S. corporations were the envy of the world. (S&P makes the same point, and it is one that is hard to argue against.) Fisher offers 15 tips for identifying growth companies that seem awfully sensible, in retrospect. And why not? The United States was enjoying a strong multidecade economic run. Pension funds and endowments were expanding, and large numbers of individual investors had returned to the market after a quarter-century absence. Fisher's writings remain popular today in part due to Warren Buffet being on record as a fan and reader.

Sarnoff's radios were now computers. Decades before Apple had taken over the known world, the stock market was crazy about IT systems and computers. The very modern and tech-sounding names—Alphanumeric, Scientific Data Systems, Control Data, and others—were on every investor's lips. The 1960s' confidence in machines just oozes from the names of even the non-computer companies: Tektronix, Liquidonics, Solitron Devices, Xerox, Victor Comptometer, Transitron, etc. There was no jet pack (yet), but George Jetson was flying around on the family's new Magnavox color TV in the living room; why wouldn't he be in the family's brokerage account?

The Swinging Sixties Culture of Investing

The financial journalist George J. W. Goodman, writing as "Adam Smith," captures the "Swinging Sixties" spirit of the time in much the way that LeFèvre's derring-do and Gibson's optimism reflected the wild 1920s. His erudite and witty accounts of the period—*The Money Game* (1967) and a follow-up volume, *Supermoney* (1972)—vividly describe the mantra of "performance" for those seeking to grow assets. It was an age before benchmarks and clear peer groups, so the success or failure of "growth" tended to be measured more anecdotally and in terms of individual stock picks. In that vein, Goodman tells tale after tale of managers chasing stocks that had already rocketed up—a metaphor that meant a lot during the moonshot era—or were soon expected to lift off. Change a few details (and metaphors), and *The Money Game* of 1967 could easily be Jesse Livermore's confessions from the 1920s. As in the earlier version, so too in Goodman's account, the market is a big game to be figured out. And it is to be enjoyed immensely. Goodman quotes approvingly from Keynes about "the game of professional investment" and even more approvingly of the superstar academics John von Neumann and Oskar Morgenstern, who came up with modern game theory as it applies to economic matters. Consistent with the game metaphor, investing for Goodman was as much a matter of popular psychology as counting: "The irony is that this is a money game and money is the way we keep score. But the real object of the Game is not money, it is the playing of the Game itself. For the true players, you could take all the trophies away and substitute plastic beads or whale's teeth; as long as there is a way to keep score, they will play."[60]

Goodman's version of "behavioral finance" is present throughout his works as pop psychology, including ink-splotched images and personality types. Being a growth investor at this time was about having a "feel" for the game. Goodman quoted Edward Johnson II of Fidelity—already the 500-pound gorilla of the investment management industry—on what constituted good managers: "What is it the good managers have? It's a kind of locked-in concentration, an intuition, a feel, nothing that can be schooled. The first thing you have to know is yourself" with the follow-on corollary that "if you don't know who you are, this is an expensive place to find out." Smith characterizes Johnson as a Zen-like character, a philosopher king, not a mere successful bean counter.

In this subjective world, the metaphors of choice reflected the times. Goodman is an educated and sophisticated writer, but in regard to women, there is more than a touch of Mad

Men and even cringeworthy Austin Powers in his account of the Swinging Sixties. The market, he tells us, is an "alluring woman" to be conquered. Goodman purportedly quotes Johnson again as saying that

the market is a like a beautiful woman—endlessly fascinating, endlessly complex, always changing, always mystifying. I have been absorbed and immersed since 1924 and I know this is no science. It is an art. Now we have computers and all sorts of statistics, but the market is still the same and understanding the market is still no easier. It is personal intuition, sensing patterns of behavior. There is always something unknown, undiscerned.[61]

Another observer of the market wrote a passage about stock trading in 1973 that would make a modern late-night cable TV writer blush. When no one is looking, go to pages 101 and 102 of the original edition of Burton Malkiel's *A Random Walk Down Wall Street*. (The scene may have been edited out of subsequent editions.)

Moving in and out of stocks quickly, the prominent performance managers of the 1960s would, like the syndicates of old, push share prices around a lot. The *New Yorker*'s business writer, John Brooks, borrowed an image from contemporary pop culture and called these the "go-go" years, a style of investment that "was, to be sure, free, fast, and lively, and certainly in some cases attended by joy, merriment, and hubbub. The method was characterized by rapid trading of huge blocks of stocks, with an eye to large profits taken very quickly."[62] "Manipulate" is an ugly word, and it has legal connotations, but it is clear that quickly buying and selling 10,000-share blocks of a small number of securities resulted in material share price changes. The behavior of the leading managers put all that more pressure on the other would-be performance managers or even just investment bystanders to buy or sell the same stocks that they felt the big boys were moving. You didn't want to be the last one into a stock, and certainly not the last one out, so you'd better move quickly, a process made easier by new computer-based trading platforms. Volatility of share prices and turnover necessarily increased. Annual turnover rates of 100% or even 200% among the leading portfolio managers were not uncommon. In addition, because many of these institutions were not subject to immediate capital gains taxes on their assets, playing the market aggressively made sense in a way that it might not for individual investors or trustees. The Prudent Man managers who might have 10% annual turnover at most were stunned. Holding on to old economy names like AT&T—commonly known just as Telephone—offered little room for profit for the new era traders. Instead, "unseasoned" or newly issued stocks were preferred. They were smaller and could be more easily moved around.

Market Participants

By the 1960s, the syndicates of the 1920s had been replaced by institutional investors—pension funds, mutual funds, endowments—as well as plenty of punters, the individual investors who had returned to the market in numbers after a multidecade hiatus. Mutual fund assets grew dramatically from $1.3 billion in 1946 to $35 billion in 1967. At that time, institutions were managing another $150 billion. Though nominally more professional than the big boys of the 1920s, the institutional investors of the 1960s were still colored by the personalities of their superstar managers. By the 1950s, Fidelity had already emerged as a dominant mutual fund company, under the guidance of Edward Johnson II, a Boston attorney who had taken over the company in 1943. Johnson had read Edwin

Lefèvre's account of the speculator Jesse Livermore when it was serialized in the *Saturday Evening Post* in 1922 and 1923 and had been smitten by the markets ever since. Coming from the most conservative of backgrounds, and from the very location where the Prudent Man Rule for trustees had emerged a century earlier, Johnson facilitated the rise of a new type of investing around "unseasoned" issues and lots of turnover. It may have been heresy to his fellow Brahmins, but Livermore-quality speculation took on a new life under Johnson's direction, and it seemed to work well in the postwar period.[63] His protégé, Gerry Tsai, was the undisputed star of Wall Street, the face of the unapologetically growth Fidelity Capital Fund from its launch in 1958. Tsai happily ran a concentrated fund holding assets "that were then thought to be outrageously speculative and unseasoned for a mutual fund (Polaroid, Xerox, and Litton Industries among them)."[64] Tsai later ventured out on his own, starting the Manhattan Fund, another pedal-to-the-metal momentum (buy what's already going up) investment product. During the bull market of the mid-1960s, the superstars managed funds that might grow 100% in a single year. In 1967, the Winfield Growth Fund under Dave Meid and the Enterprise Fund under Fred Carr both did so. Fred Alger went out on his own in 1964, and his firm is still in existence more than 50 years later. His Security Equity Fund rose 260% in a four-year period in the late 1960s.[65]

Almost all of these individuals (other than Johnson himself) were in their thirties at the time of their ascendance; they were a new generation of young, glamorous daredevils. If World War I had caused a "lost generation" of young men in Europe, so too did the 1929 Crash and the Great Depression lead to an absent cohort of professional investors. Come the resurgence in equities in the 1960s, the pre-Crash generation was already retired or not ready for the rough and tumble of this new bull market. And so it was up to an entirely new crop of young guns whose relative investment inexperience seemed well suited to (and facilitated the return of) the 1920s' investment climate. By one account, half the salespeople and analysts working on Wall Street in 1969 had joined their enterprises after 1962. "The positions were being filled . . . by the soon-to-be-celebrated, sideburned, young hotshots of the late nineteen sixties."[66]

For retail investors, it was the golden age of the broker, led by the "thundering herd" of Merrill Lynch, the "A&P"[67] of the investment world, serving smaller investors around the country. Seemingly in parallel with the broker culture of the day, investment newsletters offering the not-so-secret formulas to instant or near-instant riches prospered in the postwar period as they had in the 1920s. The *Capital Gains Report* purported to offer substantial trading profits to its 5,000 subscribers, each of whom paid $18 per year in 1963.[68] The *Dines* weekly newsletter ($75 for an annual subscription) offered technical, fundamental, and psychological views on the market and individual securities. Other newsletters included the *American Investors Service, The Insider Report* (offering "5 sleeper stocks for wide gains in '65"), the *Granville Market Letter, Babson Reports,* and the industry leader—the *Value Line Investment Survey* (founded in 1931, having 50,000 subscribers paying $167 per year in the late 1960s, and still in business today)—among many others.[69]

Diversification?

For the 1960s' investor, the sober (if unquantified) diversification of the Prudent Man sort was out; Carnegie was back in. In this instance, however, the Scotsman took the form of veteran E. F. Hutton broker Gerald Loeb, whose widely distributed *The Battle for Investment Survival* was explicit in arguing for concentrated portfolios, 6 to 8 stocks for smaller accounts, 10 to 12 for larger ones. Loeb's definition of risk is quite different from the standard of MPT. Rather than "safety first," he thought that too much diversification limited the "upside" without good justification. Loeb was unencumbered by any investment theory; he was the Nike of the golden age of brokers—"Just do it!" You might as well get on the bandwagon, because the market was going up. And there is no point in the exercise unless the investor has "anticipated large gains": "Aim for a real profit. Reject everything that does not promise to advance generously in price."[70] Risk in Loeb's world meant missing a big move up in an asset price—an opportunity cost that would regularly be debited from the accounts of the excessively cautious. He (and others) also pointed to inflation—an increasing concern in the postwar period—as another reason to go for growth, and why swinging for the fences could be safer than sitting on the sidelines with go-slow income stocks. While not exactly copying Carnegie's all-your-eggs-in-one-basket approach, Philip Fisher's take was similar: too many investors owned too many stocks and actually encountered

the disadvantage of having eggs in so many baskets that a lot of the eggs do not end up in really attractive baskets, and it is impossible to keep watching all the baskets. . . . An investor should always realize that some mistakes are going to be made and that he should have sufficient diversification so that an occasional mistake will not prove crippling. However, beyond this point, he should take extreme care to own not the most, but the best.[71]

I reference this mid-century take on diversification because it was made just a few years before the academics would leave their ivory towers and begin their assault on Wall Street. One consequence of their victory (á la Bernstein) has been a dramatic shift away from concentrated portfolios. Concerned in the 1960s that portfolios might *already* be too wide and not deep enough, Fisher (and Loeb) would be utterly shocked to see today's portfolios with hundreds if not thousands of individual holdings.

Analysis

In the 1960s culture of performance, there was no time for Benjamin Graham's dividends. In retirement at that time, Graham told Goodman that he had generally stopped investing in stocks. He owned some municipal bonds and was generally trying to give his money away, not make more of it. Instead, the new generation was all about figuring out which stocks were going to go up the most, and perhaps push them in that direction. As Goodman sarcastically writes: "Dividend returns! Dirty words to an aggressive investor in the fifties, and certainly to a swinger in the sixties. . . . And ignore the market! Not watch the tape? Not trade stories? Not press the button on the quote machine?"[72] As we've seen, the disconnect of dividend from share price had occurred in the 1920s, and that had not ended well then. But that was before (once again) investors properly "understood" the market. Groucho Marx's branch manager was probably long gone by the 1960s, but his words about "a new world" echoed 40 years later—and in that new (old) world, all that mattered was share prices. Actually getting something for one's capital, other than a slip of paper that repriced daily, was just not part of the new (old) equation. History repeats itself when we are not paying attention, and apparently few in the 1960s investment community were paying attention.

The notion that it might be helpful to view investments from the perspective of portfolios rather than individual holdings and that some idea of risk might be applied systematically was rarely encountered in the investment climate of the 1960s. The work of Markowitz and his colleagues remained safely ensconced in the academy. More generally, it's hard to find a lot of systematic, marketwide analysis in the 1960s. Data itself was still a big problem. While narrow market indexes had been in existence for decades, what we today consider the broad market benchmark of the S&P 500 Index companies had only just come into being in 1957. And it wasn't until 1964 that a detailed study of market returns allowed investors to start talking about "the market's" 9–10% annual return. Lorie and Fisher's study of the average returns for all the stocks listed on the NYSE from 1926 through 1960 (and updated regularly thereafter) was originally funded by Wall Street itself, by Merrill Lynch, but the work was conducted at—yes, you guessed it—the University of Chicago, where the authors of the study taught.[73]

Well into the 1960s, what we might consider portfolio analysis appeared to be a rare activity. In a speech given to the New York Society of Security Analysts in 1966, Richard Jenrette (cofounder of Donaldson, Lufkin & Jenrette) had to lay down the basics: "Portfolio management is probably the most neglected phase of the investing process. Little has been written on the subject, and at our industry's study groups and seminars, we typically concentrate either on economics or on industry and company analysis. *Little attention is given to how these portfolio components fit into a logical whole*" (emphasis mine). He dismisses picking "hot" stocks—the reigning style of the 1960s—as a satisfactory substitute for systematic investment, and goes on to suggest that investors need to agree with clients on the portfolio's goals. With indexes only just coming into being, it was too early for a casual "choose a benchmark," but that was, in essence, what he was recommending. His suggestion that managers need to have an "investment philosophy" highlights how little the industry had come from the 1920s. He outlines DLJ's preferred approach at the time, what might now be considered GARP (growth at a reasonable price). His next observation is absolutely stunning in light of investment trends over the past 50 years: "Over-diversification is probably the greatest enemy of portfolio performance. Most of the portfolios we look at have too many names." I can only imagine what the Mr. Jenrette (88 years old in 2017) thinks now. He wrote that 25 to 30 holdings would work for a $100 million fund (the equivalent of $750 million in inflation-adjusted dollars today), and that for a $1 million account ($7.5 million in today's dollars), he could see holding 10 to 15 different securities.

Jenrette's final observation speaks volumes about the state of the art at the time: he suggests portfolio managers "keep score": "Buttressed by a 30-year bull market, the investment community, at least until recently, has seldom found it necessary to report results to its clients."[74] Robert Kirby, chairman of Capital Guardian Trust Company, echoed that sentiment in 1979, observing that the "most significant and influent invention of the investment management business during its long delayed, post-depression renaissance has been the concept of continuous, systematic measurement of investment performance. I supposed it is incredible to realize that portfolios . . . were not really subject to performance measurement prior to about 1960."[75] In this regard, industry and investors have come a long way, perhaps too far. We can and do check the performance score every day. What would Mr. Jenrette and Mr. Kirby say to that? Their characterization of the investment management industry in the mid-1960s strongly implies that the advancements in the academy had not made it yet from gown to town. The focus remained on stocks, not portfolios.

Dissemination

The circumstances that led investors to continue in their established ways through the 1960s did not last. Two primary developments led to the change. The first was the aforementioned rise of the institutional investment business. Aggregated money—insurance companies investing their premiums, mutual funds garnering assets from a rising middle class, brokerages pooling the assets of their customers and investing them according to models, and perhaps most importantly the growing pension plans of an expanding industrial postwar America—brought with it a class of intermediaries, professional analysts, and consultants, who eventually adopted the new and complex tools to manage the large sums that they were increasingly responsible for. The performance chase naturally led these practitioners to look for ways to help them in the daily struggle to win and maintain client assets.

But the real catalyst was much simpler: another major drawdown in the market. The first crash of the modern era motivated Graham, Keynes, and Williams (and many others) in the 1930s to try to figure out the market, and that pursuit was continued by Markowitz, Sharpe, and the rest in the postwar period as they brought their linear programming skills to bear in the computer age. By the late 1960s, a coherent "system"—really two closely related but separate systems—had been worked out by the academics. As long as the market hummed along, however, there would be little call for the application of either Markowitz-Sharpe or the EMH approach. The old investment tools—if they can be called that—still seemed to work. But the exuberance of the mid-1960s didn't last. The bull market took a pause in 1969, when inflation, monetary tightening, and a modest recession pushed the S&P 500 Index and the Dow Jones Industrial Average down by a quarter. The broader New York Stock Exchange composite index retreated by a third. Many of the notable story stocks of the 1960s crashed. The big conglomerates that had been hastily put together with debt and stock the previous few years (Litton, Gulf & Western, and Ling-Temco-Vought) fell sharply, as did the very popular computer, computer leasing, and other nontechnology growth names. Teleprompter went from 44 to $1\frac{7}{8}$. Avon dropped from 140 to $18\frac{5}{8}$. Best Products fell from $66\frac{3}{4}$ to $3\frac{1}{4}$.[76] On the other side of the transaction, Merrill Lynch "agreed" to take over the failing Goodbody brokerage, the nation's fifth largest, as hundreds of smaller brokerages around the country failed.

Bad soon turned into much worse. The market rallied quickly in 1971 and 1972, but the next round of challenges that hit starting in 1973 proved far greater: High unemployment, even greater inflation, the institution of price and wage controls, the OPEC oil embargo, the collapse of fixed exchange rates, and the removal of the United States from gold convertibility, not to mention a society in turmoil over Vietnam, Watergate, and the counterculture generation—all of these finally sapped the strength of postwar investors. From the market peak at the end of 1972 to mid-1974, the S&P 500 Index fell 46%. The Dow retreated by a similar amount from peak to trough. The New York Stock Exchange composite fell 44%.

No one needs help when things are going just fine. But when the pros began to appear incompetent, they had little choice but to take a hard look at the investment tools that had been quietly manufactured in the academy over the previous two decades. Even then, their acceptance of these tools was relatively slow, perhaps because the new methods came from without and were dramatically different and more complex than what had come before. And remember, the academics were outsiders; rarely were they businesspeople or investors themselves. Eugene Fama and Burton Malkiel notwithstanding, they were not parading up and down Wall Street demanding that their classroom models be implemented. But many professional investors realized that things were broken and that some sort of new method was needed. And so Wall Street was finally willing to reach beyond the confines of its own community for an explanation and a plan.

Peter Bernstein was not a neutral observer of this process, and he admits to being a cheerleader for the adoption of the new techniques, so much so that in 1974 he decided to push history forward by creating the *Journal of Portfolio Management* "to help others to learn what the new theories were all about. My goal was to build a bridge between town and gown." The first issue led off with a rallying cry from an early convert, James Vertin, CIO of trust accounts at Wells Fargo, who pointed out that customers were not satisfied with what they were getting at the time and that the industry needed a new approach. Fast-forward nearly a half century, and I couldn't agree more. After another financial crisis largely the result or at least exacerbated by the ideas introduced to the marketplace in the 1970s, it's time for a new approach. To paraphrase Vertin from four decades ago, it doesn't have to be this way. [77]

Regulatory Push

Washington also played a role. By the early 1970s, the country was in turmoil, and the stock market was down by nearly half from its peak. Industrial unions were still powerful, and their members were rightly concerned about the pensions they were supposed to receive from America's leading manufacturers. In 1974, Congress passed the Employee Retirement Income Security Act (ERISA) to create basic operating standards for private pension plans. A decade earlier the Studebaker Corporation had closed its remaining automotive plant in South Bend, Indiana, leaving a pension plan with a $15 million deficit. The default that soon followed started the legislative process that resulted in ERISA. As a consequence of the new legislation and follow-on rules and clarifications,[78] culminating in the Uniform Prudent Investor Act of 1994, the staid world of managing money on behalf of others— the world of trustees and fiduciaries—was essentially turned upside down. The Prudent Man Rule had governed the activities of the trustees of pension funds, trusts, and endowments for over a century. As a practical matter, for much of the late nineteenth and early twentieth centuries, being a prudent trustee meant limiting investments to the highest-quality bonds, and, depending on the time and location of the trust, perhaps a very short list of the bluest of blue chips, preferreds, and a handful of exceptional common stocks approved by state regulators. All other common stocks were simply out of the question. The "list" era, however, failed to protect trust beneficiaries during the Depression and was clearly not an adequate approach to investing. After the Second World War, trustees were given a bit more flexibility to own stocks and even mutual funds, but they very much had to remain in the spirit of the original 1830 Prudent Man Rule. And that meant focusing on capital preservation of each individual investment. Speculation and all the tools of modern investment were off limits. But this approach served trustees ill in the postwar decades when inflation eroded the purchasing power of bond-heavy portfolios. By the early 1970s, with inflation really raging, the old Prudent Man Rule was perceived to be a straitjacket leaving trustees with too few options.

The new body of legislation and rulings upended the existing notion of prudence. Trustees were now allowed—and over the subsequent decades were increasingly expected—to use all the new strategies and tools that had been worked out in the academy. And not using them—sticking to the old Prudent Man Rule—could render the trustees liable to being considered risky or imprudent. Whereas the prior standard was based on the risk of capital loss—hence the focus on owning bonds—trustees increasingly moved toward the new definition of risk provided by Markowitz, that is, variability of expected return around a mean. Where previously there had been a bright line between investment and speculation in trust work, now there would be a spectrum of acceptable outcomes. Key from our perspective is the redefinition of prudence from consideration of the investment at the individual security level to its impact at the portfolio level. Going forward, diversification would be of paramount importance. This is straight from the Markowitz playbook. Finally, the new legislation and the growing acceptance of MPT more broadly heralded a shift from judging the activities of the fiduciaries by the outcome—was money lost?—to considering whether the trustees followed a reasonable process of consideration and implementation. Prudence was no longer a list of bonds, but a series of steps and analyses.

Tools: How's the Torpedo?
Where Are You in the Box?

Having the ability and the computer power to analyze quantitatively current portfolios and possible future ones was a key hurdle to be cleared before MPT could be implemented in the marketplace. While the computers were being provided by IBM and its mainframe peers of the time, the analytics came from academics such as Barr Rosenberg, a Berkeley-based professor who in the 1970s and 1980s developed the "factor" analysis that is now regularly used to parse and judge the performance of mutual funds and individual portfolios, as well as pension funds and endowments. The goal was to understand what types of risks a portfolio was taking. But the meaning of the word "risk" was evolving. Risk in Sharpe's early work was understood simply as exposure to the overall market (beta). Sharpe's CAPM provided a basic analytical and predictive framework based on one factor—the market—but little means to explain why an individual portfolio deviated from that prediction.

Rosenberg expanded the list of individual factors that might be driving portfolio outcomes and by which they could be measured. Importantly, he included factors beyond the stock market—he initially called them "extra-market covariances."[79] Rosenberg's original model included 39 inputs such as size, sales growth, profit margins, balance sheet, etc.[80] At least for a while, business had snuck back into stock market analyses. (The portfolio that I manage is regularly analyzed to determine which of 21 separate factors explain its total return performance relative to a benchmark or an index. My favorite factor is the "EPS Torpedo." I have no idea what it is, but it sounds ominous.) More importantly, using these historical inputs, Rosenberg's models could supposedly predict future portfolio risk and therefore help managers estimate future performance. That presumed that the factors held steady and were themselves the underlying driver of performance, not just a reflection of some other factor. Knowing for certain which factors to consider remains a challenge to this day. I read recently of one study where portfolios were analyzed by 319 factors.[81] That may be more than the securities in the actual portfolio. It may or may not include the phases of the moon and the scores from the local bowling league. Is it possible to have too much information? Can having 319 separate analytical factors get in the way of owning a business and making investing decisions? I should think so if you have to spend all your time managing your factor exposure as opposed to managing your business.

The dissemination of factor analysis led quickly to the creation of a whole new generation of benchmarks by which investors and institutional consultants—a profession just coming into being to provide all these services—could evaluate portfolios. If a manager said he was a "growth" investor, how could one measure his performance without some sort of benchmark consisting of "growth" stocks? The same was true of value, large cap, small cap, etc. Russell introduced broad-based benchmarks in 1984 and added style benchmarks in the years thereafter. Today Russell offers over 80 different indexes for the U.S. market alone. Look closely at your brokerage statement, and you'll see the Russell 1000 Value Index or Russell 1000 Growth Index, among many others, used to provide a comparison for how your particular portfolio or fund is doing on a total return basis for any given measurement period.

By the early 1990s, "style investing" had been transformed. If the 1960s had just growth and everything else that was not explicitly growth, three decades later institutional investors had access to a large number of different styles, each with its own benchmarks and driven by its own specific set of factors. This in turn led to a business opportunity to introduce a simplified version of these institutional tools to the retail investment community. And for that purpose, Joe Mansueto created Morningstar. He started with a mutual rating system—the stars—in 1984 and then in 1992 introduced the Morningstar Style Box, the now omnipresent way of characterizing mutual funds by style (value, blend, growth) and size (small, mid, large) to create a nine-box matrix into which one's equity investments necessarily fell. The intention was to provide a simple, nonacademic tool for retail investors to help them understand the risks that they were taking and to allow them to measure their returns against similarly oriented funds.

The emergence of style characterizations, benchmarks, and factor analysis has contributed significantly to the proliferation of minuscule-weighted positions in client portfolios that I referenced earlier. The new tools allowed brokers and consultants to tap into numerous categories of investments, now that they had a way to measure each one against its appropriate benchmark and peer group. This opened the door to investors large and small having multiple managers or funds because each could be measured for its efficacy. Why does your financial advisor recommend a half-dozen specific mutual funds or individual managers for your account? Because he or she has the tools to judge and allocate among them. As I suggested earlier, this trend has now gone to potentially absurd lengths. I recently advised a professional association that had a small, $2.3 million investment fund. That endowment was invested in an institutional fund with a well-regarded advisor that used 24—yes, 24—separate managers, each investing a small amount—a sleeve—of the fund. Each individual sleeve had its own benchmark, and the manager was trying to generate alpha versus that benchmark. Not surprisingly, the fund generated about the same as the overall market—sometimes a bit better, sometimes a bit worse. It could have done so with a fraction of those investments and much, much less complexity. In the same vein, a leading vendor of the newest "smart beta" benchmarks offers (as of mid-2015) some 2,750 different benchmarks based on various factors.[82] Investors and portfolio analysts can now slice and dice to their heart's content. I see the minutiae, but where is the business in this microscopic analysis? To me, it's all trees and no forest.

Product Implementation

The trust department at San Francisco–based Wells Fargo Bank moved out front in the late 1960s and early 1970s as the leader in the practical application of the new approaches to investment management and analysis. In Bernstein's account, having trust departments in the vanguard of new investment styles was surprising given their conservative mandate and the legal constraints on their activities. At that time, a typical trust account would consist of a dozen or so different securities, with limited if any reporting or analysis provided on a regular basis. In retrospect, however, that backwater approach may be exactly why they jumped the queue. Given the new legal pressure on fiduciaries—being a trustee is serious business; you can readily end up in court if things go wrong—it is less surprising that MPT made its first inroads in the trust departments of regional banks.[83] Those that were last shall be first.

At Wells, James Vertin was joined by William Fouse, another academic enthusiast who was, according to Bernstein, basically kicked out of Mellon Bank in Pittsburgh for his effort to create an index product to test the new approaches. Together at Wells, Vertin and Fouse did just that, putting a portion of the Samsonite pension fund into 1,500 NYSE stocks on an equal-weighted basis. After two years of operational challenges, the assets were merged into a common fund for Wells Fargo trust clients based on the S&P 500 Index.[84] So started the multidecade flood into broad index funds.

The quantitative investing business of the Wells trust department eventually became its own business unit, Wells Fargo Investment Advisors. That was sold to Barclays Bank in the mid-1990s. It in turn was purchased by Blackrock in 2009. So if you own an index fund or, more recently, an ETF from Blackrock, you can trace the lineage of that investment back to the earliest implementations of Modern Portfolio Theory.

This initial activity at Wells spread quickly. Barr Rosenberg got American National Bank to begin measuring and managing money along the lines of his factor model.[85] Rosenberg's original business—Barra—met the needs of an increasing number of pension funds newly challenged by ERISA to adopt MPT, and to do so quickly. That meant being able to explain to trustees and regulators how a portfolio "behaved," not just due to a high or low beta, but also due to exposure to small-cap (or large-cap) stocks, high (or low) dividend yield, positive momentum (share prices going up, or not), high (low) sales growth, and many other basic business factors, as well as more esoteric inside-baseball, stock-market ones. Barra provided that explanation.

Not everyone welcomed the new way of doing things. The idea that risk was variance of expected return and could be expressed in a single figure—Sharpe's beta—or even a combination of statistical factors was not well received. Goodman quotes a market observer dismissing it: "These people with math and computer background who think they can assign precise degrees of risk to five or six decimal places are nothing but charlatans."[86] Noted market strategist at the time, Barton Biggs, wrote of the new approach, "I think it's just a lot of baloney."[87] Robert Monks, a Department of Labor pension administrator in the 1980s, went further: "Modern portfolio theory is absolute horse manure. I had to take a year to stop being bullied by it. I don't believe that just because I, as a trustee, have a low beta in my portfolio, I should sleep better at night. Much of MPT is ratification after the fact. We do not use MPT in the regulatory process here."[88]

Despite the initial resistance, the adoption of Modern Portfolio Theory progressed apace. By the late 1970s, the Markowitz-Sharpe paradigm of the risk and return was widely accepted in the institutional investment community and was making strides in the retail market as well. In a guide to Modern Portfolio Theory published by Dow Jones in 1979, the author Robert Hagin, director of quantitative research at brokerage firm Kidder, Peabody & Co., declared boldly that "MPT provides the ability to classify, estimate, and hence control, both the types and amounts of risk and expected return."[89] Kidder's retail clients would be getting the best the new science had to offer. And the confidence wasn't limited to just the Markowitz-Sharpe propositions. A whole new range of tools to analyze and value "derivatives" (options, swaps, futures, etc.) were becoming available at the same time. The key one—the Black-Scholes method for pricing options—was worked out in the mid-1970s just as the need for complex new investment tools was being felt in a routed market. It did for derivatives what Sharpe et al. had done for basic stock portfolios. At the time (and to this day), the entire slate of new tools was often sold as a way to lower stock market volatility and reduce the risk of big drawdowns during future market corrections.

It didn't hurt that the new tool kit had a very mid-century "whiff of truth" about it, in line with the broad acceptance of the mathematical simplification of human existence. Science could put people on the moon. Similarly, it was the heyday of the application of social science to real problems: school busing to assist in desegregation, modern housing projects to address aging slums, and welfare programs to eradicate poverty. A proper understanding of risk and return, complemented by reasonably priced derivative instruments, meant that market volatility could be substantially if not entirely suppressed, or so it was believed. For Bernstein and the other cheerleaders, it was "mission accomplished." Starting in 1985, the Nobel Prizes began appearing—for Modigliani in 1985, for Markowitz, Sharpe, and Merton Miller in 1990, and for Scholes and Robert C. Merton (also involved in the options formulas) in 1997. Surely if these guys had received the biggest academic prize of them all, they must be right.

Given the absence of a systematic investment framework that went before, it's not surprising that there were more than a few success stories of MPT implementation. Yale's David Swenson applied the core insights of MPT to the university's endowment and went further down the path of getting non-traditional and less correlated assets into the portfolio. That got him closer to the diversification Promised Land of the entire universe of investable assets. Swenson's rigorous due diligence process and a willingness to have more equities and fewer bonds than most of his peers didn't hurt either and allowed the Yale endowment to post many years of excellent relative and absolute returns.[90] (It probably did not hurt Swenson's cause that Yale had earlier come off several decades of losing money with a prior "Yale model" that sold equities and bought bonds in an inflationary environment.)

Even where the investment returns numbers were not as impressive as Yale's, or the process as well defined and measured as Swenson's, that is, for pretty much the rest of the investment community, the implementation of MPT created a far more coherent portfolio management narrative than had ever existed before. Clients knew whether they were leaning harder on value or growth, whether they had more small caps or a larger international allocation, how they had fared on a total return basis against a certain benchmark, etc. Many investors have come to know their portfolio's beta the same way they know their HDL cholesterol or A1C numbers. In this regard, Bernstein was right. The darkness had been vanquished, and it had been replaced by a factor-filled spreadsheet. Those numbers led many investors to believe that they were in control of where they stood on the risk and return spectrum and that the formulas worked. The entire system—now that there was one—created a certain comfort throughout retail brokerages across the country as well as in the offices of institutional investors and their consultants.

So by the mid-to-late 1960s, the outlines of MPT were in place, as was the notion that the markets could not be gamed. A decade later, implementation began in earnest. Investors following the academics were assured that they could safely focus on share prices and not insist on cash payments in return for their capital outlays. The following decades would bring significant revisions and improvements, but the underlying intellectual framework remains in place to this day. It is not much more than an intellectual hop, skip, and jump from these basic models to your quarterly brokerage account statement, your 401(k) style box choices, the barrage of ETF and index fund e-mails you receive daily, and even the near-term relative benchmark approach to equities in the typical pension fund or endowment. The intellectual framework for your hard-earned money is wearing bell-bottom jeans and humming Mamas and Papas tunes. Modern Portfolio Theory isn't modern any more. It's middle-aged. AARP is knocking on the door. And the theory doesn't look as good as it did 50 years ago . . .

One task of this work is to remind—in many cases inform—investment professionals and investors themselves that the framework under which they operate did not emerge from the primordial mist and that it should not be confused with something that is perfect and eternal. It was developed in a particular time and place and for a particular purpose fit to that time and place. As I'll argue in the remainder of this work, these tools just don't work anymore. It is time to develop new ones.

4

The (Nonexistent) Paradigm That Fails Investors Every Day

That place is so crowded, nobody goes there any more.

—Yogi Berra

In finance, we seem to have a chronic love affair with elegant theories. Our faculties for critical thinking seem to have been overcome by the seductive power of mathematical beauty.

—James Montier

All of this has been said before, but since nobody listened, it must be said again.

—André Gide

Does MPT Still Exist?

It took me several years to put this study together. During that time, I discussed the nature of Modern Portfolio Theory with many colleagues and peers. Their response was nearly universal: few admitted to believing in MPT. They were all aware of the shortcomings of the CAPM, that beta and the numerous follow-on factors are poor predictors of future outcomes, that the style box is not a helpful tool for investing, that relative benchmark investing doesn't meet real-world client needs, and that retail investors and many institutions get nowhere near the returns that they should if the system worked as advertised. And the litany of known problems goes on. Some practitioners might acknowledge the occasional utility of mean variance optimization (or MVO, the heavy statistical name for applying the Markowitz propositions) and the goal of making portfolios as Markowitz-efficient as possible, but that is as far as they are prepared to go. Most portfolio managers claim to be and genuinely are doing something a little different, in order to generate alpha, investing with a particular twist that takes it beyond the realm of standard MPT. Indexers and ETFers generally accept the notion of a broadly efficient market, but they still aim for achieving alpha or for getting an edge by focusing on narrower slices of the market.

So while many if not most professional investors keep some distance from the classic MPT or CAPM approach, *that overall Greek-letter investing framework remains firmly in place.* Despite the denials, the system sketched out in the 1950s and 1960s, and implemented in the 1970s and 1980s, lives on decades later in just about every single dollar invested by you or on your behalf. Alpha has managed to become a virtue disconnected from its origins. Investors seek it out, but they utterly ignore if not completely reject the relevance of the intellectual framework whence it came. Beta remains the casual way to discuss risk. Near-term relative benchmark performance is the high hurdle for professional investment managers. The newest variants of the classic model—portable alpha, smart beta, and ever-narrower benchmarks turned into an even greater array of ETFs—show that Modern Portfolio Theory is alive and well and trudging on in your retirement account or pension fund. The overall system remains focused on asset prices, with the goal of expected total return variance management, and risk-adjusted "excess returns."[1]

An alternative is needed, and that is what I propose in the final chapter. In this chapter, however, I want to provide an updated bill of indictment. The academic literature abounds with math-heavy challenges to some specific part of the theory itself or to MPT in practice. In contrast, my purpose here is to list all these challenges together and to not get lost in the esoteric details that characterize most academic commentaries on modern investment theory.[2] I would like to think that putting all the shortcomings in one place might shake the passivity of those who have heard the separate charges before but have not been moved by them. In addition, my intention is to make those weaknesses of MPT as relevant as possible to your financial life. It's not why the current system is flawed from a theoretical perspective; that's a matter of concern mostly to the academics. They can fight it out on the pages of finance journals only they read. Why MPT is flawed from a practical perspective and is threatening your financial well-being in retirement should be of more general interest.

Rational Actor Theory and Reality

Having just stated that I want to keep the list of problems focused on practicalities, I can't help but start with the basic issue that generates a majority of those practicalities. And that is the assumptions about investors that underpin the rules of MPT. The very nature of scientific advancement calls for taking shortcuts. It is done in all disciplines. Those assumptions can be justified if the outcome has real-world implications that are not undermined by those very same shortcuts. But in regard to the theoretical choices made on blackboards in ivory towers a half century ago, we are suffering the consequences in our brokerage accounts today.

In his early work, Markowitz went to great lengths to lay out in precise mathematical terms how a theoretical investor would and should behave. He had to do this because ideal investor behavior—rational investment decision making under conditions of uncertainty—was largely uncharted territory at that time. (Recall that in 1938, Williams had put forth a few simple assertions, but he did not elaborate on them.) For the whole thing to work, Markowitz and his postwar peers had to get rid of as much of that uncertainty as possible. In Markowitz's hands, it's really quite a lovely approach: describing rational investment behavior through a series of axioms and likening it to Euclid laying out the rules of geometry:

In the modern manner, we can drop the distinction between axioms and postulates (used by Euclid) and refer to the initial propositions of our deductive system as either axioms or definitions. . . . The axioms are offered as basic principles which we would expect to be consistent with the choices of a rational man or perfect computing machine. We cannot "prove" our axioms: if we knew more plausible principles from which they could be deduced, then these more plausible principles should have been used as axioms instead.[3]

Among those axioms, we find this: "Rational Man or Perfect Computing Machine is not subject to indecision." In addition, there is a clear ordering of probability distributions—that there is no "fuzziness in the perception of preferences" about what choices Rational Man would make. Specifically in regard to the generation of efficient portfolios, Markowitz assumes that the investor owns only liquid assets (bought and sold at the exact same price, and any amount can be transacted), that he is a utility-maximizing investor (defined intricately throughout his work and the main purpose of the axioms), and that the probability of expected outcomes from the portfolio investments does not change during the investment period. At the very end of his treatment, Markowitz does address some real-world circumstances that could affect the generation of efficient portfolios, and he concludes in regard to the vexing issue of taxation that "perhaps future conceptual research plus practical experience can produce improved procedures in this area."[4] A half century later, we can judge if that has indeed come to pass. Markowitz's early work reads less like an investment theory and more like the working out of the math of rational actor theory with a particular application to investments: "It may be thought of as a procedure which a Rational Man might employ in determining his course of action. This exact method of analysis is well beyond the capabilities of real men and real machines."[5] To my mind, his greater enthusiasm appears to be for the overall logic of his system, not the particular application of it: As Jerry Seinfeld might say, "Not that there is anything wrong with that . . . ," but it does bear pointing out.

Miller and Modigliani's blackboard exercise consisted of "an ideal economy characterized by perfect capital markets, rational behavior, and perfect certainty."[6] Treynor acknowledges that "in a real market, institutional complexities, frictions, taxes and certain other complications which are absent from our model may have a significant effect on share prices," but he makes his simplifying assumptions nonetheless: no taxes, no frictions (costs), maximization of expected utility, risk aversion, a perfect lending market, "perfect knowledge of the market," and finally "equal intelligence and equal effort to all investors."[7] Lintner writes of "idealized conditions" that are too long to post here but amount to detailed versions of the same assumptions made by the others.[8] In laying out his own assumptions for CAPM in 1964, Sharpe writes that they are "highly restrictive and undoubtedly unrealistic." He soldiers on by shifting the burden of relevance from the weaknesses of the inputs to the quality of the output, and we agree with this notion wholeheartedly. For Sharpe, "the proper test of a theory is not the realism of its assumptions but the acceptability of its implications."[9] Here too, more than 50 years later, we should be in a reasonably good position to judge that acceptability. Markowitz acknowledges that "the Rational Man, like the unicorn, does not exist. An attempt to see [the] general principles by which he would act, however, can be suggestive for our own actions."[10] Suggestive, perhaps, but not the binds that they have become.

More than a half century after rational actor theory conquered academic investment analysis, there is simply little to no evidence that it exists in practice, and its use has created more problems than it has solved. (Its main virtue remains that is permits grand, generalizing, macroeconomic theories . . .) While most investors are not overtly "irrational," they are simply not up to the exacting standards of rational actor theory. We are not machines, we do not have perfect information, and we have a variety of goals and fears and expectations, and they all change over time. In eco-speak, the latter are individual and unstable utility functions that Modern Portfolio Theory and a lot of other modern quantitative theories of human behavior prefer not to have. Importantly, these abstract constructs generally cannot work as advertised in the presence of frequently changing individual behavior and preferences. In this algorithmic world, the people are the problem, not the formulas.

Do We Really Live in a "Normal" World?

Our shortcomings as individuals and investors challenge the underpinnings of basic MPT, but that is not all. There are real data problems. Most (but not all) of the underlying models of modern investment theory demand data sets based on "conventional market assumptions that prices vary mildly, independently, and smoothly from one moment to the next." We know these as "normal" distributions (called Gaussian in the field of statistics) which bunch relatively smoothly around a central tendency—the bell curve. In this world, extreme events are rare. More or less all of the tools in modern investment theory assume that data pattern. "If those assumptions are wrong [as Benoît Mandelbrot and others have strongly argued], everything falls apart: Rather than a carefully tuned profit engine, your portfolio may actually be a dangerous, careening rattletrap."[11] Nassim Taleb has adopted part of Mandelbrot's mantle, and in two popular works, *The Black Swan* and *Fooled by Randomness*, Taleb rages against normal distributions of security price changes and the underappreciation of risk in the financial markets resulting from extreme events. He gets downright nasty on the topic of giving Nobel Prizes to the purveyors of finance theories based on normal distributions. He writes scathingly:

After the stock market crash [1987], they [the Swedish National Bank] rewarded two theoreticians, Harry Markowitz and William Sharpe, who built beautifully Platonic models on a Gaussian base, contributing to what is called Modern Portfolio Theory. Simply, if you remove their Gaussian assumptions and treat prices as scalable, you are left with hot air. The Nobel Committee could have tested the Sharpe and Markowitz models—they work like quack remedies sold on the Internet—but nobody in Stockholm seems to have thought of it.[12]

Subsequent extreme events—1998, 2000–2001, 2008–2009—that might not fit a bell curve and could not occur in a system in structural "equilibrium" suggest a real problem with the assumptions underpinning modern investment theory. Taleb finishes with an assertion consistent with a central argument of this work that the current approach was adopted not because it was correct but because it was available. In his words, "It is contagion that determines the fate of a theory in social science, not its validity."[13] Nassim Taleb is not a popular figure in the academic finance community, and while he comes off as a colorful character in his books, he seems far from genial. Still, with your retirement funds at stake, you might want to take his concerns about the shaky statistical underpinning of the standard financial model into consideration.

The CAPM and the Efficient Frontier

Setting aside robots as investors and bell curves and other statistical assumptions, there are other, more commonsense issues that need to be addressed. For instance, the CAPM component of the current framework makes assumptions that can only work in the ivory tower. One of them is that investors can borrow an unlimited amount at the rate of U.S. Treasuries (the risk-free rate) in order to invest and sell short investments by the same infinite amount. None other than Harry Markowitz observed that this clearly nonsensical premise had profound implications for the conclusion that the market itself was the most efficient portfolio that everyone should own. "The world does not work this way," he drily noted. "When one clearly unrealistic assumption of the Capital Asset Pricing Model is replaced by a real-world version, some of the dramatic conclusions no longer follow."[14] In its purest form, CAPM also has everyone holding the market in the same proportion as the market. Despite the advance of index funds, it has been noted frequently that that condition "cannot be obtained in the real world."[15] (I would add that it should not be obtained, even if it could.) Another catch-22 is that the more people who index, the greater the systematic risk to everyone indexing. And that was observed over three decades ago, well before indexing took off and dominated Main Street and institutional investing.[16]

Fifty years after the young Markowitz started the revolution in finance with some stunningly simple precepts—what matters is the portfolio and variance from expected return—the father of MPT was having doubts about the actual formulas that were developed to implement his ideas:

The CAPM is a thing of beauty. Thanks to one or another counterfactual assumption, it achieves clean and simple conclusions. . . . Now, 40 years later, in the face of empirical problems with the implications of the model, we should be cognizant of the consequences of varying its convenient but unrealistic assumptions. . . . My own conclusion is that it is time to move on.[17]

Here again, we find ourselves agreeing that Harry Markowitz is a very wise individual, even if we distance ourselves from how his original propositions have come to be used in the marketplace.

But what about those original propositions? Does Markowitz's own efficient frontier exist, even if we don't get there via CAPM or a related approach? Is there an easily accessible continuum of risk and return, predictable to three decimal points? No, there is not. MPT's efficient frontier is a fairy tale, a Shangri-la for mathematically inclined people, a place where historical data accurately predicts the past, a realm in which pure math, with its alluring simplicity, holds sway and banishes uncertainty from the human experience. It is comforting, but it does not exist. Then again, like Santa Claus, if enough people believe in the efficient frontier, perhaps it springs to life? For nearly 50 years now, people have been striving to get to that magical place. It cannot be proved to exist, but it is also very hard to prove that it doesn't exist. And if tens of thousands of individuals spend their professional lives making decisions based on factor analysis and historical return covariances projected into the future, can it really be said that the place doesn't exist? Yes, Virgina (look it up!), there is an efficient frontier. It lives on in the computers of institutions up and down Wall Street, and in the portfolio recommendations of Main Street brokerage offices.

Are we not in the realm of some sort of quantitative philosophy, where human behavior has been reduced to an unprovable (but also hard to deny) set of mathematical equations? The issue goes well beyond investment finance. First principles about human behavior when pushed to an extreme can be very dangerous, as the twentieth century has demonstrated. At points Nassim Taleb seems to blame all the shortcomings of twentieth-century politics and economics on aggressive professors relying on normal distributions. Even if you do not go that far, his point is profoundly important: if the data does not "act" in the way that the academic mandarins say that it must, then the resulting outcome—the stuff of most current investment theory and practice—is just plain bunk. My industry peers will reject this notion out of hand. They will do so for the same reason that the "powers-that-were" rejected the notion that the Earth revolved around the sun. It throws their world into tumult, steals their certainty and their purpose. My assertions may be presumptuous, even arrogant, but just because they are inconvenient and challenge the status quo does not make them incorrect. The alternative world-view that I am about to sketch out in the next chapter may not be "correct" either. Indeed, there will be many flaws in it. But that does not make the existing worldview correct. It only makes it the existing worldview.

Defining Risk

Beyond the problematic assumptions outlined above, there are significant costs associated with building an investment theory on key constructs that are completely unrelated to the underlying businesses, to their operations, and to the cashflows that determine ultimate values. Markowitz chose to define risk in a very specific manner: variance from an expected total return, using a statistical construct—standard deviation—as the measure of that risk. That simple choice set in place the basic outlines for how money is managed more than 60 years later. (Sharpe's beta now passes as a shorthand measure of risk, but it is similar in nature to Markowitz's.) As a practitioner, I object to MPT's definition of risk. It speaks to the price of assets, not their utility. It separates the price from the asset—the underlying business really doesn't matter—and severs it fully from the present and future cashflows that ulti-mately support the asset price and the long-term trajectory of the asset price.

Moreover, having a single, narrow definition of risk may be fine for *Homo economicus* but is less likely to suit real individuals and institutions that might have a variety of con-cerns about their investments and ways of defining risk. For some of them, risk may indeed be variance from an expected median total return of market assets from one single point in time to another single point in time. In that case, MPT looks like a pretty good way to manage financial investments. For some others, it may be the cashflows that I emphasize. For others it may be "drawdown" of asset levels, and for still others, it can be "volatility," however that is defined. For some, it will certainly be the more subjective "sleep-at-night" test of risk. Risk, like beauty, is in the eye of the beholder, and investors should not assume that some canonical academic definition of risk is the only one. Having multiple ways of defining the success or failure of an endeavor creates big challenges for the academics trying to build universal models of investor behavior, but that is their problem, not yours.

Within CAPM and most other means of valuation, there is also a second definition of risk, or lack of risk, that warrants closer examination. For stocks, CAPM explicitly starts out with a risk-free rate and then adds a bit extra—the equity risk premium, adjusted by the investment's beta—to compensate investors for taking risk (and expecting return) above the risk-free rate. Even outside the constraints of CAPM, most discount rates, however they are calculated, also generally rely on a risk-free base rate, topped off by an additional amount. For U.S. investors, the rate of interest on U.S. Treasuries at any particular time is and has long been considered by market participants to serve as the risk-free rate for that moment. While it is true that if the U.S. government defaulted on its debt obligations, the world would likely be in a bad place, that does not make U.S. government securities risk-free in any absolute sense. Nor does it make any particular yield-to-maturity number a bona fide risk-free rate. In fact, Treasuries change price (and prospective yields) every day the bond market is open. Indeed, it is no harder to lose money in Treasuries than it is to lose it in any other type of investment. For the past several years, the price of the 10-year Treasury note has been extremely high (and the yield extremely low), suggesting that "risk" is itself very low. But few people are borrowing. Businesspeople intuitively understand the real level of risk, even if the risk rate on government debt appears to be quite attractive. Or in plainer English, you can lead a horse to water, but you can't make it drink. The U.S. Federal Reserve (and the ECB and the Bank of Japan) has pumped money in recent years into the global financial system only to see it flow mostly into the financial markets, rather than into the real economy. The situation in Japan is instructive: the official level of "risk" in that country has been exceptionally low for decades, and yet Japan has been mired in an economic funk for much of that time.

Diversification

Modern investment theory and practice is a sober and measured exercise built up over numerous decades and the result of literally tens of thousands of very smart people contributing to its continuous improvement. I do not take that lightly, and I have tried to present my criticisms at an equally high level. But in regard to diversification, I must resort to plain statements: MPT has led to absurd, *utterly absurd*, levels of diversification. In the 1950s, Harry Markowitz rightly encouraged investors to think in terms of the portfolio, not individual stocks, and how to define and measure risk at the portfolio level. In his time, the absence of diversification was a serious investment issue: portfolios with just a handful of securities would have been common, so Markowitz's injunction was wholly needed. Not anymore. In the form to which it has come to us today—relative benchmark performance exercised through vast holdings in numerous style boxes— Markowitz's approach more or less compels investors to own a ridiculously high number of tiny stakes in businesses they might not want to own, and certainly in amounts that make no sense to own, all in the name of risk-reducing diversification at the theoretical level and in the goal of relative bench-mark outperformance at the practical level. That is, MPT discourages investors from thinking about what they own in any absolute sense—a stake in an ongoing, prospering real business. Instead, it encourages them to think in terms of whether they are "overweight" (have more) or "underweight" (have less) than the benchmarks and what others might own or not own. Remember that these benchmarks and the sectors into which they are divided are not carved in stone. They are a relatively recent phenomenon, developing necessarily hand in hand with the implementation of MPT.

Thinking about one's investments as a businessperson really helps in this regard. If investors thought of their hold-ings as stakes in enterprises rather than as betting slips, they might realize that having so many small positions in a single portfolio does not really have much value. At the other end of the quizzical spectrum, the still-dominant market-cap-style benchmarks can force the same investors who own thousands of meaningless stakes to own a handful of very large weights in companies that everyone else owns in the same amount: To wit, Apple is 3.7% of the S&P 500 Index and 11.8% of the Nasdaq 100 (as of October 2017). If you own an index fund or ETF based on that benchmark, you own a large slug of Apple whether you think that desirable or not.

In practice, we have "Markowitz-gone-wild" diversifica-tion. An investor individual with $500,000 allocated to equi-ties might have a "separately managed account" overseen by a financial advisor with perhaps as many as 5 individual portfolios covering different parts of the style box. Each of those silos might have around 50 to 60 stocks in the portfolio. So the client would own at least 250 to 300 stocks, and pos-sibly many more if the individual managers were so inclined.

Amazon and Merck and a few others (certainly Apple) would be in several of the portfolios at the same time, so the total number of individual equities might be a bit lower. If the client had an allocation to small caps, as many investors do, the numbers move up well above 300 or so, as small-cap products typically have many more holdings. For investors who have index funds and ETFs, you can possibly add a zero to these numbers. Those clients will have potentially *thousands* of small "investments," which amount to no investments at all in the sense of directed ownership of a business.

Let's just take the very conservative 250-separate-stocks number. The mathematics of price return diversification are quite simple at the basic level, even if calculating individual stock covariances is a time-consuming process. The core benefits of diversification materialize with a few dozen holdings. According to one controversial study, most of the benefits are realized with just 10 stocks.[18] A more persuasive analysis suggested that the benefits of diversification were substantially achieved by having 20 to 30 holdings. In that study, a 1-stock portfolio had a standard deviation—a measure of volatility—of 49.24%. At 4 stocks, it fell to 29.69%; by 20 stocks, it was at 21.68%; and for 30, it fell just a bit more to 20.87%. From there on, the incremental benefits of diversification became marginal at best. At the 1,000-stock level—common in so many portfolios today loaded with ETFs and index funds—the standard deviation was 19.21%, just barely lower than that of the 30-stock portfolio, and hardly worth the extra complexity and cost of the additional 970 stocks.[19] So remember that analysis the next time your financial advisor says you need a bit of this, and a bit of that, and a dollop of Chilean copper futures, and a Japanese bank ETF, all in the name of diversification.

Whatever the right number necessary to achieve basic price diversification, it is nowhere near 500 or 1,000. With that number of stocks, the client is just exposed to the overall market and will do a little better or a little worse than the market portfolio. That's not diversification. That's a closet index fund, even if none of the individual managers is remotely indexlike. Even though each component of the portfolio is trying to do something relatively narrow (beating the mid-cap-value benchmark, generating large-cap growth alpha, targeting a particular beta, getting "exposure" to international financials, having a stake in small-cap growth, etc.), put them all together and you have *the* stock market. The most extreme case I saw recently was an institutional endowment fund that had approximately 1,000 securities in it. Not surprisingly, it did somewhat better (or worse) than the market, depending on the measurement period. When the indexlike returns were pointed out to the fund's salesperson, he rejected the notion entirely: each of the managers of the fund's two dozen separate "sleeves" had a specific, narrow mandate and was actively pursuing alpha versus the manager's narrow benchmark. The salesperson could not see the forest for the trees.

That is not an isolated instance. In managing client portfolios to meet the needs of style-specific benchmarks, investors—including the "smart" institutional money—have also lost sight of the broader forest as they wander within their favorite grove of stocks. In recent years, the diversification fetish has failed a basic commonsense test: if the market portfolio is filled with modern-day "fancy" stocks—as it periodically is—owning the market doesn't seem like a great idea. One answer to that challenge is to suggest that you go short the entire market when you feel it is unattractive. That is not a reasonable solution for the overwhelming majority of investors, including institutional ones with specific mandates. Even many of the largest institutional investors do not have that option, and I doubt that they would want it. Instead, most investors just own a lot of small positions, the good and the less good, to mitigate risk. For them, Markowitz diversification has degenerated into carelessness, an unwillingness to make choices.

This assertion that most investors have too much diversification—and are using diversification to avoid decision making—will ruffle many feathers. The standard wisdom remains very much that if there is an asset class out there—Martian real estate, Nepalese government bonds, Pokémon GO futures—then you should have a slice of it. No, you shouldn't, and don't let a consultant tell you otherwise. The extreme diversification one encounters today gives investors the sense that they are in control of risk, when in many cases it turns out to be the exact opposite—opting for a lot of small choices that amount to not making any big decisions. As I'll suggest in the next chapter, the desirability of an asset should be determined by its present and prospective cashflow to the owner, not its position in an enormous covariance matrix.

The Expected Rate of Return

Modern investment theory is based on two key pillars: diversification (Markowitz) and a CAPM or ultimately CAPM-derived expected rate of return (Sharpe et al.). In many ways, the expected rate of return may be the more crucial of the two. Markowitz doesn't come up with his own, but defers to the prevailing framework of his day—Williams. Thirty years after Williams, Sharpe came up with a much simpler, less company-specific formula for expected return. Without this critical input, none of the math of modern investment theory really works. Yet, to this day, and despite the existence of formulas designed to generate or describe an expected rate of return, it is still a mysterious element. In a recollection near the end of his life, Merton Miller joked that he still remembered

the teasing we financial economists, Harry Markowitz, William Sharpe, and I had to put up with from the physicists and chemists in Stockholm [where Miller et al. had gone to collect their Nobel Prizes] when we conceded that the basic unit of our research, the expected rate of return, was not actually observable. I tried to parry by reminding them of their neutrino—a particle with no mass whose presence is inferred only as a missing residual from the interactions of other particles. But that was eight years ago. In the meantime, the neutrino has been detected.[20]

Another 15 years later, and the expected rate of return remains as elusive as ever, even as another proposed and very hard-to-detect particle from the natural world, the Higgs boson, has been properly welcomed. Fifty years of algebraic formulas in finance journals have not succeeded in making a physics-like *science* of human behavior, and harder yet of collective human behavior (the stock market) involving expectations and decision making. While it might have provided some insight, it has fallen far short of the promised mathematical precision. Indeed, the notion that the formulas are increasing certainty in the choices we make may well make some of that decision making even worse, because we fall into the trap of assuming that the formulas are infallible.

The consequences of this fallacy go further. The CAPM-derived rates of return are not limited to the academics arguing about the stock market. They directly affect your . . . monthly utility bills. The capital asset pricing model filled an enormous business void, allowing your state's public utility commission to mathematically forecast rates of return. Since the 1980s, those commissions have had an academically blessed way of reviewing rate cases and setting reasonable rates of return for the utilities to provide the public service of generating and delivering electricity. It sounds good, and it certainly marks an improvement over the lack of a system that preceded it, but the tail now wags the dog. Even private companies use CAPM—with either made-up betas or the adjusted betas of similar publicly traded entities—to assess the expected returns and cost of capital for projects.[21] This stuff matters. At a minimum, those who rely on CAPM should know where it came from. And I would hope that some investors, businesspeople, and public utility commissioners would want to go the extra mile and at least question whether it actually is the end-all and be-all approach that it is assumed to be for forecasting future returns.

Near-Termism and the Relative Benchmark Performance Game

Prior to the introduction of a wide range of indexes, benchmarks, and Rosenberg's tools in the 1970s and 1980s, it was very hard to tell how institutional portfolios were doing relative to other portfolios or even the broader market. The introduction of these means was an unalloyed good. The push for style diversification, once that was possible, soon followed. For the retail investor, the now famous Morningstar style box was introduced in 1992. (If you don't already know the style of your various managers or funds, you can quickly determine it on the Internet and quite easily at Morningstar.com.) Fast-forward several decades, and these initially very reasonable and innovative measurement tools have too often become the means for short-term decision making by institutions and individuals as they play the relative benchmark game. Measuring total return performance every day, every month, every quarter against a style benchmark encourages near-termism by professionals who are expected by their customers to generate stock market "outperformance" in just about every measurement period. Performance measurement is a great idea, but doing it every day for what are meant to be long-term business decisions undermines its purpose.

Short-termism is an unintended though inevitable consequence of modern investment theory because it is based on paying close attention to daily stock market total return. Since the stock markets are open on a daily basis, you get a new total return figure every weekday, 250 times per year. Why not measure it? The magical number tells you "how you are doing," or at least that is what investors are led to believe. If it is up today, you are doing fine. If it is down, you are ailing. In contrast, most of the businesses behind those stock prices really don't change that much on a daily basis. Take that Coca-Cola bottling plant in your nearby industrial park, the one that has been there for 30 years. It's been pumping out bottled and canned beverages for decades—initially mostly soda, now more water, tea, and sports drinks—no matter what the share price of Coke was. KO goes up, KO goes down. Regardless, the plant produces and the people buy. There can be trends in consumer preferences, in packaging costs, in labor relations, in profits and capital expenditures, but they occur over months and years, not days. In contrast, the KO shares reprice daily. Of course, there are times when the share prices do contain important information about a company's genuine business conditions; they are, as a wise friend observed, "a real-time barometer of collective expectations about a company's prospects." Those expectations need to be taken seriously, especially when they move sharply. There are also supply and demand issues—money flowing into or out of the stock market—that might justify and explain material price swings. I'm not suggesting that markets shouldn't be open daily to provide liquidity, but investors should realize—really think about—the unintended consequences of otherwise stable business assets repricing every 24 hours. Should their portfolio management system be based on the underlying business conditions of the companies or on the flickering numbers on the computer screen? Contemporary practice, informed by MPT, focuses more on the latter. That is unfortunate.

The pressure on investment managers to "perform" and to "perform now!" can be intense. One client of ours at a large bank managed money for wealthy individuals but also for institutions and endowments. Both populations were conservative. The wealthy individuals were content to keep receiving a steady stream of rising checks from our dividend-focused strategy. The advisor left that allocation alone; the clients left him alone. But the institutions were guarded by gatekeepers who were tracking performance every month. And they were indifferent to cash generation, even though as endowments and charities, they had a cash distribution mandate. We happened to meet the bank after a period of relative benchmark underperformance of eight months. This was during a Federal Reserve–induced strong market rally. It was a market melt-up during which our conservative assets had melted up less. The bank official indicated to me that while a high and rising income stream from low-volatility assets was just what both sets of clients needed, he was going to have to reduce our weight in the institutional accounts, because the pressure to perform *now!* and do something about underperformance *now!* was intense. In short, if he didn't fire us or at least shift money away from us, he was at risk of getting fired himself.

At our meeting, he threw up his arms and acknowledged that he was doing the wrong thing at the wrong time, and he knew it. As a result, those endowments got "hot-money" products and perhaps suffered the typical consequence of chasing near-term stock performance.

That's the typical outcome of a system based on short-term relative benchmark performance. Most institutions claim to invest for the long term, but too many of them behave like near-term traders, to the detriment of their goal of meeting the needs of the ultimate owners of the assets. It's fair and appropriate to measure the performance of a product against its peers, but how appropriate is it during a marathon to bet on one runner and then check every quarter mile and shift the bet to the runner that was in the lead for the previous brief stretch? Come the twenty-sixth mile, the investor-turned-punter has only managed to generate a lot of money for the bookie. When Michael Dell took his eponymous computer company private in 2013, he stated that the move would allow the company to change "from a quarterly focus to a more of a longer term, five-year, 10-year focus, doubling down on the investments that are really needed for this company to be able to serve its customers."[22] Time will tell whether Dell is able to achieve that goal in the brutally competitive computer industry, but he is clearly right regarding the risks of baring all every quarter. A movement to step back from quarterly reporting is growing, with major commentators and investment houses pointing to the business damage done by the need for publicly traded enterprises to "make" their quarterly EPS estimates.

Looking at near term and seeing long term are not limited just to the relative benchmark performance game. They actually make up an important component of the data issue, which I took up originally in *The Strategic Dividend Investor*

(2011). Mathematically, dividend yield + dividend growth = total return from an equity over the long term. Add what turns out to be a small factor for yield compression (P/E expansion) or yield expansion (P/E compression), and you get the actual total return. However, the industry measures returns on a daily basis and then geometrically links them (dig out your high school math text) for as long as you want: a month, a quarter, a year, a decade, a century. That math— using short-term swings in share prices to explain returns over much longer periods—effectively masks the role of dividend growth in capital appreciation, and it pushes people to focus on the stock price, not the cash that is actually received from investment in a business.

Drawdowns and Cyclicality

MPT doesn't really foresee market "corrections," sharp but temporary downward moves in the market. Instead, it is a point-to-point framework for investing, one that largely ignores the market's ups and downs that actual investors must necessarily experience. Recall that Lorie and Fisher's average 9–10% positive annual returns from the stock market have some wild swings in them. Markowitz diversification is supposed to mathematically protect investors against extreme downdrafts at the company or sector or overall asset level by making sure that the covariances are as low as can be vis-à-vis other investments. The problem with that approach is very simple: During periods of financial crisis, the correlation of financial assets tightens sharply. Everything moves together so there is no "port in the storm," which is exactly when you most need the protection that MPT is supposed to offer. During the stock market drawdown of 2008–2009, we saw this failure of diversification play out in real time.

Companies such as Verizon and Johnson & Johnson, which were as remote as possible from the Lehman Brothers and Bear Stearns of this world, were nevertheless sold off with a vengeance. The VZ shares traded down as much as 44% (from October 2007 to October 2008); stodgy JNJ was bid down 35% (from September 2008 to the market bottom on March 9, 2009). Why? Because fully diversified investors who could not get their money out of the financials turned to the nonfinancials to raise cash. Other investors who may have sidestepped the worst of the financials also decided to cash in their chips because they didn't like what was going on in the marketplace. So the out-of-the-danger-zone investments sold off sharply, perhaps not as much as the financial institutions that were on their way to zero or a bailout, but a lot more than their historical betas or covariances would have suggested.

The fact that nearly all stock prices move together during crises is widely known by most engaged investors, but to my mind it represents a fascinating Achilles heel for one of modern investment theory's main claims: making the stock market experience less volatile for investors. I'm particularly intrigued by MPT's attempt and ultimate failure to mitigate volatility through diversification, because the effort is based on marketplace prices and their *historical* relationship. Over time the covariances (Markowitz) or betas (Sharpe) may be stable, but during crises, those defensive properties diminish. The good get sold along with the bad. And it is precisely during those times when too many investors, many of them passive, start looking at the whole exercise and get justifiably scared. Telling them to hold on in order to get the average 10- or 20-year return can be cold comfort for many during these drawdown periods. The Markowitz diversification framework can be particularly dangerous when coupled with the notion of an efficient market. In that world, the S&P 500

Index could trade at some crazy-high P/E multiple, with no or minimal cash distributions, and the MPT/EMH/CAPM/indexers would happily buy it (and many of them did in 1999).

In short, *MPT doesn't work when it is most needed.* Defenders of the canon would reply that true Markowitz diversification includes owning all sorts of publicly traded assets, not just equities, and that full diversification would protect investors if one particular asset class, say stocks, was overblown. But what if, after years of financial stimulus, all financial assets look bubbly? The defenders of the current approach will also point out that diversification is only designed to minimize *nonsystematic* or *company-specific* risk, and that *systematic* risk (in this case, market risk) is unavoidable to some degree or another as long as one holds financial assets. That may be narrowly true in an academic court, but in the court of public opinion, it does little to console investors. MPT may be not directly guilty of overall market drawdowns, but as the reigning investment paradigm, it cannot claim complete innocence either. When it became part of the official canon, Markowitz diversification was considered the "last free lunch" in academic finance because it purported to offer investors a measure of riskless return—getting company-specific risk out of the portfolio without sacrificing any return. But the remaining systematic risk, when combined with the occasional crazy markets and extreme diversification, can turn that supposed "free lunch" into a nasty case of indigestion or worse all afternoon. In contrast, actual business operations tend to be more stable than the stock market prices they are supposed to represent. Verizon connected the usual number of calls during the financial crisis—perhaps even more—and J&J sold roughly the same amount of baby powder, Band-Aids, and Tylenol as expected. Perhaps an investment theory might be more closely tied to those business operations?

Modern investment theory came out of the substantial efforts of curious and concerned individuals, initially in the 1930s, trying to make sense of the 1929 Crash and the Great Depression. One of the leading issues at that time was the economic cyclicality that loomed large for businesses and stock market investors alike. The advances continued in the postwar period with the new tools to manage risk and volatility. Nearly a century after the initial events, stock market crashes aren't really supposed to happen anymore. Federal Reserve activity should theoretically limit the cyclicality of the underlying economy, and increasingly efficient markets should play their role in controlling market volatility. At the portfolio level, Markowitz diversification shields investors from excessive variance of return by having stocks with the right covariances or a good mix of betas. I somewhat overstate the case, but MPT offered the prospect of banishing stock market cyclicality to the dustbin of history. Well, that didn't happen. After MPT was developed but before it was implemented, 1969 happened. Then came 1973–1974, by which time market efficiency was already somewhat known, and that big drawdown ushered in the tools and framework of MPT. Thereafter big drawdowns have followed with disconcerting regularity: 1987, 1998, 2001 (preceded by a vast bubble), and 2008–2009. The challenge of asset price cyclicality remains essentially unresolved. Mathematical formulas have not tamed it; Federal Reserve Board credit loosening and tightening cycles have not eradicated the business cycle. Tens of thousands of MBAs and CFAs running around the investment industry have not gotten rid of the business cycle or its appropriate reflection in asset values.

Let us be a bit more humble than the theories suggest we need to be and acknowledge the ups and downs of life. Yes, science led to the eradication of polio and smallpox. Yes, traveling on an airliner is a lot safer and faster than it was five decades ago due to advances in airplane and, in particular, turbofan technology. Car insurance, building design, and a multitude of other pedestrian elements of the human experience have benefited substantially from the quantification of risk over the past century. But uncertainty remains a key component of the human experience. Investment risk in its many forms is still out there, and decades of new formulas and products to control it have done little to change that reality. In fact, they may have made matters worse, not by increasing volatility, but by conveying to investors the idea that they are insulated from that volatility when they are not.

Nearly 200 years after it was written in 1830, the Massachusetts Supreme Court ruling behind the Prudent Man Rule remains sound: "Invest as you will. The capital is at hazard." That is the nature of life. Mathematics may improve the odds a bit. Self-awareness can definitely help us navigate the choices, but the fundamental reality of uncertainty confronts us all. Better to acknowledge that than to delude ourselves. Industry pioneer Barr Rosenberg was fined several million dollars and barred from the securities industry for life in 2011 for failing to banish uncertainty. He had an investment model that he used to manage client assets. When his team discovered a computer coding flaw in the algorithm, "Rosenberg directed [his team] to keep quiet about the error and to not inform others about it, and he directed that the error not be fixed at that time."[23] When the mistake was ultimately revealed, the SEC investigated and tossed him out of the industry. Depending on your politics, you may view his fate as a case of nanny-state overreach, but I would argue that the key issue is the current system's implied claim to effectively quash uncertainty. That expectation raises investor expectations too high. And we live in a litigious society. The two together make a dangerous combination.

Supply and Demand

When you walk into your financial advisor's office and tell that person what you'd like to achieve from your capital, he or she will discuss your tolerance for risk, put a number on it, and then have the firm's computer spit out an allocation of stocks and bonds and other assets that should deliver the MPT-optimal combination of expected return and tolerable risk. Step two involves buying a mix of stocks, bonds, funds, or strategies, or—as is quite common now—ETFs or index funds. That's all well and good, but it's all on one side of the equation: the demand side. It's telling you what you should own, not necessarily what is out there in the marketplace. Models address the demand for certain types of assets, not their availability or quality. Models are based on expectations of returns and volatility, but what if the supply of said constituents just isn't there?

Once again, we run into an important theoretical hurdle. MPT describes a world that ought to be, not the rather messy world that is. If the marketplace is filled with junk—as the stock market was in the late 1990s, and will likely be again at some time in the future—then a typical asset allocation model isn't going to help investors much. Efficient market folks will say that quality will eventually chase out the junk, but that is small solace for investors who bought tech in 1999 and financials in 2007. Let us set aside the EMH for a moment and consider that there might be an ideal portfolio for clients that is not just the market portfolio. The identification of that portfolio doesn't mean that those assets are available for purchase, particularly if everyone is using the same (or similar) asset allocation models. For instance, just because you as an investor should have—given your age, asset level, and risk tolerance—a healthy dose of dividend-paying stocks in your retirement account does not mean that there are enough dividend-paying stocks out there to satisfy the demand of you and 50 million fellow baby boomers eyeing retirement. If enough people buy up those assets, then the yields will drop and they become less attractive. Supply and demand may work well over the long term, but the idea that if demand for dividends is high, companies will immediately start paying more dividends so they can get and retain share-holders has not borne out in the marketplace, at least not in recent years. For the better part of the past decade, demand for income has been high and supply has been insufficient. In short, a portfolio theory that tells you what you should own really ought to take into account what you realistically can own. MPT does not.

Passive Investing *Isn't*

Many people conflate the emergence of the efficient market hypothesis and the wisdom of "passive" investing, on the one hand, with the triumph of Modern Portfolio Theory, on the other. Although they were developed at roughly the same time, they were separate efforts, and it is important to go back and get the sequence of events correct. The statisticians came to the fore—bringing with them the prior work of Bachelier—in the 1950s and 1960s. Markowitz published his landmark article in 1952 and refined it in 1959. The emergence of CAPM in the mid-1960s essentially joined the two ideas together when the academics determined that if everyone is on board, then the most efficient portfolio is the market portfolio of all stocks and, by extension, all investable assets. That is, CAPM works best in an efficient market with everyone behaving in more or less exactly the same way. In the succeeding decades, much of investment theory and a good portion of its practice have leaned in the direction of unbeatable markets. The academic community voted strongly in favor, at least initially.[24] The professors have been joined by the perhaps less vocal retail investment community that has also shifted toward broad-based index funds and, more recently, ETFs. Most practitioners, not surprisingly, continue to believe that they can do well and add value to client portfolios by making explicit investment choices.

Interestingly, the Nobel Committee recently hedged its bets by having the original efficient markets guru, Eugene Fama, share his prize in economics with Yale professor Robert Shiller, who is one of the few academics not in the efficient markets camp. Much as Irving Fisher had the bad timing to state that the stock market was at a permanent plateau in September 1929, Shiller had the good fortune to go mainstream in 2000 in his book, *Irrational Exuberance*, with his argument that securities can be dramatically mispriced. Even before the Internet bubble, in the aftermath of the 1987 stock market jolt, Shiller was quoted characterizing EMH "as the most remarkable error in the history of economic theory."[25] He is not alone. The ever-eloquent Roger Lowenstein noted that in regard to EMH, "observed experience has undermined a beguiling but simplistic theory that has charmed the economics profession."[26] Lowenstein continues, "If behavioral theory, with its messy, imperfect view of investors, has won in the real world, the efficient-market hypothesis has long been trumps in academia as an elegant theory that offers a pleasingly ordered view of the world. People are deductive; prices are rational."[27] The equally eloquent Jeremy Grantham has observed that "at the top of the list of economic theories based on clearly false assumptions is that of Rational Expectations, in which humans are assumed to be machines programmed with rational responses." It is not at all realistic, Grantham continues, but it sets the stage for nice formulas and simple conclusions, and "it did leave us, though, with perhaps the most laughable of all assumptions-based theories, the Efficient Market Hypothesis (EMH)."[28]

These occasional dissenting comments aside, the broad index funds offered initially by Vanguard and then by numerous other vendors have done very well in the financial marketplace over the past few decades. When the EMH was being worked out and disseminated, the steadily rising market, the high fees for the traditional investment products of the day, and a lot of naturally bad investment timing made index funds—first, the clones of the S&P 500 Index and then products mimicking narrower, style-specific slices of the market—look attractive. The lower relative fees of the index products did not hurt their cause. Fama, Jensen, and Sharpe (and Malkiel in his summary version of the argument) made it clear in the 1960s and 1970s that it is very difficult to beat the market, but they assert with equal emphasis that it is nearly impossible to do so after the hefty investment management fees that were common in the immediate postwar decades. In these analyses, fees are the issue as much as the random walk or Brownian motion. Jack Bogle's proposition as he launched the Vanguard 500 Index Fund in 1976 was about cost. Yes, he viewed the markets as largely efficient, but he really got (and still gets, now in his late eighties) agitated about costs. As a result, Bogleheads (the fans of Jack Bogle) abound, and passive investing is now *de rigueur* up and down Main Street and much of Wall Street.

Ironically, the greater the percentage of assets that are in passive products, the easier it becomes for an investor to distinguish the bad individual security from the good. Be careful what you wish for. The great paradox of the EMH is that it requires a lot of people to *not* believe in it. From Bachelier to Fama to the Bogleheads of today, the argument is that having many market participants—all trying to beat the market—is what makes the market efficient. If you don't have those people—if they have thrown up their arms and just buy index products—the argument falls apart, and securities can easily be mispriced. The very success of the EMH as an idea over the past several decades is what undermines it in application today. Even the academics are beginning to wonder. After a round of backslapping and high-fiving in the 1960s, the academics have spent the subsequent decades discovering and explaining away more and more "anomalies" that directly contradict the idea of an efficient market. The stalwart efficient marketers continue to argue that, in aggregate, the potential anomalies seen in the market offset one another or cannot be profitably exploited and therefore we are still left with a generally efficient market. That is a poor sort of defense for a grand theory. This is not to say that securities are widely mispriced and that successful stock selection is easy. It is not, in the same way that being a successful businessperson is full of challenges. So while it may be hard to take advantage of the long list of observed stock market anomalies, that difficulty does not make the market somehow correctly priced.

Due to its very success in the marketplace over the years, passive investing no longer really is. If you don't believe that, take a look at your index fund. If it is anything other than an S&P 500 Index fund, ask who created it, how the index is defined, what's included, what's excluded, what's the methodology for making changes, etc. There will be answers to those questions, and they add up to the fact that all but the broadest index products do in fact reflect choices made by "portfolio managers" or index designers behind the scenes. One of the benchmarks used to track a portfolio that I manage recently dropped a 5.3% position during its semiannual rebalancing. The weight was not shaved, trimmed, or adjusted. It was taken to zero from one month to the next. As far as we can tell, the company that was removed is in fine shape. That act of rebalancing on the part of a so-called passive index provider was about as active a step as one can imagine in the investment business.

The move away from passive investing is also reflected in the proliferation of ever-narrower index ETFs. For example, you can purchase FirstTrust's SmartGrid Infrastructure Index Fund ETF, the Global X Fertilizers/Potash ETF, the Powershares Cleantech Portfolio ETF, the iShares MSCI Belgium Capped ETF, and, closer to home, the LocalShares Nashville Area ETF for those of you wanting to focus on central Tennessee. In choosing to invest so narrowly, the investor is making very specific decisions to sharpen his or her focus and accept the choices made by whoever designed the index in question. If deciding to invest in Music City companies is not active, I do not know what is. As such, this new generation of investment products is a direct *refutation* of the original Vanguard hypothesis and of the EMH. Why buy a focused slice of the market if it does not offer some sort of advantage to the investor?

From my perspective, the "Is the market efficient?" question is beside the point of trying to make good business decisions through the stock market. Fifty years after the emergence of the idea of unbeatable markets, a vast amount of time and energy has been and continues to be spent arguing whether or not investors can find undervalued securities, or traders can find profitable patterns in stock prices. Some still see patterns and opportunities, and others see randomness, with no point of parsing. From Bachelier, whose work on the French bourse appeared over a century ago, to my hedge fund friend in New York—a highly talented computer scientist who swears he can write programs that profitably trade ever so slight patterns in prices—*most participants in the debate agree on one critical point: they care only about the price data. The point is to profit from those disembodied numbers. The enterprises behind those share prices might as well not even exist.* In the case of trading commodities, where the nominal dollar value of outstanding contracts vastly exceeds the amount of physical commodity in existence, there is very little there beyond the prices. Trying to make a buck out of random or not so random data series—stock or bond or commodity prices—can be a fine and profitable endeavor, but I think we can agree on one point: it's not business ownership. The same can be said of the efficient market indexers. Is buying the market through indexes really investing? Does it involve decision making under conditions of uncertainty, like the human experience? Does it involve the ownership of actual assets?

For a businessperson investing through the stock market, the question needs to be different. *It is not whether the market is or is not efficient in terms of share prices, but whether it is efficient for pricing cashflows to investors.* Even the slightest market experience over the past 30 years makes it clear that the answer is no. An efficient market for businesses does not have a dot-com bubble and does not reward cashless businesses with vast market capitalizations. In a market focused on share prices, but paying little attention to distributed cashflows, opportunities abound for the genuine business investor to tap into income streams while others focus on share prices. Don't be dissuaded by your MBA finance professor who coolly informs you that the market is efficient and that your choices in life do not matter.

Investor Returns

All of the above may be of interest to academics and practitioners with a nit to pick. What matters to investors, however, is whether the system works or not. It's that simple. And perhaps the most damning indictment of Modern Portfolio Theory is that it has broadly failed to do what it was supposed to do: establish predictable and steady investor returns in line with a clear understanding of risk and return. Lorie and Fisher outlined the stock market's 9–10% returns in the 1960s. Their work has been updated periodically ever since, and the long-term return pattern from the U.S. stock market has been reasonably stable. The starting and ending dates for measurement matter a great deal, as does whether one is looking at a large-cap benchmark such as the S&P 500 Index or a narrower market measure. Recall that these returns are over long measurement periods. In most years, the stock market offers a total return that is quite different from the 9–10% standard. In 2008, the market (defined as the S&P 500 Index, the main large-cap benchmark) declined by 37%; in 2013, it rose by a total of 32%. And so forth.

So the question becomes, Has your personal stock market portfolio done as well as the overall averages? The Dalbar measure looks at typical individual investor returns based on an "average asset allocation" return that is then annualized and measured over a 20-year rolling period.[29] And according to those figures, how have typical investors fared? The answer, I'm sorry to say, is not very well. Average individual equity returns—depending on the starting and stopping period—have come in at around 4.7% annually, a bit better than half the large-cap market's return. Total investor returns, from all financial assets, have come in at just over 2% per year. Said investor results are worse than the category returns of stocks, bonds, gold, and homes. That's a strikingly poor result. Even if one adds an extra 100 basis points (1%) to the return to cover fees, you still get just a 3% return, lagging everything other than inflation and home prices. Let's just step back and appreciate the magnitude of this shortfall. If the Dalbar measure is correct (and there are a lot of assumptions embedded in it), individual investors moving in and out of investments at just the wrong time have done worse than every major investment category. That is astounding. Modern investment theory makes a claim to assist investors in getting a maximum amount of return for a given amount of risk. Either U.S. investors have tolerated little to no risk, all evidence to the contrary, or the reigning theory is a failure in practice. Data issues abound here, and I'm sure there are many investors who did a lot better than the 4.7% in the stock market, but the fact that the average individual experience *may* have been this poor—a full half century after the introduction and dissemination of MPT—is an abomination. It's time for a new way to approach our financial investments.

Defenders of the academic castle will taunt me from the parapet—Monty Python style—that the theory is fine; it's just that the investors are flawed, because they move in and out of their investments with abysmal results. I would respond that *any theory that is subject to such a prolonged, substantial shortcoming in its application is a problem for the theory.* It's time to stop blaming the victims. Four decades after the widespread dissemination of Modern Portfolio Theory, the fact that investors have not enjoyed anywhere near market returns is explained away because they have succumbed to those behaviors that do not exist in MPT: emotion, bad timing, imperfect information, inaccurate forecasting, cash needs, taxes, transaction costs, home purchases, retirements, divorces, and college educations. If investors would only get with the program—and avoid the distractions of being human, of needing shelter, education, and companionship while at the same time maintaining steady and common investment expectations and preferences for 40 years—and get on the efficient frontier, they would enjoy the best that MPT has to offer! That is a woefully poor justification for a theory. As the supporters of the status quo would be quick to point out, shortcuts are necessary to create a generalized theory. They come at the cost of some precision in application. That's fine. But how much precision can be lost in application and still have us support the original idea?

MPT Revisions and Alternatives

Am I the first to point out the critical shortcomings in how your retirement fund is set up? No, not even close. There were revisions from the get-go due to problems identified almost immediately. Indeed, MPT has necessarily been a moving target.[30] In 1973, two of the new model pioneers—Jack Treynor and Fischer Black—tried to bridge the gap between traditional security analysis (Graham) and the purer forms of MPT/CAPM, in which security analysis plays little to no role.[31] In their peacemaking effort,

portfolio selection can be thought of as a three-stage process, in which the first stage is selection of an active portfolio to maximize the appraisal ratio [the author's measure of additional return], the second is the blending of the active portfolio with a suitable replica of the market portfolio to maximize the Sharpe ratio, and the third entails scaling positions in the combined portfolio up or down through lending or borrowing while preserving their proportions.

That's a mouthful, and it tries to do the nearly impossible: combine a market-beating individual stock portfolio, a market portfolio for efficiency, and a cash or borrowing level to toggle risk. There have been numerous other efforts to improve MPT and make it more practical. This section reviews just a few of the more notable developments.

Fixing the CAPM

To the extent that Markowitz's MPT has come to be implemented, it has substantially been through the conduit of the capital asset pricing model, its variants, and follow-on approaches. Over the years, most of the academic challenges to this system have not been to Markowitz's core idea of linking risk and return at the portfolio level—which remains intellectually robust to this day—but to its implementation, usually via CAPM in a largely efficient market setting. MPT really doesn't exist independently of those parallel constructs, and problems with them cast a long shadow on MPT itself. Robert Merton tried to address a key flaw in the CAPM approach early on: time. CAPM and most currently applied analytical tools are point to point. They analyze returns or volatility or the role of any other particular factor from one moment in time to another, without consideration of what the experience in the "middle" might be. For instance, a portfolio might have a 6% compound annual growth rate over a 10-year period, but if you are the investor and your annual returns are as follows: +10%, −10%, +5%, +20%, −10%, +25%, −25%, +5%, +25%, +30%, you will end up at the exact same place, but your very bumpy ride won't feel at all like a smooth 6% annual return. Merton's intertemporal model also captured the fact that market sensitivity (beta) and the other important factors used as inputs can change over time. They are not static.[32] In the mid-1970s, Stephen Ross's arbitrage pricing theory (APT) tried to integrate external economic factors (and the sensitivity of financial assets to changes in those economic influences) into a broad asset pricing framework. His APT model was also not reliant on as many handcuffing restrictions—normal distributions of returns and uniform investor preferences and expectations—that made the pure CAPM so difficult to accept or even test properly. Instead, it was based on a simpler, more intuitive assumption—the law of one price—that means an asset cannot sell for two separate prices at the same time and at the same place. If it did, there would be a simple arbitrage opportunity—or riskless profit—which does not exist in active markets.[33]

Perhaps the greatest amount of time since MPT was introduced has been spent by the academics and a fair share of practitioners on "factor analysis" to determine which factors drive superior investment outcomes. Through the 1970s, academics observed that the market factor alone—Sharpe's beta—was an insufficient explanatory (for the past) or predictive (for the future) tool. In particular, the academics quickly observed that low-beta stocks did better than the original CAPM would have predicted. Alongside growing dissatisfaction with the original single-factor model, Ross's APT opened the floodgates to having multiple factors used to explain and perhaps forecast returns. As referenced in the prior chapter, Barr Rosenberg built a substantial business around identifying significant factors and assessing portfolios based on them. In the early 1990s, none other than Eugene Fama (along with Kenneth French) expanded the original single-factor model with the addition of two general stock market factors beyond beta: company size (small beats large) and price to book (lower beats higher). The resulting Fama-French three-factor model claimed to improve upon the basic CAPM and explain 90% of equity returns. More recently, the authors went to five factors.[34] Other academics have also developed robust factor models that are used by some practitioners to analyze and manage portfolios.

Indeed, in today's stock market and asset management industry, it is possible to see just factors, no businesses, no cashflows, no real economy. Take the following example of a weekly update that I receive from a respected brokerage: "All major U.S. equity indices are positive over the past week as small-caps outperform large-caps and mid-caps while value indices outperform growth indices across all capitalization ranges. Within the S&P 500 Index the top performing factors over the past week are Earnings Momentum, and Earnings Quality. The worst performing factors are Price Reversal, Relative Value, and Price Volatility."[35] How much progress have we really made over the reports a century ago when "Lead was simply heavy"? Stephen Ross was a pioneer in the area, but he admitted in 2017 that "we're in a frenzy of factor-focused investing" with an "irresistible . . . tendency" to add new factors, many of which "lack a strong economic foundation."[36] In 1984, even before the factor craze got completely out of hand, the creator of the first "uber" factor (beta), William Sharpe, sounded a note of caution. He acknowledged that factor models were far from perfect but that improvements were constantly being made. "Meanwhile," he wrote, "we can use the tools we have, as long as we use them intelligently, cautiously, and humbly."[37] While the factor models have undoubtedly gotten better over the years, are they used in the circumspect manner that Sharpe encouraged? I don't know.

One factor that has gotten a lot of attention in the past few years is volatility, specifically ways of generating and maintaining "low-vol" portfolios. Indeed, low vol is now all the rage, where investors seek to capture most of the market's upside while limiting the downside risk. Data studies have suggested that low-vol portfolios outperform in terms of total return. That's all good and fine, but the approach is not much more than a kissing cousin to the early critique of CAPM that low-beta portfolios seemed to have an edge. Other innovators have taken on the tax problem, that is, that modern investment theory would only work in a tax-free environment. Fifty years later, reasonably "efficient" portfolios can be and have been structured to take into account varying individual tax rates. At the other end of the spectrum, some investment advisors refuse to take taxable assets, or if they do, they put them exclusively in index products. As far as they are concerned, the efficient frontier exists only in the realm of retirement accounts. Otherwise, it doesn't work. And then there are the numerous other revisions and efforts to go beyond basic MPT. Call up your local financial advisor or asset manager, and he or she can provide details.

Coming from a completely different, nonfinancial origin, the polymath Benoît Mandelbrot created a unique approach to investments based on his view that prices and price changes are derived from a fundamental condition of nature—the world of what he calls fractal geometry. On the way, Mandelbrot eviscerated the underlying math of both MPT and CAPM, specifically, arguing that "prices do not follow the bell curve and are not independent."[38] In the absence of those two conditions, modern financial theory really can't get much beyond the classroom, as it materially mismeasures risk. Mandelbrot sketches out his alternative approach, but it too is basically a theory of numbers rather than a theory of business ownership. Delivered in witty and flowing prose, his key takeaway is that investment in securities is a lot riskier than the computers would have you believe. Even if you don't agree with Mandelbrot and see fractal-based patterns everywhere in nature and human activity, that is still a wise observation from one of the twentieth century's leading intellectual iconoclasts.

Behavioral Finance

Perhaps the most productive effort at revision in recent decades has been at its underlying core—the rational actor theory that underpins MPT, CAPM, and the EMH, and without which it will not work. For decades, the academic finance journals have been filled with efforts to get past the impossible restrictions that come along with basic rational actor theory and the assumption of perfect markets. The emerging alternative framework of "behavioral finance" is not so much a comprehensive theory of portfolio management as an analytical framework that takes into account human subjectivity, human foibles, and the reality of life as it is lived. Most of the key takeaways from behavioral finance undermine one or another element of current investment theory. For instance, numerous studies have shown that investors experience more distress from a loss than they do joy from a gain, even in the same amount and with the same probability of either occurring. This "loss aversion" stands in direct contradiction to the standard mean variance investment framework of classic MPT.

The literature on behavioral finance is large and has crossed over the line from academic to popular during the past decade. And in comparison to the algorithmic descriptions of how *Homo economicus* invests, the literature on how real *Homo sapiens* actually behave in the market is lively and great fun to read, so much so that that it is worth highlighting here rather than relegating it to the small-print endnotes. The pioneers are the eminently readable Daniel Kahneman and Amos Tversky, captured in Kahneman's *Thinking, Fast and Slow* (2011). Jason Zweig, the *Wall Street Journal*'s

"Intelligent Investor" columnist, has distilled the neuroscience down in *Your Money & Your Brain* (2007). One of the intellectual founding fathers of behavioral finance and 2017 Nobel Prize winner Richard Thaler of the University of Chicago has produced a history of the art in *Misbehaving: The Making of Behavioral Economics* (2015). Robert Shiller of Yale has written widely on behavioral investing, and it informs his well-known popular work, *Irrational Exuberance* (2000), which was published just as the tech bubble was about to burst. James Montier gives a pithy version in *The Little Book of Behavioral Investing* (2010). Meir Statman's *Finance for Normal People* (2017) just joined the canon and is an excellent survey of the current science. Go read these books;[39] you will be glad that you did. But beyond wonderful anecdotes and much greater self-awareness about subjective decision making in regard to investments, it is hard to turn the insights of behavioral finance into a broad-based theory or practical guide to portfolio construction, management, and measurement, though there have been efforts in that direction, notably by Statman.[40] Model portfolios from a number of investment advisors and mutual fund complexes also take into account many of the takeaways from behavioral finance, but they still remain focused on asset prices and generally oriented toward Markowitzian mean variance optimization. Nevertheless, whether just in anecdotal form or in a full-fledged effort at portfolio management á la Statman, it is clear that knowing one's own biases (and those of others) will likely lead to better outcomes. Behavioral finance offers those insights.

Given the constant stream of revisions and updates, it's understandable why many current practitioners would claim that they are operating remotely from Modern Portfolio Theory. But the key ideas—the Euclidian axioms of MPT—

remain firmly in place: that asset price is the focus of the efforts, using the same or related definitions of risk and deploying the same basic tool set, much expanded over the past half century. I recently solicited proposals to manage a small endowment fund for which I sit on the investment committee. The decks from the institutional consultants and RIAs (registered investments advisors) trumpeted the efficient frontier (Markowitz) and proclaimed how their particular collection of passive investment products (EMH) got the portfolio to a good position on said frontier depending on our expectation of total return and tolerance of risk (standard deviation). They gave me the prospective alpha, the historical beta, the expected return, and the expected volatility. They did not reference MPT and probably would have denied any association, but it was pure MPT. What they didn't necessarily indicate until we prodded them was how much cash the portfolio would generate to meet the institution's spending goals. That little bit of reality was not initially of interest to them. Not only is MPT alive and well; it remains well disconnected from the real needs and expectations of many investors.

The Tally

So let's tally up the assets and liabilities of this half-century-old intellectual paradigm that frames how we invest and how we head into retirement. On the asset side of the ledger, MPT achieved perhaps its most important goal: shifting investors from thinking narrowly about individual securities to thinking about combinations of securities and how they operate at the portfolio level. This was an unqualified good, a massive achievement over then-current practices, and a sea change in investment culture. Prior to MPT, the basic, non-quantified notion of risk management through diversification existed, but

MPT institutionalized it and rooted it deeply in the psyches of investors. Second, MPT took the age-old understanding that risk and reward were correlated and brought it into the modern age, asserting that in a reasonably diversified portfolio of assets, higher reward could come only from taking higher risk, defined in this case as variance from an expected return. And the linguistic panache of that risk-reward spectrum— "the efficient frontier"—all but guaranteed that this approach would garner attention if not acceptance.

A decade later, CAPM emerged as a somewhat more practical means of implementing efficient portfolios by offering an easy-to-understand formula for expected return, integrated with an even simpler measure of risk than used in the original MPT. CAPM took on the still greater challenge of trying to quantify and, by implication, to control and dampen risk. These advances were quickly followed by insights into different reasons why investor returns might vary from the CAPM's single-factor explanation of returns and by the less restrictive APT and its introduction of additional factors. Emerging at the same time as the CAPM, the EMH reminded investors that choosing stocks is very difficult. Whether in its pure Brownian motion, physics version or just the more down-to-earth, commonsense Paul Samuelson version, the conclusion was the same: in a frequently traded and transparent market, it is not easy to consistently beat the house by a material margin. That insight led initially to the development and flourishing of broad index funds, and more recently to ETFs providing access to narrower slices of the market.

There can be no doubt that MPT and its associated models get an A for effort. Some of the best minds of the twentieth century spent a lot of time on this issue and came up with elegant and relatively easy-to-understand solutions for decision making under conditions of uncertainty in an area that people were interested in—their own wealth. The academics behind the paradigms represented the acme of mid-twentieth-century social science confidence—and late-twentieth-century computing power. They quantified what previously had been qualitative notions of good decision making and proposed degrees of precision unimaginable in the pre-MPT world. It is a great narrative, made even more compelling and comforting by sideline cheerleaders such as Peter Bernstein.

On the right side of the ledger are the liabilities, summarized in this chapter. I have been told that Markowitz, gracious as he clearly is, has acknowledged that genuine application of his version of MPT in investor accounts is essentially impossible. Now to be fair to the academics, it is possible too much was asked of them. Most of the pioneers were attempting to create equilibrium-based models that were not really meant for implementation or scrutiny at the retail investor level. That being said, they succeeded perhaps beyond even their own expectations, and now our pension funds, retirement accounts, and utility bills have been substantially organized along their recommendations. That broad-based real-world test of their theories necessarily raises the bar. It is too late to claim an ivory tower defense.

Many of the titans of MPT have parried the criticisms of its inapplicability by observing that, at a minimum, MPT is very good for teaching purposes—which it clearly is—with the implication that it is less good in practice. Laurence Siegel, director of the CFA Institute Research Foundation, rightly points out that for all its flaws, MPT forms a "base case or null hypothesis" from which to begin the journey of analysis and decision making. "Without it, we are lost."[41] That is an excellent notion—MPT as an intellectual starting point—but after a half century of this framework, we can do better.

CAPM has fared less well. It was oversold as a means of vanquishing risk and came with a degree of precision that the subsequent decades have shown to be false. That there are parameters for risk and return is undeniable. That the CAPM or the less restrictive APT can tell you exactly what they are and will be in the future is completely deniable. Two of the high priests of academic finance, Eugene Fama and Kenneth French, have concluded that "the problems [of the original CAPM] are serious enough to invalidate most applications," despite it being a theoretical "tour de force."[42] Keep that in mind the next time your investment advisor suggests a particular expected total return or riskiness from an asset or portfolio based on a historical beta.

As for efficient markets, the academic evidence was initially entirely in favor. Now the opposite is true. There are just too many anomalies. They may be hard to exploit year after year, à la Samuelson, but they are there. And then there are the periodic market bubbles and busts, which should not exist in a properly efficient market or an economic system in equilibrium. Investors don't seem to care. Passive investing through index funds and less passive investing through narrower ETFs have enjoyed a monster, 40-year run. Now that they have become the base-case investment strategy for so many Americans, it is far from clear that they will work as well in the next four decades. Index funds and ETFs have become the "crowded trade." What comes around, goes around.

MPT and the subsequent doctrines grew out of a genuine desire by several generations of academics to understand stock price movement and, by derivation, to understand the puzzle of the 1920s and 1930s and subsequent stock market history. MPT harnessed the analytical tools of the postwar period—a conviction that human behavior could be quantified and the computing power to do it—in an effort to create an investor experience that was less volatile and more rewarding than the Wild West approach to stocks that dominated theretofore. Eighty years after the attention-getting event (the Crash of 1929), 75 years after the first analytical efforts (Graham and Dodd, Keynes, Williams), 60 years after the first meaningful go-forward proposal (Markowitz), 50 years after the key simplification and extension of the Markowitz idea (Sharpe and Treynor), 40 years after broad-based implementation of MPT in bank trust departments, and more than 20 years after the introduction of the retail style box by Morningstar and a clear shift from do-it-yourself portfolios to highly constructed models designed to produce maximum return for a given amount of risk—after all these developments, in your best Clint Eastwood voice, you just have to ask yourself one question: Did it work? Well, did it? Did the system smooth out investor returns, protect them from the dips, maximize return for a given level of risk, and vice versa? Did it create certainty where there had been uncertainty? To judge by investor returns, the answer is no. To judge by the stock market of the past two decades—the tech bubble, followed by a crash, the financial asset bubble, followed by a crash, the quantitative easing bubble, followed by who knows what—the answer is a resounding no. To judge by popular sentiment toward this core institution of Western capitalism, the answer is an even more strident no!

Critics will charge that I have created a "straw man" MPT that can easily be criticized, that it does not exist in the rigid form I suppose, and that the collective investment framework has moved well beyond its starting axioms and addresses many of the concerns raised over the years. That is true, to some extent. It has gotten better over the years, more flexible and more applicable. Many of the original highly unrealistic constraints—for instance, about an investor's lending and borrowing—are no longer really required to create practically efficient, if not exactly theoretically efficient, portfolios. Practitioners now have access to many risk reduction tools beyond mean variance optimization. Within the academic community, the shortcomings of MPT are well known, and a new generation of insight based on behavioral finance is making inroads and attempting to make portfolios more consistent with real investor behavior and preferences. (That is, if the fundamentally opposite underpinnings—rational actor theory and efficient markets—can be reconciled to their respective opposites in the real world.)

These efforts should be applauded, but the basic disconnect between theory and reality, between expectations and outcomes, remains vast. The defects of a system do not necessarily make it entirely wrong, particularly in the absence of an alternative that is clearly superior. There is no perfect static solution to the human condition. There is a constant need to revise, to improvise, and to improve. Modern Portfolio Theory is not evil; it is just wildly inaccurate and misleading. Even more importantly, it has outlived its genuine usefulness. It has become an intellectual zombie, clumsily lumbering along in our retirement accounts and underfunded pension plans. If we stick with it much longer, we will be lost in the false comfort of algorithms rather than commonsense definitions of risk and business practices, and lost in the grand casino where enterprises once upon a time raised capital to advance new ventures and where investors shared in the successes and failures of those ventures. It is time to move on.

5

Getting Back to Business

*There is nothing more difficult to carry out, nor more
doubtful of success, nor more dangerous to handle,
than to initiate a new order of things.*
>   —Niccolo Machiavelli

Do what you will, the capital is at hazard.
>   —Judge Samuel Putnam,
>   *Harvard College v. Amory*, 1830

*If the stock market were to take a breather . . . then
perhaps corporate managers would return to the
basics of their businesses—that is, earning a profit,
and passing on a reasonable portion of that profit to
their owners.*
—President's letter, Smith Company 2000 annual report,
Journal of Portfolio Management (2001)

Outlining an Alternative

Having investors adopt a new way of imagining, managing,
and measuring investment portfolios is no small task. MPT
and its follow-on approaches have a 50-year head start. My

goal here is more modest: to outline an alternative narrative about investing, particularly in regard to public equities. If you are looking for specific stock picks, you will not find them here. What you will find are some general guidelines about how you might apply a "getting-back-to-business" approach to your financial assets. I start by reviewing "first principles." They include viewing your stocks as ownership stakes in ongoing enterprises and understanding that their ultimate value is derived from what you actually receive from them, in cash. Compared with the current system focused on daily share prices, that can be a jarring adjustment, and it requires some elaboration. Having made that leap, however, the businesslike investor is ready to reconsider risk, discount rates, expected returns, valuation, asset types, and diversification. Those are vexing issues under any system, and the treatment here is meant to be preliminary, not exhaustive. I then pause to consider some implications of this approach for companies, investors, and the markets themselves. The next section starts the process of portfolio construction by characterizing companies by income types and addresses how non-income-paying, "lottery ticket"–like securities can fit into an income-focused system. This is followed by a very basic asset allocation exercise and an acknowledgment that there are other investment professionals already thinking along these lines. Finally, space is provided for the boo-birds and academic mandarins to make their obvious criticisms. Their inputs are welcome, as they should contribute to the ongoing discussion about how to move beyond the tired narrative of MPT and toward using the stock market once again as a business investment platform.

First Principles

There are many ways in this world to make money. Having ownership stakes in successful enterprises is one of them. Speculating in share prices is another. I believe in and encourage our clients to believe in the former. In contrast, Modern Portfolio Theory more or less dictates the latter. MPT treats stock market investment as a mathematical puzzle to be figured out, not as a means to invest in businesses, engage businesses, and benefit from their ultimate success (or suffer from their failure). Investors need to consider moving from the now fashionable numbers game back in the direction of the rather less fashionable business ownership proposition. The purpose of this effort is not to replace one overreaching and ultimately failed paradigm with an equally complex but different one, but rather to shift the discussion from the world of daily asset price changes, if not entirely, then at least a lot closer to that of ownership of working enterprises. The choice is as much philosophical as it is mathematical. It is a matter of subjective preferences. Twentieth-century mathematical finance has turned those fundamentally human choices into restrictive formulas, but it is important to repeat that those subjective preferences come first, not only in my assertions, but in MPT itself. Individuals still have to *decide* how they are going to invest, and make those decisions under conditions of uncertainty. There is no way to avoid making choices in life.

The hagiography about Harry Markowitz—specifically what he achieved in his 1952 article and 1959 book—is quite correct in at least one respect. Notwithstanding the contributions of the founding fathers outlined in Chapter 2, Markowitz created a system where none had existed before. He brought order to chaos. To do so, he laid out his own series of subjective preferences and assertions. He had to.

Without them, he would have been building his system on not much more than air. They include his famous dictum in the first paragraph of his landmark article that "the investor does (or should) consider expected return a desirable thing *and* variance of return an undesirable thing." He considers this a rule or a "maxim." It is not argued or proved; it is asserted. It is not an unreasonable assertion, but let us all agree, it did not come down from the mount with Abraham, it is not in the U.S. or any other constitution, and it is not part of the DNA of humans or in the geological structure of planet Earth. It has effectively become a hard-and-fast rule for most gatekeepers, analysts, and consultants focused on the U.S. stock market, but it was at the time, and remains to this day, simply an election made by a 25-year-old graduate student who apparently had little if any direct engagement at the time with the actual stock market or business ownership. More than 60 years later, there is no one holding a gun forcing investors to speak the language of mean variance optimization. It is still a choice.

Markowitz follows with another assertion in 1952 that "diversification is both observed and sensible; a rule of behavior which does not imply the superiority of diversification must be rejected both as a hypothesis and as a maxim." I do not dispute this assertion, but I do want to note that it is no less a subjective choice than his other first principles. And I would repeat my earlier observation that in practice, having 30 or 40 stocks versus 3 or 4, as was common then, is indeed risk-reducing diversification, but that having many hundreds or even thousands of holdings in one's portfolio, as is common today through index funds and ETFs, is not. While sitting at his desk at the University of Chicago in the early 1950s, Markowitz could never have imagined nor could he have intended such an absurd state of affairs. Worse, the extreme diversification so popular currently is a form of self-deception in that the overdiversified investors are really choosing not to choose, while all the time thinking they have made very responsible decisions.

In his 1959 book-length elaboration of Modern Portfolio Theory, Markowitz stated several other first principles.[1] Investors wanted two things: return (however defined) to be high and to be "dependable, stable, not subject to uncertainty."[2] It's hard to argue with the latter, but there is a bombshell in the former. And that is that Markowitz defines his return, without much ado, as the combination of share price movement and the dividend payment in any given period, as a percentage of the initial share price. That is the correct definition of total return for a stated measurement period, and it is innocent and sensible enough at the theoretical level. But here is an instance where we reach a limit of academic theory, where it works out quite differently in practice. That is because the cash payment is received a few times a year (quarterly in the United States; usually semiannually or annually outside the United States), but the share price changes (or at least can change) continuously for 6½ hours, 5 days a week, around 250 days per year. With the share price resetting that frequently, total return can be calculated by the hour, day, week, and month. You can see how you are doing in the market all the time, and too many investors do exactly that.

In that "check-it-every-day" environment, however, it is easy to lose sight of the significance of the less frequent cash distributions. Historically, the dividend payment represented about 40% of the annual total return from U.S. stocks. If you attribute long-term share price appreciation to dividend growth—we do, as there is a clear correlation and logical causal relationship between the two—the ratio grows to around 90%.[3] If you look just at long-term real (inflation-adjusted) returns, the situation is much the same: most of the annual return from stocks comes from the basic dividend payment. The growth in the dividend, or share price, is largely offset by inflation.[4] Yet the existing formulas draw little distinction between the nominal daily price reset and the cash-on-the-barrel payments. Indeed, in practice, the cash payments made by successful publicly traded businesses to their owners are lost in the daily flurry of green and red stock price changes. At its core, MPT does not help investors distinguish between what is fundamental—business outcomes—and what is ephemeral—the ever-changing prices.

Businesses First; Prices Second

So I offer my own first principles, not with the assertion that they are objectively superior to Markowitz's, but with the acknowledgment that, as with all first principles, they are subjective preferences. If there is an implied claim, it is simple: that the 60 years since the articulation of MPT have shown serious shortcomings in how Markowitz's assertions have come to be applied in the marketplace. Therefore, it is time for a fundamental rethink. My first and most important maxim is this: *Investment in publicly traded stocks should first and foremost be based on ownership of the underlying asset.* That's what the stock certificate—if you have yours—actually means. That's what the line item in the brokerage account signifies. More simply, you are a company owner; act like it. Fractional ownership and daily stock repricing are prominent obstacles to investors understanding that when they hold the KO shares, they really are an owner, albeit a very small one, of the Coca-Cola Corporation, a successful global beverage company based in Atlanta, Georgia. It seems obvious, but to judge by typical investor behavior, it's as if the stock has a life of its own separate from that of the company, and that investors don't really know or care too much about the company behind the stock, the goods that it produces, the services it provides, or the future of either. To some degree, that is understandable. If you just invest in KO, you probably don't make the concentrate, fill the bottles, drive the red trucks, restock the shelves, or come up with the jingles. Most of what you see and experience, beyond the occasional refreshing beverage—I am quite fond of Coke Zero and the company's coffee drinks sold in Japan—is just the share price moving around. But that is a matter of perception. In fact and in law, you still have a legal stake in the business. That simple reality is obscured by a blaze of numbers, the daily share price. And Modern Portfolio Theory has contributed to this loss of clarity by ensnaring investors in a theory of numbers rather than a theory of business ownership. If you need courage to be a business owner rather than just a stock owner, you can take it from Warren Buffett. In one of his annual letters to his investors, he wrote:

Whenever Charlie [Munger] and I buy common stocks . . . , we approach the transaction as if we were buying into a private business. We look at the economic prospects of the business, the people in charge of running it, and the price we must pay. . . . When investing, we view ourselves as business analysts—not as market analysts, not as macro-economic analysts, and not even security analysts.[5]

The second maxim is in regard to the value of an investment. Like the first maxim, it is not new, but instead a restatement of what was formulated by Irving Fisher, more than 50 years before Harry Markowitz, and practiced daily by most successful businesspeople the world over: *"The fundamental principle which applies here is that the value of capital at any instant is derived from the value of the future income which that capital is expected to yield.*"[6] More simply, it's worth what it's going to make. That assertion applies equally well to individual amounts of capital (a single stock or bond) and to collections of capital (a portfolio). Any reasonable portfolio construction and management system should be structured around this axiom. In contrast, the current model is based mostly on the nominal price change of the assets, not the distributable cashflows that they generate.

It's easy to understand why "price," and a system designed to optimize expected price changes, has had the upper hand over cashflow in recent decades. It can be found every day at the marketplace, and many investors may be happy to focus only on changes in price as an investment strategy. Outside the stock market, house flippers may fall into the same category. But even stock speculators and house flippers are businesspeople at the end of the day, and their success or failure is reflected in the distributions that they generate from their enterprises and can take home to spend as they wish. If there were no take-home cash from the exercise, they wouldn't do it. No one would. Still, it can be hard to appreciate why distributable cashflow matters when there are so many mature, highly successful U.S. companies—marquee businesses such as Berkshire-Hathaway and Facebook—that make no dividend payments whatsoever to company owners or have such low dividends that the cashflow component really doesn't matter in the investment decision. Almost no such enterprises exist outside the United States; it would be all but inconceivable in Europe for a large, established company not to make a profit distribution unless it were in significant distress. Most of the relatively young but successful, large Chinese companies with listings on Western exchanges pay dividends. Not so in New

York or Silicon Valley. In today's U.S. stock market, investment return is perceived to be mostly if not entirely share price driven. Lots of demand and the screen is green. Little demand and the screen shows red. Eventually the market price has to represent the genuine condition of a business—reflected in its distributable cashflows—but it is obvious that the daily repricing of otherwise generally stable operating assets means Graham's "Mr. Market" is pointing an unsteady, often wildly shaking finger at the value of an enterprise.

Despite the popularity and durability of various price-based investment strategies, all serious analyses of asset valuation highlight the centrality of a cashflow-based calculation of worth, á la Fisher and Williams. There is just no other reasonable way to do it. All my written work on investments—this book and two prior ones—serve only to remind investors that it is worth recommitting to this businesslike approach. Shifting from prices to cashflows is not that difficult for privately held assets—where it is commonplace—but it is hard for publicly traded ones due to that daily striking of a new price. For some investors, particularly those who are in and out of the market frequently or those who will soon need to sell their assets for whatever reason, price may genuinely matter a great deal more than cashflows. That is granted without reservation. But for most long-term investors, there is simply no reason why their accounts shouldn't be invested, managed, and measured according to the income generated, just as in a real business.

(Re)Defining Wealth: Synchronic Versus Diachronic

Unless you just took the SATs, don't feel bad if the words "synchronic" and "diachronic" don't roll off the tongue. But they represent two different ways—first principles—of viewing the world: one is a snapshot *in* time (synchronic), and the other is *through* time (diachronic). One is a photograph; the other is a video. The same can be said of wealth. For some, it is how much you have in the bank or in your brokerage account or in a 401(k) at any given moment in time. Does it add up to a quarter million, a half million, a million? That is a static view. The other approach is dynamic: what's coming in the door, through time. Or to put it crudely, what are those assets making for you? The question sounds less crude when posed in Jane Austen's world where wealth was defined diachronically, as the amount of annual income the various characters had at their disposal, usually but not exclusively from their land holdings. In *Pride and Prejudice*, the attractive Mr. Bingley had 4,000–5,000 pounds per year to spend at his leisure.[7] The even more attractive Mr. Darcy enjoyed an annual income of 10,000 pounds from Pemberly, his magnificent estate in Derbyshire. Alas, the Bennett's lesser estate, Longbourn, in Hertfordshire, generated a mere 2,000 pounds annually. Those numbers are laid out early in the novel and frame the relationships as they develop.

Nowadays it is more common to link the value of an asset to its market price, not its income generating ability, but from my vantage point, the diachronic approach to wealth is axiomatically superior to that of the synchronic snapshot. While Irving Fisher lacks the elegance of Jane Austen, he wrote just as pithily when observing that "the stock of wealth is called capital, and its stream of services is called income. The income is the more important concept of the two, for the capital exists merely for the sake of income, and the ownership of the capital has no other significance than the ownership of possible income from that capital."[8]

But what about principal? What about that synchronic sum in the bank or the brokerage account, or the amount put to work in any particular venture? That notion is deeply enshrined as an independent variable in the investment equation. We talk about the principal (or capital) that we put into our homes, into our businesses, into partnerships (the principals). In trust law and practice, the principal can be legally separated from the income generated by it, with different beneficiaries for both. So in the real world, principal matters. The other term for it—"capital"—is everywhere, up to and including the name of our overall economic system. It would be utterly naïve to think that investors do not or should not think about the bottom line, about the total amount of assets at their disposal, about their financial target needed to buy a house, pay for a college education, etc.

Rather than challenge that notion, I would simply point out that the stock market has made a hash of the notion of principal over the years. The problem is that the stable capital level described in the terms above reprices every day in the stock market, so it doesn't seem very principal-like. It is a moving target, and the movement is seemingly unrelated to the asset's underlying distributable cashflow, it if has one. That is not the case in real-world businesses, where, from an accounting perspective, "book value" can come close to representing the current value of the principal in any given enterprise. Accounting conventions can easily distort book value, but it's nothing like the daily roller-coaster ride of the stock market. One can put $100,000 of principal into the stock market, and 6 months later it can be worth $80,000 or $120,000. Technically, the amount of principal has either declined or increased. But in most cases, that decrease or increase is simply a stock market phenomenon. The long-term prospects of the underlying enterprises are unlikely to have changed by 20% in either direction in such a brief period of time.

Monitoring the amount of capital one has, even down to the minute, may seem to some a reasonable endeavor. Indeed, some principal, when it is sitting in commodities (or my vice, vintage timepieces), can only be measured as a price, as it is not producing anything, and those amounts may fluctuate dramatically. But by deploying an entire portfolio management system based on the amount of capital at any given minute, we have botched up the formula, creating an investment framework that puts the price cart before the income horse whose sole purpose is to draw the cart. A diachronic cashflow approach to portfolio management would relieve some of that daily repricing pressure. If one accepts the axiom that the value of principal is and should ultimately be equal to the present value of the future cashflows that can be derived from it, then the notion of principal is returned to the investors, but in a much less volatile form.

There is a simple elegance in a cashflow-based portfolio system. Even the most jaded traders know down deep in their psyche (where it remains firmly suppressed) that the value of any asset— public, private, large, small, tech, real estate, oil and gas royalties, a fast-food franchise, or a lemonade stand on the street corner—is necessarily based on the diachronic view. It is the amount of future distributable cash discounted back to the present time. This is Fisher's law of present value. It isn't actually a law, but it ought to be. It is repeated in the first chapter in every serious book on investments, and then dutifully ignored by most price-focused stock market participants, including professionals. Whether a business is owned in perpetuity or held for a nanosecond to be traded to someone else, it is the underlying truism that an enterprise's distributable cashflow determines its value.

Coca-Cola may trade daily as a stock (synchronic), but inside Coca-Cola, managers are making investment decisions and assessing their operations not on the price that they might get were they to sell each division 6½ hours every day, but on the capital invested in that business and the long-term cashflows generated by it (diachronic). As I write this in late 2017, Coke pays a $1.48 annual dividend. It will rise next February, as it does pretty much every February, to approximately $1.56. Coke's shares trade around $46. They can trade at $46; they can trade at $40. What's important here? What would you rather pay for that income stream? $40 or $46? A businessperson would say $40. But in today's stock market, investors are encouraged to pay $46, because it appears that the stock is "going up." Thus everything must be well with the world. Chase those rising share prices, and you too can underperform the long-term returns of the underlying assets and end up with a Dalbar-like 2% return. Do not fear; over time, the KO share price will follow the dividend up, as the value of any business follows the direction of its cashflows. That is, KO's price will very likely continue its decades-long gradual appreciation. That is as it should be, but let's make sure we understand what's driving the value of the business up—rising cash distributions, just as in any other venture.

Hedge fund traders who care not a whit about cash payments and may own shares only for a few seconds will logically prefer the synchronic share price–based system, and the more volatile the prices, the better. For them, Coke's $1.48 dividend means nothing as long as the share price toggles back and forth between $40 and $46 so they can trade it to their heart's content. But Grandma doesn't really care about trading range–bound stocks. She cares about paying her bills from the income stream of assets left to her by Grandpa after a lifetime of hard work. And John Q. Public, owner of a small business or executive at a large corporation, may have an understanding of the mean variance optimization of price-based returns, but he too really needs to focus on managing the operations and the cashflows of his own enterprise.

Our third maxim, therefore, is that *investment in a publicly traded business, or a portfolio of such businesses, should hold to the same diachronic standard of investing in enterprises in general, and only secondarily should be shaped by the synchronic reality that the assets may reprice frequently.* A portfolio analysis and management framework based on this view is more likely to be satisfactory than the by-the-minute price-based one that too many professionals currently use. It's just common sense, and it is yet another recollection of Benjamin Graham's distinction between price and value, albeit expressed in a somewhat different way. In this instance, Graham's "intrinsic value" becomes our diachronic income stream versus the more fickle synchronic price offered by Graham's Mr. Market, the cheery but not very sensible fellow who reprices your assets anew every day the market is open. Or as Graham's purported heir, Warren Buffet, famously put it, "Price is what you pay, but value is what you get." These important distinctions are well known in the investment community; yet they must be mentioned again and again and again.

My stock market friends will ask at this point, perhaps in great distress, whether current asset prices—the synchronic view—are a reasonably good proxy for assessing cash streams—the diachronic view—in a businesslike manner? It's a fair question. My answer is that in some instances at the present time and more generally in the decades prior to the 1980s and 1990s, share prices were often an approximate measure of business conditions and long-term distributable cashflows for many publicly traded assets. And at some time in the future, I am quite certain they will be again. And at that time, a mean variance optimization framework or some other asset price–based approach might form the basis for a sensible portfolio management system. That was the case in the 1950s when Markowitz came up with his system. But that is simply not the case now, particularly in regard to equities. We live in an upside-down age where making a profit distribution to company owners is viewed, incredibly, as a failing by many S&P 500 Index companies and nothing less than heresy by the overwhelming majority of new economy companies.

I've addressed how this came about elsewhere, but suffice it here to note that a major change in the U.S. market occurred in the 1980s and 1990s that put asset prices structurally front and center and asset utility in the background. MPT blessed the new system and gave it deep roots. That's the difference between the speculative bubbles of the 1920s and 1960s, on the one hand, and the cashless system starting in the 1990s, on the other. In the former instances, there wasn't a grand theory justifying the manner of investment. In the latter, MPT and orthodox finance doctrine in general have given academic credibility to a very unbusinesslike manner of investing.

It would be silly to assert that there was some halcyon, ideal period prior to the acceptance of MPT during which all financial investments were approached soberly and in a businesslike manner. Open financial markets have always had and will always have an element of speculation and exaggeration to them. There is nothing wrong with that. And even in supposed "businesslike" periods, there can and should always be investment without regard to income streams. For start-ups and early-stage ventures, that is healthy and necessary. The capital markets should continue to provide resources to said companies without expectation of a distributable cash stream anytime soon. That is the original and still important purpose of the capital markets—to raise funds to invest in actual businesses. But as I pointed out earlier, the major part of the U.S. stock market no longer really serves that function, and it hasn't for decades.

(Re)Defining Risk

As in life, so in investing, there is an undeniable relationship between risk and reward. Harry Markowitz may have put some numbers around the idea, but since our ancestors stumbled out of the cave to consider taking on that mastodon, humans have intrinsically understood that higher reward is usually attended by higher risk. Still, from the perspective of asserting first principles, it is worth stepping back and considering how we define risk in the context of the supreme human challenge of decision making under conditions of uncertainty. When confronted with investment choices, the questions and potential outcomes are numerous. If you are considering taking a stake in PepsiCo versus Boeing versus Facebook—or some combination thereof—you get to ask whether people will continue to eat Doritos, whether the 787 can become the standard wide-body jet and if it can be profitable, whether Facebook will become our society's Deathstar, if the "multiple" of stock A will expand while the one of stock B contracts, and how stock C will move in regard to the others. Throughout that analytical exercise, these are "uncertain" matters, and there is "risk" associated with these choices. A century ago, the economist Frank Knight distinguished between the two challenges.[9] Simply put, risk could be calculated quantitatively and assigned various probabilities; uncertainty could not. (More recently, we have Donald Rumsfeld's easier "known unknowns" and harder "unknown unknowns.") You don't have to accept this typology, but it is clear that academic finance as it is practiced currently has subsumed the entire range of human decision making under Frank Knight's category of risk, leaving little room for uncertainty. In contrast, I would argue for some degree of true uncertainty. Even if we would like to know the odds, we should still acknowledge that investment entails not only quantifiable risk but also unquantifiable uncertainty.

Do not despair. There is intellectual and personal upside to uncertainty that the quants cannot imagine. Peter Bernstein, to his great credit, welcomed "the great gift of uncertainty" and derided a fully mathematized world, with only probabilities and no meaningful individual choices:

What a bore! In that system, innovation and change are impossible, creative destruction unknown, risk-taking nothing more than a numbers game. Thank goodness the world of pure probability exists only on paper and has little to do with breathing, sweating, anxious, and creative human beings struggling to find their way out of the darkness. No, we are free souls. Our decisions do matter. We can change the world. Whether that turns out to be for worse or for better is up to us. The rules that determine the next throw of the dice have nothing to do with it.[10]

Bravo. In contrast to that exuberance, Modern Portfolio Theory operates very narrowly, and entirely at the level of risk. But let us be very clear that Markowitz's specific definition of portfolio risk—variance from an expected total return, and by derivation, the standard deviation of total return—is also just a choice. There was and is nothing absolute about his definition, nothing preordained about it.

Other very successful investors have kept their distance from this approach to risk. Benjamin Graham, you recall, had an entirely different approach. For him, it was about effort and the willingness and ability of an investor to put forth that effort. And he went out of his way to suggest that fluctuating share prices—at the core of the current definition of risk—need not be considered risk at all by the serious investor. (Granted, he made that point before MPT's even narrower definition of risk had become the standard.) More recently, famed investor David Swenson of Yale University seemed to echo Graham's definition of risk as return for effort. Higher effort and risk are for professionals; lower effort and risk are for those without the time and resources to invest as professionals.[11]

Even lower-profile academics and practitioners have had the nerve to put forth different definitions of risk. In 1984, Robert H. Jeffrey argued for a paradigm shift away from risk defined as volatility of portfolio total return to one that links the portfolio to meeting its objectives, the owners' expected liabilities or "consumption" (eco-speak for expenditures or bills to pay): "The real risk in holding a portfolio is that it might not provide its owner . . . with the cash he requires to make essential outlays."[12] (Not surprisingly, the present author is sympathetic to that version of risk.) Even certain textbooks accept the idea that price movement is not necessarily the exclusive basis for risk: "If the investor is not in need of high liquidity and is truly a long-term holder, then price volatility per se does not really pose a risk."[13] Other commentators such as Ashvin Chhabra have sought to introduce different, nonmarket forms of risk, such as "personal and aspirational risk," that take portfolio construction and analysis beyond the confines of traditional MPT.[14] Chhabra's approach amounts to an acknowledgment of the cereal-box wisdom that life is a journey, not a specific destination known decades in advance. Did you plan on those triplets? Did you plan to lose your job? Did you plan on divorce? Did you plan on supporting your elderly parents? Did you need cash right in the midst of a market downturn? Perhaps not, but life as it is lived outside the realm of MPT is full of this type of risk. Understood broadly, behavioral finance can be seen as being about *all* the forms of risk other than MPT's mean variance.

Adopting a businesslike approach to the ownership of equity assets leads to my definition of risk, and it is one that any businessperson can appreciate. Let me be as axiomatic as Markowitz: *I propose that investment risk be associated with that which ultimately determines the worth of an asset, its utility. And that utility is the cashflow that the asset or portfolio generates and can be distributed to the owner. Risk then becomes the chance that the income stream might not materialize or grow as fast as expected.* Paraphrasing Markowitz, we can state then that "the investor does (or should) consider expected [cashflow] a desirable thing and variance of [expected cashflow] an undesirable thing." In simpler terms, investment risk is the chance that the check might *not* be in the mail.

As a practical matter, one can as readily choose cashflow as market price as the basis for both risk and return. In fact, the industry standard definition of total return—the combination of actual cash distributions plus change in the asset price, itself driven by the trajectory of the cashflow—need not change at all, but the emphasis would be quite different. More importantly, the alternative definition of risk shifts the investor's concern from the daily share repricing game, over which he or she can have little control, to the reasonably judgeable business risk that the actual cashflows might not materialize—in the case of stocks, that the dividends might be canceled or not grow as expected, and in the case of bonds, that the interest payment might not be made or principal repaid. This cashflow-based risk can also take the form of inflation that would erode the buying power of those cash distributions. Here the check is in the mail, but by the time you get it, it is worth less than you had hoped it would be. That type of prospective risk can be accounted for with an appropriate discount rate. Bond investors would say that they already do this; stock investors rarely do.

Moreover, this definition of risk would bring stock market investment a good deal closer to the idea of risk that is standard in any private business. In that world outside Wall Street, where people invest their daily labors, financial risk is associated with the paycheck at the family level and with making payroll and paying vendors at the business level. The other risk, that on any given day the bid price from a broker for a stock or a bond (or your business or your house) might rise or fall from the bid price the prior day, is certainly worth noting. But in most cases—unless you are intent on selling your stock, bond, business, or house that very day—it is a secondary concern. In the U.S. stock market today, these two notions of risk have been reversed. We spend too much time considering market risk and insufficient time assessing genuine business risk. Shifting to a cashflow-based investment theory would close the intellectual gap—or at least narrow it—between business analysis and public company business analysis. Why should they be so dramatically different? Procter & Gamble and Apple may be storied stocks, but at the end of the day, they are businesses and need to be judged as such. Let me reiterate that Harry Markowitz's choice in 1952 to define risk as variance from a total return expectation was not explicitly designed to get away from a businesslike approach to investment. Indeed, the opposite is true. Many of his assertions in 1952 fit in very nicely with a cashflow-based rather than share price–based approach to risk. But at that time, working as a young academic and not a businessperson, and looking at a stock market that still valued cashflows, his approach did not necessarily contradict a businesslike approach to investing.

Viewing equity risk through the prism of distributable cashflows is not entirely new, but it has become somewhat of a lost art. There has been little appetite to apply these concepts for the past 30 years while Miller and Modigliani dominated the intellectual ramparts and everyone was focused on share prices. Compared with the voluminous literature on share price movements, the academic literature on the right discount rate for dividends barely rises to the level of sparse, and most of it is from the 1970s and 1980s.[15] By the 1990s, the sway of M&M was absolute, and dividends were in a full and hasty retreat. Perhaps it is not surprising that what little recent work has been done on the subject comes from England, where businesses are still measured by their distributable cashflows.[16] But the math is not that difficult—although, alas, it is still rooted in risk-free rates—and should be a topic of future research should the stock market once again become a serious business investment platform. The infrastructure for considering equities in this manner is already in place in the bond world where analysts are accustomed to assessing the "term structure" of interest rates used to discount future coupon payments. Another bond calculation, "duration," is used to measure how soon one gets one's money back in income. These concepts can and should again be applied to the dividend distributions from publicly traded stocks.

So how does one come up with a reasonable discount rate, particularly if one is not inclined to use CAPM or a CAPM-related expected rate of return, which is the mathematical flip side of a discount rate? At the end of the day, how do we quantify risk? This takes us back to the big picture behind all of investing and what Modern Portfolio Theory purports to address: decision making under conditions of uncertainty. CAPM is an elegant solution to that profoundly difficult problem, and it solves for multiple factors in the investment equation. But just because it is an easy solution does not make it the right one. Not using it means a lot more thought needs to go into the process. Prior to the creation of CAPM-based discount rates, these important formula inputs were still based on the risk-free rate of government or high-quality corporate bonds, and then an undefined but usually historically based equity risk premium demanded by the provider of capital to justify the incremental risk or the opportunity cost. That too is a straightforward way to derive a discount rate. It's just not a very good one.

Is it possible that there is no simple, universal formula for quantifying risk? Quantitative analysis can round the sharp edges of decision making and provide greater insight into the process, but can a single formula capture and ultimately subdue risk, particularly for individuals who might define risk in a multitude of ways? The current formula is a one-size-fits-all approach, and for now, there is no obvious alternative to it. But let us be clear: CAPM is far from a perfect formula. The risk-free rate is not risk-free. The equity risk premium remains hard to quantify and quite unrelated to real-world business risk. In a getting-back-to-business investment culture, coming up with a business-oriented discount rate should be a high priority. To my mind it should be based on (though not limited narrowly to) an estimated probability that the specific cashflows in question might not materialize as expected or that their buying power would be less due to inflation. (Alas, expectations of inflation are inexorably tied up with the rates on "risk-free" government securities. There seems to be no way around them!) I will leave it to the Gaussians and Mandelbrotans to determine whether the probabilities should be based on normal or nonnormal distributions. And can there or should there be individual rather than general discount rates? Williams says yes. Strict rational actor proponents prefer one discount rate for everyone. Beyond the statistical questions, the bigger challenge is nevertheless philosophical, not mathematical. Making decisions in life is hard. Formulas can help on the margin, but they cannot turn us all into a Mr. Spock or a Lieutenant Commander Data, and perhaps should not even try.

(Re)Focusing the Expected Rate of Return on Cash

Reward is the flip side of risk, but for all the progress of the past few decades, theoretical forecasts of expected return are still substantially based on the troublesome CAPM or CAPM-derived models, troublesome because those models have little to do with the underlying businesses of the investments in question. My experience in the market has been and the argument here is that estimating less volatile distributable cash-flows is inherently more desirable than trying to estimate more volatile share prices. In both cases, estimation is required, but the difference in volatility is critical in choosing between the two approaches. As Geoff Considine has observed:

Those who suggest that total-return investing is inherently superior to income investing are ignoring a potential crucial source of uncertainty: estimation risk. If you believe that you can estimate a portfolio's expected price appreciation as accurately as you can project its future income, you should favor a total-return portfolio. If, on the other hand, you acknowledge that past income is more predictive of future income than past price returns are predictive of future price returns, you should be biased toward income-oriented portfolios.[17]

Put another way, guessing share price changes is a lot trickier than estimating dividend payments. For equities, distributable income is generally determined once a year and is dependent on the condition of the business, which for most publicly traded companies simply does not change dramatically day to day and month to month. In contrast, share prices for publicly traded equities are set by the market 250 times per year by factors substantially external to the business. The market is a lot more exciting, perhaps even more interesting, than all but a few businesses, but I look for excitement in other parts of my life, not from my investment portfolio.

In the absence of the elegant but failed CAPM, how then would we generate an expected rate of return from an asset or portfolio? The same way any businessperson would: in terms of the cash generated and, for equities, the prospective growth of that cash stream. Yes, that approach de-emphasizes the everyday price changes in both, but that's the point. The basic expected annual total return for a fixed income investment becomes the coupon or yield-to-maturity figure (that takes into account bond purchase prices other than par). Bond prices, just like stock prices, can change every day, and one's realized total return from a bond can be quite different from just the yield, particularly for higher-yielding bonds. But let's set that aside for now to focus on the cashflow-based return. For equities, the cashflow-based return is the combination of the dividend yield at time of purchase and the expected annual dividend growth rate. The market sets the yield at time of purchase. It is there for all to see. As long as the dividend is secure, that part of the cash return is a given.

The key figure, however, is the dividend growth rate, which over time is reflected in share price appreciation of the same amount. This is the Gordon constant growth dividend model. It is a good shorthand tool for larger, mature companies—with CAPM-like simplicity—but can only be viewed as approximate. The growth figure still needs to be forecast "by hand," but if you can reasonably hold just 50 or 100 such equity investments rather than 500 or 1,000, the task is less taxing for your financial advisor or the money manager(s) and the analysts entrusted with your assets. And it is a company-specific exercise, native to and reasonable in a business environment, based on the company's actual conditions and commercial outlook: sales, margins, product development, labor costs, profits, taxes, inventory, industry trends, market share, cashflow from operations, capital expenditure needs, the balance sheet, debt coming due, etc. Given our stated preference to invest as a businessperson, the fact that the key input into the expected return formula is business-based, rather than stock market–based, makes it necessarily more attractive.

Critics will jump in here on the need for additional complexity to support multistage growth dividend figures and various discount rates. That is certainly true, but John Burr Williams's complexity is not the goal. Investors should have an approximate expectation of distribution growth over the intermediate and long term. They do not need (and are unlikely to be able to get) forecasting precision to the third decimal. The same critics will observe that the flaws of the current system—notably the astoundingly poor forecast records of market participants of company sales growth, EPS (earnings per share), P/E multiples, price targets, etc.—would transfer over to the exercise of forecasting distributable cashflows. Yes, a degree of error—likely excessive optimism—is to be expected, though some of the risk of poor forecasting would be diminished by the lower variability of income streams, as Considine noted earlier. And at least the matters being forecast concern the business, not the stock market where entirely different matters are being forecast. To borrow from Keynes's famous analogy comparing typical security selection in the stock market to a beauty contest: "It is not a case of choosing those which, to the best of one's judgment, are really the prettiest, nor even those which average opinion genuinely thinks the prettiest."[18] Instead, we are left with the challenge of trying to figure out what other people might think other people (etc.) might think about a stock. That can be entertaining, but it certainly introduces substantially greater forecasting error than focusing on business trends.

But of even greater importance is simply letting go of the assumption that we need to and can forecast the future precisely. Forecasting the free cashflow necessary to support distributions *adequately* is a much more reasonable standard. Modern finance wants mathematical precision. Everything should add up just so. That's just not realistic when imagining the future of collective human behavior or specific business endeavors. My solution to forecasting dividends—the specific form of decision making under conditions of uncertainty that confronts the cashflow investor—is not to come up with a better algorithm, but to realize that mathematically perfect forecasting is simply not necessary to make good business decisions.

Having returned to a pre-CAPM, more business-based way of deriving an expected total return, we can, however, take a page from the CAPM playbook and offer a shortcut for those individual investors who may not have access to company databases or third-party analysts or not have the time to come up with cashflow forecasts for their holdings. As William Sharpe observed more than 50 years ago, most companies' shares move up and down in line with their sensitivity to the market (beta). As a business investor, we can also observe that most established companies' dividend growth prospects will likely bear some relationship to the overall level of economic activity in their regions or industries. One could take a forecast of nominal GDP growth and then add or subtract an amount for each company to acknowledge that individual holdings will likely do a little better or a little worse than the overall economy or their particular slice of it. This approach amounts to a very distant cousin to Ross's APT from 1976.[19] Here, too, you won't get precision to three decimal points, but you will have an adequate, do-it-yourself estimate of dividend growth for most larger companies in a position to make distributions to company owners. For smaller, rapidly growing enterprises and even large companies that do not make profit distributions to their owners, such as Berkshire-Hathaway, this approach is not relevant. In the same vein, I have been told by critics of a cashflow approach that companies like Netflix and Facebook are paradigm breaking and cannot be valued or even assessed by the tools of a century ago or even a decade ago. Perhaps that is the case; perhaps not. Time will tell. For now, however, these companies must necessarily be treated separately in the asset allocation framework that is proposed later in this chapter.

Whether through third parties building company-specific models or with do-it-yourself shortcuts, it should not be that hard to come up with dividend growth forecasts for reasonably sized equity portfolios. If you can put in the time to forecast how far your favorite sports team is likely to go this season, you can do the same for your financial assets. If you cannot or wish not to, you can pay your financial advisor or money manager to do it. That's what he or she is there for. However derived, that simple growth figure plus the yield at time of purchase gives you a basic, approximate annual return expectation. It makes only one significant assumption about the market, and that is that the yield of the investment will remain relatively constant over the forecast period. That is, that the share price gains over time will line up with the dividend growth rate. That's a big assumption given that the market is open every day and the yield of stocks necessarily changes slightly every time the price goes up or down.

Over longer measurement periods, however, the correlation of share price growth and dividend growth is, as one would expect, very tight. At the same time, for those investors who can't help but look at their screens every morning and every evening, have no fear. The daily stock and bond prices will still be there. Graham's Mr. Market will give you his opinion of your investments as frequently as you wish. The daily (weekly, monthly, quarterly) calculations of total return will still be present. They are all certainly worth noting, but they are not worth making the centerpiece of a portfolio management system, and they would not be the focus of obsessive investor behavior. Instead, investors would track the income stream and the change in that income stream, just like in a real business.

Not (Re)Defining Valuation, but Shifting the Emphasis to Cash

Viewing an individual investment or a portfolio of them from the perspective of the distributable cash that it generates is not difficult. It's just a matter of orientation. Even a portfolio of low-yielding holdings can still be viewed from a cashflow perspective. It's just that the numbers will be very small, counting the pennies that come in rather than the dollars. The trickier part—as in any investment—is to determine the amount of distributable cashflows, of cash-based return, that one would like to see. That is, what makes an attractive investment? Obviously, more is better than less, but more comes with greater risk that the expected cashflows might not materialize. So how much is enough? In Benjamin Graham's day, a 5% dividend yield and a P/E of 10 was normal. In contrast, the current base numbers are shockingly paltry. The dividend yield of the S&P 500 Index is 2%, and it trades around 20 times earnings. Granted, the S&P 500 Index's income stream has grown robustly in recent decades, at a compound rate of 5.7% from $9.75 per unit in 1988 to $48.93 in 2017, and perhaps can justify a higher P/E (and lower yield) than would otherwise be desirable. The question is one of degree. And note as well that all other major stock markets—except Japan's—offer higher cash yields to their business owners.

So what is an attractive yield of a public equity portfolio? Who is to say? Beauty is in the eye of the beholder. There really is no standard measure of what stocks should yield. Instead, they are, once again, traditionally measured relative to the opportunity costs of forgoing other outlays or, as we discussed above, via a CAPM or CAPM-like calculation. It is instructive to step back from the public markets and take a look at how privately held assets are viewed. For those assets, the cashflow-based return is called an internal rate of return (IRR). It is the discount rate that makes a set of future distributable cashflows equal to the current purchase price. Here, too, higher is better than lower. But even in the private realm, it is hard to get away from a relative approach when the base rate of return for private and public company debt is still U.S. Treasuries plus a spread, and U.S. Treasuries plus a risk premium for equity stakes. That is, you are not likely to find many low-risk, large public equity investments with a 20% cashflow-based IRR when Treasury notes sit at 2% and the broader stock market's own cash yield is also at 2%. The market may not be efficient, and it certainly is not from a cashflow (as opposed to price) perspective, but lots of very low-hanging fruit are hard to come by. That fact does not make the rate on Treasuries risk-free or the market equity risk premium the right one. They are just the current ones that we use. So though an IRR approach is not without its flaws, it is still business-based and cashflow-based, rather than strictly stock market–based.

Whatever difficulties might be encountered valuing cash-flows, they pale in comparison to the carnival sideshow that currently passes for valuation in the stock market. There are three main textbook ways to put a price on an asset. First, there is the cost of physically replacing or rebuilding said asset. This approach dates from the industrial age and is less directly relevant in a service economy. The next approach is a discounted cashflow (DCF) exercise. That is our preferred method and one largely ignored in the current marketplace.[20] The third is comparing what an asset sold for recently or what similar assets are trading for currently. That is usually done by taking the share price and dividing it by a company's current or future EPS to derive the famous P/E multiple. Although a measure of cashflow can be backed out of a P/E multiple, that is not how it is used. Instead of focusing on cash actually received by company owners from their investments, P/E multiples and their cousins purport to measure nominal profits available to company managers. That creates a vast array of opportunities to manipulate earnings, and to adjust what is an acceptable P/E ratio.

The financial shenanigans behind EPS calculations are legend. There is an entire financial and accounting literature on all the ways companies make their earnings look higher so that their P/E ratios become lower.[21] They include using adjusted earnings rather than reported. That usually gets rid of all the bad stuff and keeps the good. And then there are the exceptional and unusual charges that seem to recur every year. More prosaically, companies can recognize sales and profits from goods that will be delivered in the future. That is known as "channel stuffing" and is easy to do: just ship goods to a distributor before the end of a quarter. The items have not been sold to the end user and can be returned, but for now the manufacturer can book the profits. Companies can also amortize various costs over multiyear periods that should be expensed. (For tax reduction purposes, many small businesses do the exact opposite—expense costs that should be amortized on the balance sheet.) Selling a building or an investment near the end of a quarter to realize a profit needed for that quarter is a common and uninspired practice. The list goes on. The market's obsession with EPS numbers and P/E ratios feeds directly into near-term price speculation, not long-term business ownership. The culture of P/Es is part of the problem, not part of the solution.[22] That being said, a lot of people and institutions are comfortable using the P/E system. It suits the brokerages; it suits the hedge funds; it suits the traders. Enough said. I propose to put the cashflow horse back in front of the valuation cart. Company managers can still tamper with dividends. The cash to pay dividends can be borrowed, dividends can be paid in shares, etc., but it is just a lot harder to fake a cash dividend than it is to fake a noncash EPS figure.

A valuation environment focused on distributable cashflows can serve the same important market functions that the current system does, though, I would argue, in a more honest and transparent fashion. Open and liquid markets are an excellent mechanism for price discovery, putting a real-world dollar number on a good or service. For stocks, focusing on distributable cashflows—the current or prospective dividend, rather than the EPS—would allow genuine price discovery, as capital market participants offered differing views on any given company's dividend growth prospects and the appropriate dividend valuation. That would, naturally, be an easier exercise for companies with current dividends, less so for those without. (Investments without cash streams are treated in the next section.) Shifting the focus to cashflows also leaves room for what many believe to be the great allure of the stock market—security mispricing.[23] A cashflow-based approach does not assume that all income streams are priced properly. Indeed, the current system's near-exclusive focus on price changes means that, at least in my own experience, most income streams in the U.S. stock market are very much mispriced, as little attention is paid to them. The occasional high-yielding telco or real estate investment trust (REIT) might count as an exception. But for the rest of the market, there is a great opportunity to invest on the basis of distributable cashflows and benefit from mispriced securities. Markets are about having genuine disagreements and making decisions under conditions of uncertainty. They do not have to be about EPS obfuscation.

(Re)Defining Investable Asset Classes

Earlier in this work, I emphasized that until the past few decades, publicly traded securities fit more into a spectrum of cash generation, with bonds, preferred stock, and common stock forming a range of income options. All paid a coupon, and the small number of stocks without a current or prospective payment were viewed by one and all as pure speculations. In recent decades, however, stocks were largely stripped of their dividends—the S&P 500 Index payout ratio fell from around 50% to about 25%, but it has since recovered to somewhere in between; and the yield fell from 4% to 2% due to the payout ratio falling, the decades-long decline in interest rates, and the market's strong rise. That is, investors now pay a good deal more (cash) for less (cash) than they used to. Those numbers are for the market defined as the S&P 500 Index and do not include what is going on in the largely dividend-free Nasdaq land. It is true that in the past decade, many Nasdaq companies have introduced or materially upped their dividend payments, but it is still a dividend-light, if not exactly dividend-free, investment platform. In the meantime, Modern Portfolio Theory kept investors focused on prices, not income streams. To the extent investors have sought material income during the past few decades after dividends disappeared from the stock market, they have done so through fixed-income instruments (at least until yields compressed dramatically after 2008). For most investors, stocks are primarily for long-term or short-term capital gains. Except for a distinct minority of equity income investors—including this manager—the dividend is not why one buys a stock nowadays. And if you happen to need more income today than generated by the skimpy yields in your bond portfolio, you just sell shares to meet the cash requirement. Ironically, that is how pension funds and endowments that have a distribution requirement (that could be aided by income-producing stocks) go about meeting their regular payments: they sell assets. It makes little sense, but it is the way business is done.

Against that current bifurcation of purpose, viewing portfolios from the perspective of distributable cashflows creates the opportunity of once again seeing a broad spectrum of asset types rather than a few distinct types. Yes, bonds still generate fixed coupons, but stocks can and should be viewed in terms of their fluctuating coupons—rising, one hopes—like they once were. Taking this approach to the portfolio requires that one rethink exactly what purpose all those large non- or minimal-dividend-paying stocks serve. In a cash system, what is one to make of the zero-dividend technology companies, as well as the biotechs and the social media stocks? Where do they fit into this puzzle if we no longer base portfolio construction and management on having a share price alone? Well, the answer is not as shocking as it might seem. It turns out that they can all be viewed in terms of their *future* distributable cashflows. Writing over a century ago, Irving Fisher answered the "What about Amazon?" question when he observed:

When capital is for the present yielding non income, as, for instance, vacant land, it nevertheless is expected sometime [emphasis in the original] to yield income, and it is the discounted value of this remote income which alone [my emphasis] constitutes the present value of the land. It is true that a speculator may prize the land simply because he thinks he can sell it later to someone else, and to him it may seem that its value is independent of any future income, and depends only on the future capital-value at which he expects to sell. But it is clear that this future capital-value is itself the discounted value of the income which the then purchaser will expect. Or, if he too be a speculator, and his valuation, like his predecessor's, depends on a resale, the dependence on future income is merely again postponed to the time when some purchaser shall buy the land for the income it will yield. This ultimate expected income gives the basis for all prior capital valuations *[again, my emphasis]. . . . Capital-value, independent of expected income, is impossible.*[24]

So take that, Jeff Bezos! You preside over a dividend stock; you just don't know it yet. Thinking about Amazon's future dividends allows the investor to figure out where, if any place, it and its dividend-free brethren fit in a portfolio. Are Amazon's future dividends worth the current price of $1,181 (December 2017)? Well, time will tell. According to Fisher, "Actual income is hoped for *sometime* [emphasis in the original], even if it be not for a million years. The present [price] is the discounted value of that ultimate income, however far distant."[25] I do hope that Amazon shareholders will not have to wait quite that long to receive the income stream that successful business ownership entails.

As an aside, it is worth noting that Amazon appears to disprove the present work's anti-M&M stance. Amazon has refrained from paying a dividend and has invested any profits it has generated back into its growing array of businesses. And if Jeff Bezos had declared in May 1997, when his company first began publicly trading, that he would not make any distributions for the following 20 years while he completely disrupted retail trade in this country, well beyond just book sales, as well as lead the fields of cloud storage and cloud computing that did not even exist at the time, perhaps I and other investors might have said, sure, that sounds reasonable. Go for it. We will wait for 20 years. In retrospect, that would have been a great (cashless investment), as the Amazon shares have risen from a split-adjusted $2 per share to their current level. But do keep in mind, Amazon is a real exception. Approximately 500 companies had IPOs in 1997—the numbers vary according to the source. Few of them survive to this day, and the better-performing ones beyond Amazon, such as CH Robinson Worldwide, Ralph Lauren, the Children's Place, and TD Ameritrade, are quite notably old economy companies. The first is a shipping and logistics business founded over a century ago, the second a clothes retailer opened in 1969, Ralph Lauren is Ralph Lauren, and TD Ameritrade started as a brokerage in Omaha, Nebraska, in 1975. All currently pay dividends. A few other survivors from the class of 1997 linger on: Cerus, Casella Waste Systems, Rambus.[26] Some others may have been bought out profitably along the way, but literally hundreds did not make it, did not take over the world, and never made any distributions after taking in that IPO capital. (You can generate a partial list of them at http://www.findthecompany.com.) According to Jay Ritter, a finance professor who tracks the IPO market, "64.6% of [IPOs from 1999 and 2000] were trading five years later, or last traded before delisting, at a greater than 90% loss from the offer price."[27] For those who have the focus and resources to navigate the IPO market, the rewards can be substantial, as Amazon and, more recently, a number of social media and biotech companies have proved. But it is equally clear that there is a lot of hard work involved in finding those winners, and avoiding the rest.

So whatever the challenges of holding nondistributing assets, you can still easily justify them in your cashflow-based portfolio if you think of them in terms of their, the hope is, not-too-deferred income streams. At the other end of the ownership equation, knowing individuals and institutions were now looking for cash streams might lead some of the more successful non-dividend payers to start distributing a portion of their ample profits. That would allow investors to distinguish which of the new economy companies have the means and inclination to act as normal businesses and which of them simply cannot afford to. Or in Warren Buffett's famous analogy (applied differently): when the tide goes out, you can see who is wearing a bathing suit and who is not. In the case of his own company, Berkshire-Hathaway, Buffett thinks that it would be stupid to pay a dividend when it has so many high-return investment opportunities available to it. Like Amazon, his company may be the exception that proves the rule. In a stock price–only system, Buffett clearly has the upper hand. If investors cared more about approaching their investments in a businesslike manner—something, ironically, Buffett has excelled at—more mature, successful companies like his might make cash distributions to company owners.

Expecting cash payments from successful enterprises would clear space for and highlight the capital needs of those companies genuinely coming to the market to raise capital (the original purpose of the capital markets), early-stage companies that are not yet in a position to make distributions, distressed cyclicals that cannot and should not make cash distributions, and others in a similar predicament. Having Berkshire-Hathaway and its large successful peers not pay dividends only serves to confuse investors about the difference between the "can't-pay" and the "don't-want-to-pay" crowds. A greater emphasis on distributable cashflow in the investment analysis and portfolio construction process would draw a brighter line between the two.

One's thinking about a cashflow-based portfolio doesn't need to stop with the traditional notion of just stocks and bonds and the now much-rarer preferred equity in between the two. (Convertible debt falls into the "between" category as well.) From a cashflow perspective, the distinction between publicly traded and privately held companies becomes less sharp, which is a good thing. Both can and do make periodic distributions. One is easier to put new money into or liquidate than the other, but for long-term investors, the similarities may be as great as the differences. How is the distributable cashflow? Is it rising? Is it falling? The same is true of real estate. Your private real estate holdings may not reprice every day the way your stocks do, but from a cash-flow generation perspective, are they really all that different? Money is money. The rent check from a tenant and the dividend check from Coca-Cola have the same green color when they hit your online account. What about other types of potential investments, such as buying a fast-food franchise, or putting new machinery in the workshop, or opening up a new branch of the business? At the end of day, the health and success of all businesses is based on their ability to generate distributable cashflows.

Indeed, using income rather than asset prices as the basis for portfolio management gets investors a bit closer to one of the great unanswered challenges of Modern Portfolio Theory. By the mid-1960s, the academics had proved, at least to their satisfaction, that the most efficient portfolio was the entire universe of investable assets. In the decades since, academics and investors have wrestled with defining the universe of investable assets and then accessing it. Clearly that universe should go beyond just blue chip stocks, corporate bonds, and U.S. Treasuries. Over time, it has become easier to include small company stocks, foreign stocks, riskier bonds, precious metals, etc. There are markets for such things. Publicly traded REITs have been around for decades—as have private ones. For pension funds and endowments, large-scale direct real estate, private equity, etc., have entered the mix, getting investors closer to that promised land of all investable assets. For retail investors, index funds and ETFs have helped extend the reach of individual portfolios. Brazilian commodity companies and exotic derivatives from the leading investment banks are now just a keystroke away, even for small retail investors.

That's all well and good, but what about using the individual investor's *actual* universe of real-world invested and investable assets as the basis for a portfolio system? That would include the investor's three-unit rental apartment by the local college, the one-eighth share of an oil and gas lease, Grandpa's farm divided among the cousins, the minority stake in the pizza shop down the street, and the interest in the sister-in-law's business. None of those assets have daily prices associated with them, at least not frequently the way a stock or bond does, but if they are successful, they do make periodic distributions to the company owners. A cashflow approach brings these very important and very real assets into the investor's portfolio management and analysis structure. They can and ought to be considered together in one package. Indeed, using a cashflow approach allows the most important asset and source of income for working-age investors to enter into the mix: their paycheck. We all expect cash payment for our services, not a piece of paper that may have a greater or lesser value in the marketplace. For most of us, our labor is the most important asset in the family portfolio. And Modern Portfolio Theory has *absolutely nothing* to say about it. In that regard, is our day job really all that different from the financial assets that we hold in brokerage and financial accounts? And unlike the stock market of today, clouded by a theory of prices, the cashflow from your direct efforts is something you certainly know and understand quite well.

An Easier Diversification

Sixty years after Markowitz rightly advocated diversification for investors who had just a few holdings, the problem has been more than fixed. In fact, both Modern Portfolio Theory and the index fund/ETF movement have created the opposite problem—ownership of meaningless, excessive, minuscule stakes—by relentlessly pushing for more and more asset types to be included in client portfolios, down to the tiniest slices. This is ridiculously remote from the original goal of lowering the variance of a portfolio's expected total return. Adopting a business ownership approach makes the "let's-have-a-thousand-stocks-and-bonds-in-an-individual's-portfolio" approach much less necessary to reduce volatility. That's for the simple and obvious reason that much of the volatility of the investment process—trying to forecast or guess share prices that move around a great deal—is removed in favor of the much less volatile income stream derived from most financial assets.

Yale Professor Robert Shiller's data about the U.S. stock market from 1871 through 2015 shows that the standard deviation of annual earnings growth for the S&P 500 Index companies (and precursor groupings prior to 1957) is 32%. That is, reported S&P earnings jump around a lot in any given year. Some of that variance likely reflects accounting standards that have changed considerably over the years, and some more of it would be a natural consequence of the greater cyclicality of the industrial U.S. economy in the late nineteenth century through much of the twentieth century. Not surprisingly, share prices have evinced a similarly high level of volatility: a 17.3% standard deviation from the compound annual growth rate of 4.3%. That is to say, the stock market's annual share price return ranged from −13% to 21% for about two-thirds of the years. Those are big swings. In contrast, the dividend, which also grew at a similar annual rate, 3.6%, exhibited much less volatility, 11.7%, meaning most years the dividend growth rate ranged from −8% to +15%. Dividend growth is not guaranteed, and it is not perfectly smooth year to year, but it moves around a good deal less than earnings or share prices. For a more recent snapshot, the French brokerage Societe Generale compared the earnings volatility of the MSCI World Index companies from 1971 through 2016. It had a standard deviation of 22.3%. For dividends in that period, it was 8.2%.[28] The point can be made even more easily at the individual company level. In an earlier screed against share repurchase programs, I observed that the standard deviation of Procter & Gamble's dividend growth from 1992 through 2012 was just 2%, compared with anywhere from 7% to 19% for various measures of EPS and

16% for the annual price change. And that's for an incredibly stable company and blue chip stock.

Given the low volatility of most dividend streams compared with share prices, a far fewer number of different sources of income would achieve the peace-of-mind diversification that is now addressed by having hundreds if not thousands of individual securities. And if you could include your private assets—the rental property, the stake in the local pizza parlor, your share of your grandparents' farmland, and your own biweekly paycheck—the need to have highly volatile exotic investments and those volatility-dampening derivatives—all for diversification purposes—would diminish even further. James Tobin's heirs would argue at this point that what goes for prices goes for income as well: own all income-producing assets as the dominant efficient portfolio, and then just toggle your risk and return level by the amount of cash that you hold. The notion that everyone should hold the exact same portfolio—even in the tiniest slices—under the conditions that Tobin described in 1958 is as unrealistic now as it was 60 years ago.

In 1959, Harry Markowitz fleshed out the benefits of diversification from a total return perspective with a model portfolio of nine prominent stocks held from 1937 to 1954. The original holdings included American Tobacco, AT&T, United States Steel, General Motors, Atchison Topeka & Santa Fe, Coca-Cola, Borden, Firestone, and Sharon Steel. We can conduct a much simplified but similar exercise to highlight the virtues of viewing a portfolio primarily in terms of its distributable cashflows. Coca-Cola remains in the group, as does AT&T, even though it is a quite different company from the original AT&T. United States Steel and General Motors survive, but they are a shadow of their former selves. We substitute Disney and IBM. For the remainder, we use Johnson & Johnson, Occidental Petroleum, Southern Company, Wells Fargo, and Union Pacific. To make the math a bit easier, we add a tenth name, McDonald's. (Cash was Markowitz's original tenth.) This is far from a fair representation of the current S&P 500 Index, but it is a good sample of mature, publicly traded companies that happen to be profitable and distribute their profits to company owners. As Markowitz wrote after introducing his list, "No special significance should be attached to this list of securities other than that it will be used in illustrating principles of portfolio analysis."[29] Securities lawyers are even more aggressive now than they were in the 1950s, so let me reiterate: this is not a recommended list of any type. If you buy just these 10 securities as a result of reading this book, you will certainly lose all your money and your hair and put on a lot of weight. You have been warned.

To start, we can put together an equal-weighted portfolio (10% each). We can then measure the annual income generated, as well as the total return, for 20 years from 1997 through 2017. As is typical in these kinds of exercises—though less typical in actual client portfolios—the portfolio gets rebalanced annually back to a 10% share of total assets for each holding on January 1 of the following year.

The current approach to assessing a portfolio's performance is to look almost exclusively at the total return in relatively short measurement periods and then link them geometrically. That more or less locks investors into playing the share price game. In contrast, I suggest taking the same data but focusing on what is real, the cash thrown off by the operating assets. That means counting up not just total return (in which income is a component), but also highlighting the income stream. Note the steadiness in the growth of the cash payments. That's why younger investors might have a prefer-

With Dividends Reinvested					
Year	Starting Capital	Ending Capital	Total Return	Income Generated	Growth in Income
1997	$ 100,000	$ 133,599	33.60%	$ 2,828	
1998	$ 133,533	$ 150,221	10.94%	$ 2,973	5.13%
1999	$ 156,227	$ 152,322	3.90%	$ 3,640	22.43%
2000	$ 162,322	$ 180,076	10.94%	$ 3,988	9.56%
2001	$ 180,076	$ 181,900	1.01%	$ 3,784	–5.12%
2002	$ 181,900	$ 155,551	–8.00%	$ 3,898	3.01%
2003	$ 165,551	$ 206,739	24.88%	$ 4.457	14.35%
2004	$ 206,739	$ 234,604	13.48%	$ 5,205	16.78%
2005	$ 234,604	$ 245,716	4.74%	$ 5,930	13.94%
2006	$ 245,716	$ 307,796	25.20%	$ 6,881	10.03%
2007	$ 307,796	$ 357,750	19.48%	$ 8,150	18.44%
2008	$ 367,750	$ 315,015	–14.07%	$ 9,713	19.18%
2009	$ 316,015	$ 382,935	21.18%	$ 9,758	0.45%
2010	$ 382,935	$ 456,441	19.20%	$ 11,186	14.64%
2011	$ 456,441	$ 511,618	12.09%	$ 13,560	21.22%
2012	$ 511,618	$ 560,209	9.50%	$ 15,959	17.70%
2013	$ 560,209	$ 689,127	23.01%	$ 18,612	16.62%
2014	$ 689,127	$ 771,464	11.95%	$ 21,929	17.82%
2015	$ 771,464	$ 773,155	0.22%	$ 24,990	13.96%
2016	$ 773,155	$ 877,411	13.48%	$ 27,265	9.10%
2017	$ 877,411	$ 995,354	13.44%	$ 29,370	7.72%
Summary					
CAGR			11.56%		12.41%
Std. Dev			11.53%		7.30%
Median			13.44%		14.49%

Source: FactSet Research Systems, Inc., and Federated Investors, 2018.

ence for equity over fixed income. Coupons on bonds don't increase over time. And compare the standard deviations of the income stream versus the portfolio's total return, 7.3% versus 11.53%. They are significantly different. Here we are channeling Harry Markowitz—thank you once again—with an approach to portfolios that favors low variance over high variance of expected return, in our case, of cash-based returns. To achieve that low variance of the income stream, do you really need hundreds if not thousands of additional, tiny holdings?

The numbers above assume dividend reinvestment. While dividend reinvestment is a great tool of wealth creation, viewing the portfolio when dividends are not reinvested—imagine Grandma taking the dividends to meet her monthly cash needs—helps clarify the difference between equity portfolios constructed on the basis of share prices and those portfolios constructed on the basis of income generation. The table below does just that.

Without Dividends Reinvested						
Year	Starting Capital	Ending Capital	Stock Return	Total Return	Income Generated	Growth in Income
1997	$ 100,000	$ 130,771	30.77%	33.60%	$ 2,828	
1998	$ 130,771	$ 150,010	14.71%	16.94%	$ 2,910	2.91%
1999	$ 150,010	$ 152,367	1.57%	3.90%	$ 3,495	20.10%
2000	$ 152,367	$ 165,289	8.48%	10.94%	$ 3,743	7.10%
2001	$ 165,289	$ 163,490	−1.09%	1.01%	$ 3,473	−7.22%
2002	$ 163,490	$ 145,292	−11.13%	−8.99%	$ 3,503	0.86%
2003	$ 145,292	$ 177,528	22.19%	24.88%	$ 3,912	11.66%
2004	$ 177,528	$ 196,986	10.96%	13.48%	$ 4,469	14.26%
2005	$ 196,986	$ 201,337	2.21%	4.74%	$ 4,980	11.41%
2006	$ 201,337	$ 246,567	22.46%	25.26%	$ 5,638	13.23%
2007	$ 246,567	$ 288,066	16.83%	19.48%	$ 5,638	13.23%
2008	$ 288,066	$ 239,932	−16.71%	−14.07%	$ 7,609	16.54%
2009	$ 239,932	$ 283,332	18.09%	21.18%	$ 7,408	−2.63%
2010	$ 283,332	$ 329,442	16.27%	19.20%	$ 8,277	11.72%
2011	$ 329,442	$ 359,480	9.12%	12.09%	$ 9,787	18.25%
2012	$ 359,480	$ 382,408	6.38%	9.50%	$ 11,213	14.58%
2013	$ 382,408	$ 457,705	19.69%	23.01%	$ 12,705	13.30%
2014	$ 457,705	$ 497,827	8.77%	11.95%	$ 14,565	14.64%
2015	$ 497,827	$ 482,792	−3.02%	0.22%	$ 16,126	10.72%
2016	$ 482,792	$ 530,869	9.96%	13.48%	$ 17,025	5.58%
2017	$ 530,869	$ 584,459	10.09%	13.44%	$ 17,770	4.37%
Summary Statistics						
CAGR			8.77%		9.63%	
Std. Dev			11.40%	11.53%		7.20%
Median			9.6%	13.44%		11.69%

Source: FactSet Research Systems, Inc., and Federated Investors, 2018.

spective cashflows rather than daily, weekly, and monthly share price changes would extend the time horizon of internal investment for publicly traded corporations.

Viewing one's holdings as businesses rather than stocks would have the same benefit for investors as for the businesses themselves, and that would be reflected in much lower turnover. One owns businesses, but one speculates in stocks. Can you really say you are an investor as opposed to a speculator if you own something for a few hours, a few days, even just a few months? In the world of high-frequency algorithmic trading and performance measurement by the day, very high turnover is the norm. I have told clients that for the particular portfolio that I manage, it would be sufficient if the stock market were open three to four times each year for clearing purposes. That always gets a chuckle from the financial consultants and advisors, who find the idea absurd. But our businesses don't change day to day; why should they reprice daily? Is Coke really that different than it was a few days ago? Is Verizon? Yes, perhaps, stock market conditions might have altered a bit, but for most publicly traded large corporations, business conditions have not. (Smaller corporations may well have changed in a brief period of time. Their shares could trade every month or so . . .)

Staring at share prices that go up or down every day simply invites speculation, even among those who think that they are investors for the long run. That tug of trading gravity creates the Dalbar effect of terrible investor returns when most individuals and all too many professionals are poor at timing the stock market. By shifting investor focus to cashflows, there is less temptation to time the market, and therefore, for most investors, there is less value-destructive in-and-out trading. Indeed, one could view holding investments for longer periods as another form of diversification of investor behavior—over time—in order to capture the long-term growth of most publicly traded businesses, and to avoid the Dalbar outcome.[32]

One challenge to holding a low-turnover, business ownership view of the stock market is that there are many intermediaries—brokers, advisors, consultants, traders, portfolio managers (me)—who are paid to *do* something. The assumption is that if they *do* something, and in the case of liquid investments, it is invariably to trade them, a better outcome will result. The tonic here is the same as elsewhere in this argument: view the investment as a business ownership. Business owners generally have relatively few intermediaries and rarely find themselves flipping the businesses on a daily, weekly, or monthly basis. In short, a buy-and-hold (and closely monitored) business strategy, straight from Benjamin Graham, threatens the livelihoods of too many people in the financial services industry. For that reason alone, a shift to focusing on the stock market as a business ownership platform will be a long, uphill slog.

By design, our preferred focus on cash generation and distributions would also have an impact on how people experience and think about the inevitable stock market drawdowns that occur now and again. When the market starts going down, lots of people want to get out, even if the root cause for the decline is unrelated to the real-world condition of your businesses, or even to your particular stock market investment. Recall the prior examples from 2008–2009 when many companies remote from the financial services industry or the home mortgage business saw their share prices plummet. This was despite the fact that the crisis had little if any impact on their operations. A focus on cash would redirect investor attention away from what has become an end unto itself— share prices—to the underlying causes. If there is an issue affecting the cashflow supporting a particular company's or portfolio's distribution, that is a legitimate concern that should rightly affect how much one would pay for that business or portfolio. But just because bank stocks or tech stocks are selling off madly should not necessarily lead to a rout of food, beverage, and tobacco companies, or healthcare companies or utilities, whose businesses are largely unaffected.

(Re)Defining the Marketplace

The shift to a cashflow-based portfolio construction and management system might make the U.S. stock market look very different than it is today. Because cashflows move around much less than price changes, the latter's volatility would diminish as people focused on the former. Trading volumes might drop as well. It would be a quieter place. For traders and hedge funds and Wall Street, that would not be a good thing. For investors, it would be a wonderful development. Perhaps the U.S. stock market would appear less the national betting parlor that it has become in recent decades. And if investors started using cash returns for their portfolio construction and management decisions, some of the market's ratios and the practices behind those ratios would be due for a review. In initial meetings with clients, I often ask them what they might pay for a $2,000 income stream that would be expected to rise by 5–6% annually over a long measurement period (though perhaps not every year), with a medium amount of risk to the income stream. I define medium by emphasizing that the income stream doesn't come from a promise to pay (a bond), but also does not stem from highly volatile start-up companies. I usually get a variety of answers between $50,000 (implying a 4% yield) and $75,000 (implying a 2.7% yield). I then let them know that those numbers applied to the S&P 500 Index (with its $48.93 dividend as of December 31, 2017) would put the market in a range from around 1223 (4% yield) to around 1812 (2.7% yield). Wow. As I write in late 2017, the market is currently trading at more than twice the former value and 50% more than the latter. I'm not a bear market forecaster, nor am I a shortseller in my professional capacity or personally, but it is clear that most stock market investors are very bullish on America and are willing to pay a lot for the S&P 500 Index companies' distributable cashflows.

A shift to a more cash-based approach does not mean that the stock market needs to go down materially to increase the yield of the current income streams there. The cash distributions from the S&P 500 Index companies are simply low and could easily be raised without cutting back on a single dollar of investment. The reason? Share buybacks. In 2016, they amounted to $573 billion versus dividend payments of $435 billion. Share buybacks are a relatively recent phenomenon—they became very popular starting in the 1990s—and I have addressed in another forum why they are so devastating to investors.[33] Even a modest shift from buybacks to dividend payments could make the overall stock market a good deal more attractive to genuine business investors, not just to stock market traders.

Would shifting the orientation of investors in the U.S. stock market from share prices alone to cashflows ultimately be good for investors and for the companies whose shares trade in the United States? As I mentioned earlier, the no-rules system of the United States from the nineteenth century through the Crash of 1929 was effective in contributing to the emergence of the United States as an economic superpower. It has remained the global economic locomotive ever since. The

United States is the land of innovation and investment capital. Foreign companies list here and raise capital here. Rarely if ever does a U.S.-oriented company choose to have its initial public offering in some second-tier market or even in Europe. The question for U.S. investors and for companies is, How do we continue that tradition and position the United States as the market of choice for the next century? Making sense of the 1929 Crash and the Great Depression, bolstered by a belief that humans were fully rational and problems could be solved with dense formulas, was the basis for Modern Portfolio Theory. That approach suited the second half of the twentieth century quite well. But it is far from clear that it is the right formula for the twenty-first century. The same Massachusetts court ruling in 1830 that gave us the Prudent Man Rule perhaps also included the epitaph for Modern Portfolio Theory: "Do as you will. The capital is at hazard."[34] No amount of quantitative theorizing can take all the risk out of the human experience. There is no such algorithm. Harry Markowitz was aware of this from the very beginning:

There is no integrated theory by which we could dispense with human beings if we had a sufficiently large and fast computer. The study of rational behavior has produced only general principles to be kept in mind as guides. Even the significance of some of these principles is subject to controversy. The value of the study of rational behavior is that it supplies us with a new viewpoint on problems of criteria—a viewpoint to be added to common sense to serve as the basis of good judgment.[35]

Nearly 60 years after these wise words were written, it too often seems as if common sense has been entirely pushed aside by ever-larger and -faster computers.

(Re)Defining Portfolio Construction: Synchronic Asset Classes Become Diachronic Income Streams

Given our axiomatic preference for investing as an exercise in business ownership based on distributable cashflows, a practical approach to portfolio construction would be to categorize assets according to their income-producing characteristics. This in turn amounts to a new approach to asset allocation. Under the current price-based system, asset allocation runs something like this: You own a certain combination of stocks, bonds, alternatives, cash, precious metals, commodities, etc., that add up to 100% of your financial assets. Per MPT, the particular mix of the assets in your portfolio reflects the supposedly customizable combination of expected return and covariance (risk), based substantially on price changes. That reflects the synchronic Markowitzian world we currently inhabit. In contrast, defining asset classes in terms of their current income streams and the future income opportunities cements the association of investing with the actual ownership of businesses and puts greater distance between the portfolio construction process and the hurly-burly of the daily price changes. Is this just a matter of changing labels? I hope not, but even if it could be seen as shuffling the same deck of asset cards, the remix serves the necessary purpose of getting investors to think of themselves as business owners far more so than the current system does.

The easiest and most obvious income stream—we can call it *stable income*—would consist of stocks typical of the Markowitz-redux exercise, offering robust, steady, and modestly growing dividends. High-quality real estate or other private holdings producing gradually rising rents or profit distributions might also fall into this bucket. It could also include the coupon payments of super-high-quality, investment-grade bonds or government securities. This would be the "blue chip" silo of rock-solid payers with some growth in the overall income stream.[36] For many investors, this would be the core of their investment portfolio, to be complemented by a variety of satellite approaches.

A second allocation could consist of income streams that might not be material at the point of initial investment, but where the outlook for income growth is quite positive. This *rising income* group, consisting of equities—bond coupons are generally flat—would provide inflation protection for the investor, as the rising payments would offset rising costs. Private ventures soon able to generate rising distributions could fit in this bucket. This silo might not yield much at inception, but the expectation would be that the cash streams would gain substantially in the intermediate term. During periodic rebalancing exercises, individual holdings where the payment stream has come to offer a high and consistent yield might be reclassified into the stable income group.

A third silo could consist of *high-income* streams to meet current cash requirements, but with little to no prospect of income growth and greater risk of distribution cuts. This group would hold the high-yield stocks, high-yield (junk) bonds, and perhaps some riskier, privately held, income-producing ventures that don't fit into MPT but do fit into the lives of actual investors. This silo would be appropriate for those who understand that certain income streams are high yielding for a reason. Diversification within the silo would mitigate some of the risk that the expected payments may not materialize.

Cash doesn't currently pay much of a return, but there was a time when it did, and it might again in the future, so it is worth keeping the option of having a fourth silo for cash, cashlike securities (near-term government securities and commercial paper), or money market funds. Cash also serves the obvious purpose of having a near-term cautious view of the world while still wanting to maintain liquid financial assets.

A fifth and final silo could consist, if the investor so desired it, of *non-income-producing investments*. They could be your brother-in-law's start-up, the biotech darlings of Nasdaq, that leveraged private equity venture that you sort of understand, and other dividend-free enterprises such as Berkshire-Hathaway, Tesla, and such. The prospects or current growth rates of these ventures, if they are not making distributions, ought to be very high indeed to justify their position in a portfolio. There might be daily liquidity—as in the case of the publicly traded stocks—or their might not—in the case of the start-ups or your brother-in-law's enterprise. Either way, the assets in this silo are, as long as they do not produce income, understood to be entirely dependent on a cash transaction—selling the asset—in order to generate any cash value.

This allocation could be nicknamed the "American" silo. Decades ago, Keynes observed that Americans were more interested than English investors in investing strictly for capital appreciation rather than for yield:

When he purchases an investment, the American is attaching his hopes, not so much to its prospective yield, as to a favourable change in the conventional basis of valuation, i.e. that he is, in the above sense, a speculator. Speculators may do no harm as bubbles on a steady stream of enterprise. But the position is serious when enterprise becomes the bubble on a whirlpool of speculation. When the capital development of a country becomes a by-product of the activities of a casino, the job is likely to be ill-done.[37]

Few investors today would agree that our national "enterprise" has been harmed by the innovation coming out of

Silicon Valley, where the payoff for investors has been strictly price-based rather than reflected in distributed cashflows. So perhaps Keynes's characterization of these stakeholders as speculators is unjustified. As a historian, however, I would argue that how investors have approached and stood with the cashless Nasdaq juggernaut is anomalous. And though it has been ongoing now for more than three decades, the cashless stock investment world still bears close scrutiny. The "rules" of Business 101 could reassert themselves at any moment.

Can holding a nondistributing security be considered business ownership of the type advocated in this work? Of course it can. While the realization of value would be deferred until sale or the enterprise begins to make distributions, there is no reason the same degree of due diligence and care that one would exercise for a cash-distributing enterprise cannot be exercised over a company that does not yet make distributions. Company owners can closely monitor business developments, revenues, costs, management changes, industry prospects, etc. They can take a keen interest in corporate governance matters, as all investors should. Although the investment proposition is very different, investors can exercise the same intellectual sobriety in regard to Amazon as they do to AT&T.

An Aside: Solving the Lottery Ticket Riddle and Getting It into a Portfolio

However attractive nondistributive assets might appear to be, it is clearly the case that within an income-based portfolio construction exercise, they must necessarily be treated separately. Our income-oriented portfolio approach strictly defined has little to say, naturally, about these types of assets. I earlier characterized them as "hope" investments—the investor hopes that at some point in the future they will start making distributions—and moved on. That's where behavioral finance, specifically the Behavioral Portfolio Theory (BPT) of Statman and Shefrin, may be of use. In part, BPT answers the classic finance riddle about why people who spend money on insurance policies—a highly defensive, risk-averse choice—are also willing to buy lottery tickets, even when they know they have almost no chance of winning. The rational actor theory underpinning MPT and the rest of modern finance really has no good answer for that. BPT does. Rather than focusing on the mean and variance of expected returns—lottery tickets are basically a no-go in that environment—BPT portfolios "combine low and high aspiration [and] are often depicted as layered pyramids where investors divide their current wealth between a [larger] bottom layer, designed to avoid poverty, and a [smaller] top layer, designed for a shot at riches."[38] Many people buy lottery tickets, including those who know the very long odds of winning and are otherwise highly rational and numerate. Yet they do it. Leaving a non-cash, lottery ticket bucket in our proposed portfolio system is just a commonsense acknowledgment that investors have personalities, not just probabilities.

In the current U.S. marketplace, there are a lot of candidates for inclusion in the noncash silo. The competition would be tough. Some may be held in the expectation that they will make it to one of the other buckets. Others might be viewed strictly as play money. A handful might be held in the hope of stumbling upon the next Apple or NetFlix. That's all fine. I don't want to be a killjoy. Life would be boring without this silo. Just know why you are holding these investments. And always remember that the prospective high returns offered by these holdings are necessarily accompanied by higher risk of capital loss. Diversification can mitigate some of that risk, but as 2000–2001 and 2008–2009 show, only some of it can be offset. And untethered by any income streams, the publicly traded holdings in this silo would show enormous share price volatility. (Stocks without dividends move around more than the broader market and, as you might expect, much more than stocks with dividends.) Ironically, by putting all the high-volatility assets in the same silo, investors may actually feel *more* comfortable about the big price moves when they understand that they are not putting the overall portfolio income stream at risk. That little bit of mental accounting is consistent with behavioral finance but not with the orthodox finance model. So go for it; buy that lottery ticket and feel good about it.

Asset Allocation and Security Selection

Most readers of a work like this will recognize the standard "60% stocks/40% bonds" asset allocation model. That starting mix assumes close to zero knowledge about the actual investor. The ratio and constituents are then adjusted to reflect the particular circumstances of the people or institutions involved. So what does asset allocation look like in an income-based portfolio? A generic, starting distribution might consist of 50% stable income, 20% rising income, 10% high yield, 0% cash, and 20% non-income. This allocation would then be customized based on the investor's income (return) expectations and tolerance for income disruption (risk). Note that in traditional asset allocation, the weights are expressed in terms of the principal amount. With our focus on cash generation, an alternative option exists to weight portfolios by the amount of income generated. For the privately held assets, the latter is a lot harder, though not impossible. That's what your financial advisor is there for. He or she can help you figure out the type of weighting that makes the most sense for you.

Using just these five basic categories, you can construct a portfolio that mixes and matches a variety of sources of income and income risk. Contrast that with the asset allocation opportunities in the current system. The popular Morningstar style box has nine asset categories for domestic stocks alone. If you include fixed income and foreign and alternatives, it is possible to have 15 or more types of different publicly traded asset classes in a single portfolio. An income-oriented approach takes that number down materially, in the asset allocation described here, to four buckets plus cash. Depending on how you subdivide your income streams, there could be perhaps a few more buckets or a few less, but it would still be a far more manageable process than what passes for asset allocation today. And yet this more concentrated approach manages to incorporate income streams from privately held assets, something the current price-based asset allocation models cannot do.

Individual security selection is best done in conjunction with a financial advisor or a professional money manager, but the emphasis on defining assets in terms of their income generation also alters this part of the process. Because, as noted earlier, income streams are less volatile than asset prices, the number of holdings needed in each bucket to achieve a stable income stream that meets a commonsense standard of diversification is much lower than what would be needed to achieve the same outcome in a price-based world. That is, a few dozen holdings in each bucket would do what a few hundred are expected to do at present. If one bucket is perhaps 50% of the portfolio—as the first one might be for many investors—perhaps the number of holdings there is a bit larger. But investors don't need a thousand separate holdings in their retail accounts the way current asset allocation married to index fund and passive investing now has it. The exception would be the non-income bucket. Whether it consists of 1 lottery ticket or 1,000, it really does not matter from an income diversification perspective.

It is worth noting that the raw material for such an approach to investing is not promising at the present time. The S&P 500 Index yields only 2%, and the other corners of the stock market yield appreciably less—the Nasdaq 100 has a 1% payout, and fully half the constituents do not pay a dividend at all. The S&P 600 Small Cap Index and the S&P 400 Mid Cap Index have dividend yields in the same, miserly 1% range. There is just not much there to work with. Foreign markets offer higher yields but also additional risk in the form of changing currency rates. Perhaps if a more businesslike sensibility returned to the U.S. stock market, those numbers would move in the right direction. Bond yields also remain very low. For now, investors or their financial advisors will have to make do with a relatively paltry selection of income streams as they construct business portfolios.

As for the debate between passive and active management, you can make your own call. My day job involves overseeing dividend-focused equity portfolios, so you know where I stand. For those investors leaning in the other direction, there are income-oriented bond and stock ETFs and index funds to choose from. While they are not generally run for income in the manner outlined here, they do tilt in that direction. Still, they are necessarily caught up in the sector weighting and relative benchmark game. And remember that all but the broadest market ETFs and index funds are no longer passive at all. To have a narrow focus, such as the generation of income in a non-income-oriented stock market, means that lots of choices are being made by the ETF or index manufacturer. As an income investor, your choice is not really between active and passive, but between a person and a rules-based algorithm.

In regard to costs, active management fees have compressed sharply over the past decade, and the narrower-income ETFs have higher fees than the broad market index products. As a result, costs have become more of a neutral factor in the passive versus active debate.

Finally, while we reject as a fundamental notion the near-term relative benchmark game played today by too many retail and professional investors, that doesn't mean that there can't be better or worse ways of achieving the businesslike goal of managing income streams. If one set of assets can achieve an investor's cashflow goals with lower volatility of those cashflows, then why wouldn't the investor choose that option? Or to put it in traditional Markowitz language, for a given level of income volatility, investors would choose the maximum achievable income. And vice versa. Chasing that marginally lower volatility level down to the third decimal point is of little use given the small variances in cashflow. It is more important to understand putting together a cashflow-based portfolio as a business exercise, not a statistical one.

Is This Really New? No

This is just an initial sketch of what asset allocation and portfolio construction would look like if investors behaved more like businesspeople and less like visitors to a casino. It is meant to start a discussion, not end it. The main assertion is that it is far from difficult to put together, manage, and analyze a portfolio of income-producing assets. Nobel Prizes aside, this is not actually rocket science. It is a matter of orientation and starting propositions. And it is far from an original idea. In fact, it is a solution that is hiding in plain sight. Private businesses are usually run in this manner, as is real estate, a business that many individual investors can readily understand.

I am certainly not the first to make the link between investment in property and a businesslike approach to equities. In a rumination 50 years after the stock market Crash of 1929, Robert Kirby, of industry leader Capital Guardian, observed:

I have said often to almost anyone who would listen that if we were really in the "investment" business, a portfolio of marketable securities would be like a real estate portfolio or at least as real estate portfolios used to be run. The typical real estate commitment is made in anticipation of a projected cashflow versus expenses, i.e., the future internal rate of return. To meet his anticipated investment return, the investor does not have to assume that he will be able to sell the property at a higher price to someone else later on. Common stock portfolios should be constructed, and their future returns measured, by the same set of criteria. In the securities business, however, we still seem strongly to prefer looking for a stock that will be discussed favorably on next week's Wall Street Week *so that we can sell the stock on Monday 10% or 15% higher than we bought it on Friday.*[39]

Those words were written nearly 40 years ago, in 1979. Substitute Jim Cramer's *Mad Money* for Louis Rukeyser's *Wall Street Week* and, alas, they still apply today.

Indeed, for many retirees and their extremely conservative advisors, this approach may already be employed. To wit, two Morningstar executives, David Blanchett and Hal Ratner, have tweaked MPT to come up with efficient income portfolios. Their proposal, in a 2015 issue of the *Journal of Portfolio Management,* makes an argument parallel to the one made here that, due to the lower volatility of income streams compared with asset prices, there is a lot of benefit to focusing on income streams, particularly within a mean variance optimization framework. Similarly, the authors critique the M&M

assertion that investors can and should be indifferent to the source of their consumption income. More than a half century after M&M laid down the law and 40 years after Fischer Black reminded investors of that law, the continued existence of dividend-paying companies and dividend-seeking investors shows the opposite. Investors do appear to prefer that income be income, not just a sold asset, however irrational that view may be from the cloistered halls of the University of Chicago. Blanchett and Ratner take into account the headwind of taxes, but properly assert that many investors are willing to incur taxes in return for the sleep-at-night quality of income-oriented portfolios. Blanchett and Ratner stay rather more within a Markowitzian framework than is proposed here, but they make a strong statement in favor of redefining risk away from price volatility to income stream stability: "The income investor is indifferent to total return efficiency and more concerned with income predictability."[40] Amen.

Following the lead of Blanchett and Ratner, as well as Robert Jeffrey's much earlier commonsense cashflow definition of risk, one could easily assert that an individual's 401(k) should be designed to meet an individual's expected distribution requirement, not necessarily maximize (even on a risk-adjusted basis) total return. It is also hard not to see that liability-driven investing (LDI) and other forms of asset and liability matching—where a pension fund or endowment spends less time worrying about beating a benchmark and more time making sure that its cash inflows and outflows line up—are effectively a form of cashflow portfolio theory, albeit under a different name. And regardless of what it has been called, banks and insurance companies have been acutely aware for centuries of being able to meet specific liabilities with specific assets or cashflows.

So while running portfolios in this manner is occurring, it is as an exception to the prevailing investment paradigm. The intention here is to make this type of objectives-based, cashflow-oriented approach more visible and more accepted. If there are elements of this sensibility already dispersed throughout the investment ecosystem, one can ask whether it is necessary to upend the existing paradigm just to get people to think more in this manner. Might it be sufficient to write an opinion piece for the *Wall Street Journal*, appear on a panel at the CFA Institute annual conference, and press investors to think and behave in a more businesslike fashion? Perhaps, but the impact would likely be limited. After 50 years of the current system, the nudge needs to be more explicit and forceful, bordering on a serious-business "shove." The cashflow approach needs to be called out and identified as a distinct and separate method of portfolio construction and management.

Initial Objections

Let me stop here and address several initial objections. There will be many of them, and I do not want to suggest that shifting to a more cashflow-based approach to portfolio management is a perfect solution to the shortcomings of the current system. I just think that it is a better one than what we have now.

First, high-risk start-ups, loss-making early-stage businesses, and successful, rapidly growing enterprises reinvesting every spare penny in good business opportunities—and at the other end of the spectrum, struggling mature businesses—do not make cash distributions. Nor should they. And that's fine. A cash-based system is not designed to starve companies of capital by putting the expectation of cash distributions on their management teams when that might be the exact wrong thing to do.

In contrast, investors should look at dollars after all legitimate operating and investment costs have been deducted, including reasonable capital expenditures and even modest acquisitions. (It is a separate discussion whether the cash-rich tech companies are spending too much and getting too low a return for their acquisitions. Let us leave that topic for another day.) This view is close to the industry standard definition of free cash flow (FCF)—cashflow from operations minus capital expenditures—which is already used in the analysis of many companies. In addition, a lesser cashflow measure, EBITDA (earnings before interest, taxes, depreciation, and amortization), is employed in certain capital-intensive corners of the marketplace. EBITDA is a highly flawed metric in that it is not distributable cash and does not take into account a company's capital structure or balance sheet leverage, but at least it has a cashflow-based orientation.

Shifting the analysis of stocks from their spurious P/Es to their underlying and potentially distributable cashflows can only benefit investors. Moreover, there is plenty of cash available for distribution from the larger companies of the S&P 500 Index without cutting a single penny of investment. As mentioned above, that is the money that is currently going into share buybacks. *So let us dismiss once and for all the canard that building investment portfolios around distributable cashflows is in some way going to stifle needed investment and long-term growth.*

Depending on the investor's tolerance for risk and need for income, there can and ought to be room—perhaps even substantial room—in everyone's portfolio for nondistributive investments. Similarly, in their working lives, people make all sorts of decisions about volunteering their time and efforts—

helping manage a charity or nonprofit, assisting a friend with a new business—with no regard to income. And that of course is exactly as it should be. We are not advocating a Taylorist view that every second must be fully accounted for and that every effort must be measured to the penny. That's absurd. We are, however, suggesting that the opposite view—that making a wide range of investments in financial assets with little or no regard for the income that they actually generate—is also a bad idea, and it's one that can be relatively easily countered.

Second, commodities and currencies and other asset types do not make distributions. They are not ongoing enterprises. For the most important commodities, the size of the financial market for these materials is vastly larger than the size of the market for physical delivery. Food companies, for instance, take a fraction of the grain that is traded on commodity exchanges. Price speculation is the motivating force for many of these market participants. There is no problem there. There is always room for intelligent price speculation in someone's investment portfolio. If you think the price of grain is going to go up—by all means—buy grain futures. If you don't like the look of global currencies—and there might be plenty not to like—buy precious metals. I have some gold coins, alas just a few, stashed away. It is, as with the other non-income-producing assets one might own, a matter of degree. Ask yourself how much of your portfolio is given over to guesswork, to the everyday chaos of the market, and how much of it is run like a business. The pendulum has swung too far to the former. It is time for it to swing back to where the vast majority of investments are treated in a businesslike manner.

Third, the income approach transgresses a number of orthodoxies held dear by most investors. Near the top of the list would be that holding private (nonpriced) assets together with publicly traded (priced) assets will seem to some like mixing oil and water. Viewed from a distributable cashflow perspective, however, there is no reason that they cannot be combined. Publicly traded assets have the virtue of daily liquidity—you can sell at some price every business day— but a degree of volatility stems from that same virtue: the price moves around a lot, with little reference to the actual business. In suggesting that investors have more of a private market sensibility, I am certainly aware of what is gained by having the markets open every day—liquidity, price discovery, transparency, quick capital raising by companies when needed, and Joe Kernan's dry wit on CNBC's *Squawk Box*. They are all very much appreciated. But they come at a cost, a cost that needs to be acknowledged.

In addition, there is a practical challenge to getting all cashflow-generating assets into a client's portfolio. That is because financial advisors—the ones who have to think at least somewhat in terms of portfolio theory and have the tools to apply it to your holdings—only have access to your financial assets. You can tell your financial advisor how much a month comes in from the rental apartment or from your interest in the fast-food franchise, but there is not much more to be done with that information under the current system. Without a daily price and without the asset sitting in the brokerage account, there is little incentive or means of including it into an analytical or measurement system. Financial advisors are only paid on assets in the account that they oversee, not the franchise or the stake in a producing gas well. So there is not much reason for financial advisors to integrate those nonfinancial assets into their services. That is a shame, and I don't have a solution to that problem. But good financial advisors will take into account a client's other assets, even those they don't manage, can't see directly, and aren't paid on.

Fourth, a key problem of MPT, and more generically any investment theory, is that it describes what people should want, not what is actually available in the marketplace. Just because your asset allocation model spits out a 10% weight in small-cap growth stocks doesn't make those immediately available at a price that you might find attractive. The buy-the-entire-market academics and their heirs, now empowered by index products and ETFs, took care of that by suggesting that it didn't really matter what you owned: just buy all of it, regardless of how filled with undesirable elements the market might be at any given time. Shifting to a cashflow approach does not fundamentally fix the supply versus demand issue. The desire to have a portfolio with various types and amounts of distributions does not magically create a supply of such income streams that exactly meets the investor's need. But it does meaningfully change the terms of the debate and gives company managers an opportunity to engage company owners on a topic—distributable profits—more tangible than the ever-fickle share prices, over which companies have no control.

Fifth, I want to acknowledge right away that there is a large, hulking, immovable obstacle in the way of adopting a cashflow-based approach to investments, and that is the tax man. The U.S. tax code favors, and acknowledges the omnipresence of, the asset price–based system by allowing investors to take capital losses and gains (it is hoped) at their leisure, whereas income payments—coupons on bonds and dividends from stocks—create a tax liability each time they occur.[41] There is also the opportunity cost of losing the compound interest on the capital transferred to the U.S. Treasury as a result of those quarterly events. That is, for those investors who don't need income at the present moment and are determined not to pay the tax collector one penny more than they must, managing their portfolio from the perspective of income streams makes little sense. Indeed, they could prefer the exact opposite: a portfolio consisting entirely of nondividend-paying stocks and lots of very high volatility commodities and private equity ventures of uncertain value and making no distributions. So be it. The virtues of a cashflow-based system are not universal, and I'm not pretending that they are. But one of those virtues is that it has an empirically lower volatility than speculative asset portfolios. *Investors have to decide whether they are willing to run the risk of losing principal outright just to avoid paying the tax man his due.* For some, the answer will be yes, but for many more, having to pay taxes could be seen as a sign of success. I'm not suggesting that we all need to adopt Irving Berlin's famous answer when offered a tax shelter by his accountant— "You don't understand. I came to this country from Russia, and look what's happened to me. The country has been wonderful to me. I love this country. I love to pay taxes."[42]—but I do believe that the virtues of a cashflow approach do outweigh the burden of regular tax payments for all but the most IRS-averse investors. The rising stock market over the past decade has made that a harder argument to accept, as it seems that (deferrable) capital gains are easily and regularly available through the market. Should asset prices not continue their relentless rise in future years, however, then those same investors may well reconsider the idea that harvesting capital gains at their leisure is necessarily superior to clipping stock and bond coupons on a regular basis.

The sixth objection would probably be the first and most important one to many index investors and the academic supporters of efficient markets. Study after study has shown how difficult it is for active investment managers to beat the indexes after fees. More than 40 years ago, Paul Samuelson famously quipped that "most portfolio decision makers should go out of business—take up plumbing, teach Greek, or help produce the annual GNP by serving as corporate executives."[43] Samuelson noted—unlike the more strident polemicists of EMH—that there could be winners in his zero-sum game and that they could continue to win for an extended period of time, but that those folks would be hard to find. Samuelson's 16-inch broadside was fired in 1974, just a decade into the intellectual triumph of the efficient markets idea, a few years after Wells Fargo's initial foray into unmanaged products, and several years before the launch of Bogle's industry-changing index funds. In the subsequent decades, the fusillade has only continued to pummel portfolio managers. Fama's, Sharpe's, and Jensen's early studies of the high-fee, postwar mutual funds have been followed by an endless stream of academic attacks on active management. And for investors, the first generation of passive investment products has evolved into a full slate of index funds and an even larger number of so-called passive ETFs.

This present work advocates not shying away from the challenge of decision making under conditions of uncertainty. In this context, that is "active management." So the indexers will charge, once again, that it does not work. Their argument remains that the market is far too price-efficient for individual investors or managers to beat it consistently, and that when fees are included, the challenge is all the greater. My answer is that we can't possibly know. Genuine business ownership has not really been tested in the stock market in decades. Instead, active management has too often become a question of how close or far one is to a benchmark, not about making business decisions in light of current and future cashflows. The jury is still out about whether the market is or is not efficient when it comes to prices, but it is and has been utterly inefficient for decades when viewed in terms of distributable cash streams.

Until it becomes cashflow-efficient, opportunities for active business investment in the stock market will continue to exist, even in the current low-yield environment.

If portfolio managers behaved more like Samuelson's plumbers, corporate executives, and perhaps even money-savvy language teachers—managing their investments as they manage their own business affairs—then we would have the ability to test whether making business decisions (active) or not making business decisions (index) is a superior way to proceed in the market. At some point in the future, perhaps there will be enough businesslike investment products with sufficient historical records to judge the efficacy of such a strategy. After the 40-year ascendency of "passive," with most marginal investment dollars now flowing into indexes and ETFs, and with more than a little smugness among that part of the investment community, I am more than willing to take the other side of the bet on what the next 40 years might look like.

Finally, perhaps the most interesting objection to me is one that turns the whole idea of "getting back to business" potentially on its head. I argue in favor of viewing equity stakes as evidence of real company ownership. You may not drive the truck or bottle the soda, but if you own the KO shares of Coca-Cola, you are an owner of the company and should behave accordingly. That may be simply naïve. Ownership of a few shares of KO gives you almost no say in the management of the company. Once a year, you get to vote on a few corporate governance issues, most of which are quite perfunctory. More importantly, your votes count only in a nominal sense. In order to have a real voice in the management of the company—the ability to elect directors of your own choosing or sway other major company decisions that may come to a vote at the annual general meeting, an investor needs to have a lot of votes, a Warren Buffett lot. In addition to mega-investors like Buffett, large institutional investors have an impact on the outcome of proxy votes, as they are known, in large part because small investors either do not vote or do not vote as a bloc. So while your 100 shares or 1,000 shares or even 10,000 shares of KO stock may have the same legal standing as Buffett's 400 million shares or that of institutions such as Vanguard with 275 million shares,[44] the reality is quite different. Minority fractional-share ownership leaves real power in the hands of the big boys, a point not lost on early observers of the U.S. market. Writing in the early 1930s, Berle and Means compared the newly emerging corporate landscape to a form of industrial feudalism, controlled by a few at the top of the socioeconomic pyramid.

In contrast, when you own a few shares of KO in your brokerage account, that line item with its daily value can seem much more real than the idea of company ownership. You don't need to know or care much about the red trucks, the formula, the jingles, or the annual general meeting. You have the shares, and you have a price. There may be transaction and account service costs, but there are no agency costs per se—no intermediaries between you and "enjoyment" of the asset. If you can sell the shares for a lot more than the price you paid, great. In this environment, it's understandable why lots of investors focus only on the shares—which they can control (buy, sell, hold)—rather than the underlying company, over which they have little control. A cashflow-based portfolio management system does no better addressing the challenges of being a (tiny) minority owner than does the current share price one. Nonetheless, I would argue that being a business owner, no matter how remote from control of the asset, is still superior to focusing just on share prices with little regard for the underlying business.

It is easy to find fault with the proposed cashflow-based approach to portfolio management. It is far from perfect. But sticking with the price-based, near-term model is simply not working. In the long term, ironically, open societies are very efficient. Weak businesses (or ideas) will not prevail. One might well ask, "If MPT is as flawed as you have depicted it, and a cashflow-based alternative is not that hard to imagine, why hasn't it happened?" The existing system is just so pervasive, so heavy, and so entrenched. And the revisions and adaptations that have been applied over the past 30 years have made it, if not more useful, then at least somewhat less destructive. It also serves the financial services industry well, even if it serves investors less well. Let me paraphrase a line from the Steven Spielberg film *Catch Me if You Can*: "You know why the Yankees always win? . . . Because the other teams can't stop staring at those damn pinstripes." You know why Wall Street always wins? Because investors can't stop staring at those damn share prices. Giving the Yankees their due in baseball, it's time for investors to blink and shift their gaze beyond their TV and computer screens and look at the businesses they own and the income streams that they generate.

Conclusion

The second half of the twentieth century brought a massive wave of human behavior quantified, categorized, and optimized. There can be no doubt that the process produced a myriad of heretofore identified and probably many unidentified benefits to society. In medicine, we have a much clearer knowledge of how various behaviors can affect our health. Parsing how children study, and under what conditions, has led to a manifestly better understanding of educational outcomes. Weather and storm forecasting are vastly more accurate than they were even just a few decades ago due to the computing power thrown at that task. In a more commercial vein, Amazon and its peers crunch the numbers to generate great insight into consumer spending habits. Kroger knows more or less exactly where you will go and what you will do once you cross the threshold of the grocery store. Insurance companies are far better at estimating and pricing risk due to the quantitative tools now at their disposal. For better or for worse, the airlines employ complex algorithms to price seats during different times of the day and days of the week. eHarmony claims to bring the same rigor and forecasting ability to the uniquely human experience of courtship. Is nothing sacred? The promise of this quantification has been to offer understanding bordering on near certainty into the everyday human challenge of decision making under conditions of uncertainty. In the idealized version of this algorithmic world, we know what to eat, when and how to exercise, which highway to avoid, what to buy, where to study, whom to marry. The formulas have helped us solve all the big questions. What a relief. It is a Brave New World of human satisfaction and consumption. I'll take my soma now, thank you.

In regard to investment, Modern Portfolio Theory brought an unprecedented intellectual rigor to the near wasteland of investment practices that had characterized the period up to the stock market Crash of 1929. It succeeded in creating a discourse of risk and return, and in making investing more systematic and less like overt gambling. It offered straightforward theoretical constructs that provided at least approximate measures of expected return and risk, and it helped investors understand how different types of assets could be put together in a portfolio. In practice, MPT shed light on the benefits of diversification, on the differing types and sources of risk, and on the factors contributing to various investment outcomes.

But as with many new major intellectual paradigms, the expectations of what would be achieved proved too great. The champions of the new school of thought went well beyond the genuinely greater understanding of the markets that MPT offered to investors and made claims—sometimes explicit, sometimes implicit—that risk had been vanquished and investment outcomes rendered if not certain, than at least substantially less uncertain. Taming uncertainty was a fine goal, but the hinted-at possibility of making your brokerage or retirement account as mechanical as a physics schematic was simply too much. What started out as sensible diversification and the beneficial quantification of the investment process became a crude scientism remote from genuine business ownership. Fifty years after Markowitz's "Portfolio Selection" first appeared in print, Mark Rubinstein penned an appreciation in the *Journal of Finance* that ended with a soaring, history-ending encomium:

Near the end of this reign in 14AD, the Roman emperor Augustus could boast that he had found Rome a city of brick and left it a city of marble. Markowitz can boast that he found the field of finance awash in the imprecision of English and left it with the scientific precision and insight made possible only by mathematics.[1]

Those words were written in the aftermath of a crash that was in many ways intellectually blessed by Modern Portfolio Theory, albeit not by Markowitz himself. Fifteen years later and another retirement-destroying market crash behind us, is it perhaps time to suggest that the marble of mathematics has not aged as well as had been hoped, and that there is some room left in the edifice of investment for the old-fashioned bricks of commonsense business practices?

It's not the fault of the math. The formulas are all accurate in the sense that any calculation errors in the original works from the 1950s and 1960s have been corrected and revised with the passage of time—CAPM going from beta alone to five factors, the efficient frontier incorporating more and more asset classes, the utility curves acknowledging differing tax statuses and preferences, etc. But even with the various revisions and improvements, the real-world outcomes have been miserable and utterly remote from the promise. Periodic bubbles and crashes are still the norm. Individual investor timing is still appalling. In the name of risk reduction and diversification, Wall Street comes up with newfangled products that often end up increasing risk, not reducing it.

Subprime loans anyone? As a wise investor commented to me, "The ultimate irony of MPT is that it was brought in to answer the wild speculative frenzies of the prewar era, but it has now gone full circle and has caused its own version of price-based speculation. Meanwhile, cashflow-based investing has gone by the wayside."

While the past 50 years of experience has highlighted the *practical* shortcomings of the standard model, it is also possible to look back now and wonder at the *philosophical* underpinnings. The nineteenth-century science model upon which twentieth-century finance is based is neat and tidy. But that doesn't make it right. I am reminded of Paul Cootner's 1964 dismissal of Benoît Mandelbrot's challenge to the underlying math of the standard finance model as it was being worked out at that time:

Mandelbrot, like Prime Minister Churchill before him, promises us not utopia but blood, sweat, toil and tears. If he is right, almost all of our statistical tools are obsolete. . . . Surely, before consigning centuries of work to the ash pile, we should like to have some assurance that all our work is truly useless.[2]

The jury is still out on the distribution patterns called into question by Mandelbrot, and it is clear that modern investment theory is certainly not "truly useless." It is just that we rely on it too much and put too much faith in its ability to counter uncertainty.

Those are the internal problems. *From my perspective, MPT is a failed investment paradigm for an entirely different, and more important, external reason: because it is a theory of numbers for people interested in numbers, rather than a theory of business investment for people interested in businesses.* Benjamin Graham and Warren Buffett fall into the latter category; the vast majority of academics writing on investment themes—and too many investment professionals, I'm sorry to say—fall into the other. The irony of course is that as the academics removed the enterprises from the investment equations, it created an opportunity for genuine business investors like Buffett to do very well indeed. You can do the same. Do so by approaching your investments as ongoing businesses. How are they faring in their chosen marketplaces, and how are they likely to fare against future competitors and industry trends? Do they generate sufficient cashflow to meet their investment and debt obligations? Count up and track the profit distributions. If you can't figure them out, ask your financial advisor to do it. Know that your forecasts for future distributions may not always be precise, but that you do not need absolute precision to create a diversified portfolio of income streams that meets your real-world needs. Make sure you take into account the private income streams that you may have access to, and how they compare with those from the financial assets. If you have investments that don't make distributions, understand why you hold them and what your expectations of them are. Segregating the non-income-paying investments, whether private or public, from the others means their excess volatility and good or bad fortune will not unduly influence the main part of the income-producing portfolio.

You will run into a lot of obstacles to treating your investments in a businesslike manner, but don't let your holdings become lost in a haze of prices that change every day and in theories that focus on those prices rather than on the businesses. In that spirit, I would revisit Merton Miller's famous 1986 defense of the standard model against the inroads being made at the time by behavioral finance. He wrote that certain individual investors, untouched by professional investment managers, may see their stockholdings as *more than just the abstract "bundles of returns" of our economic models. Behind each holding may be a story of family business, family quarrels, legacies received, divorce settlements, and a host of other considerations almost totally irrelevant to our theories of portfolio selection. That we abstract from all these stories in building our models is not because the stories are uninteresting but because they may be too interesting and thereby distract us from the pervasive market forces that should be our principal concern.*[3]

Some 30 years after those words were written, they can be read with the completely opposite meaning. From my vantage point as an investor, a businessperson, and a historian, I do not want to suggest that investors should not, on occasion, be sidetracked by an intriguing investment algorithm, theories of stock market prices, or assertions of systems in equilibrium populated by utility-maximizing rational actors. Indeed, those ideas may be so interesting that they divert attention from what needs to be our principal concern, the *pervasive forces of human behavior*, particularly as they apply to the proposition of business ownership through the stock market. It is time to get back to business.

Notes

Chapter 1

1. Groucho's story comes from his son's account: Arthur Marx, *Life with Groucho: A Son's-Eye View* (New York: Simon & Schuster, 1954), 122–123. Arthur's version was written over 20 years after the fact, and the incident occurred when Arthur himself was only 8 years old. How much of it is to be believed? Arthur admits that he has taken some liberties for the sake of telling a tale. It is likely that the RCA dividend story occurred in March 1929 rather than in October on the eve of the stock market Crash. The high price of RCA corresponds to the price in March 1929 when the shares traded at the $500 level. That same month, they split 5 for 1, and the RCA shares entered the October collapse around $100. So what was in Arthur's account "the next day" was likely around six months later. See also Arthur Marx's commentary at http://www.pbs.org/wgbh/americanexperience/features/transcript/crash-transcript/ as of April 4, 2014. The story is further confused by the fact that the RCA stock was the object of a famous corner, by Michael Meehan, described elsewhere in this chapter, that occurred in March 1928.

2. Merton Miller, *Journal of Portfolio Management*, Vol. 25, No. 4 (Summer 1999), 100.

3. Edwin Lefèvre, *Reminiscences of a Stock Operator* (New York: John Wiley & Sons, Inc., 1994), reprint of the 1923 original, 188.

4. Paul Sarnoff, *Jesse Livermore: Speculator King* (Palisades Park, NJ: Investor's Press, 1967), 51.

5. Marshall Blume, Jeremy Siegel, and Dan Rottenburg, *Revolution on Wall Street* (New York: W.W. Norton, 1993), 95.

6. B. Mark Smith, *The Equity Culture: The Story of the Global Stock Market* (New York: Farrar, Straus and Giroux, 2003), 120.

7. Julia C. Ott, *When Wall Street Met Main Street* (Cambridge, MA: Harvard University Press, 2011), 17.

8. Solomon Huebner, *The Stock Market* (New York: D. Appleton and Company, 1922), 5.

9. Ott, *When Wall Street Met Main Street*, 230, citing, among others, J. L. Kimmel, *Shareownership in the United States* (Washington, D.C.: Brookings, n.d.); Gardiner Means, "The Diffusion of Stock Ownership in the United States," *Quarterly Journal of Economics*, Vol. 44, No. 4 (August, 1930, 561–600); and H. T. Warshow, "The Distribution of Corporate Ownership in the United States," *Quarterly Journal of Economics*, Vol. 39, No. 1 (November 1924), 15–38.

10. K. Geert Rouwenhorst emphasizes the Dutch origins of the modern mutual fund in "The Origins of Mutual Funds," in William Goetzmann and K. Geert Rouwenhorst, eds., *The Origins of Value: The Financial Innovations That Created Modern Capital Markets* (Oxford: Oxford University Press, 2005), 249–270.

11. *Commercial & Financial Chronicle*, Vol. 63, No. 1619 (Saturday, July 4, 1896), 2. The political condition the narrator speaks of is popular consideration of the gold standard, the pressing issue of the day.

12. *United States Investor*, July 28, 1900, 9 (953).

13. *United States Investor*, October 22, 1910, 13–14 (1889–1890).

14. The RCA corner is recounted in most accounts of the stock market prior to the 1929 Crash. For example, see Charles R. Geisst, *Wall Street: A History*, updated ed. (New York: Oxford University Press, 2012), 177, and Jerry W. Markham, *A Financial History of the United States. Volume 2: From J.P. Morgan to the Institutional Investor (1900–1970)* (Armonk, NY: Sharpe, 2002), 150.

15. *United States Investor*, July 2, 1910, 16 (1140), caps in original.

16. *United States Investor*, October 22, 1910, 15 (1891).

17. *United States Investor*, July 2, 1910, 25 (1149).

18. *United States Investor*, July 2, 1910, 17 (1141).

19. Marx, *Life with Groucho*, 122.

20. *Commercial & Financial Chronicle*, Vol. 63, No. 1624 (Saturday, August 8, 1896), 206.

21. The NYSE had 215 listed stocks as of 1893. Many more would have traded on the "curb." The count is from a contemporary source: Clapp & Co., *Weekly Market Letters*, issue of January 4, 1894, 2.

22. *Moody's Magazine*, July 1909, 1.

23. *United States Investor*, July 2, 1910, 12 (1136).

24. Editorial Review, *Moody's Magazine*, January 1912, 1.

25. From the appendix to the bound volume of 1893 weekly newsletters. No reference to the "index" is in the actual newsletters. It also includes 8 years (1886–1893) of high and low prices (monthly) for 26 major railroad stocks. Clapp & Co., *Weekly Market Letters* for 1893.

26. By one account, there were at least a fourteen U.S. index publishers operating in 1900, with one index going back as far as 1834. See Henry Shilling, ed., *International Guide to Securities Market Indices* (Chicago: Fitzroy Dearborn Publishers, 1996), 29.

27. This index was likely based on Dow's earlier venture, the *Customer's Afternoon Letter*, delivered daily in the 1880s.

It included a simple index of nine railroads, one steamship company, and Western Union.

28. *Daily Average Prices (Thomas Gibson's Figures)* (New York: Gibson Pub. Co., 1910).

29. As observed in the appendix of Huebner, *The Stock Market*. See also W. R. Lamar, *Investments: What and When to Buy: The Use of Statistics in Accumulating a Fortune* (Boston: Stock Department of the Babson System, 1907), in which Babson offers a simple index of railroad stock prices back to the 1860s.

30. For instance, see the *New York Times*, April 16, 1912. This seems to be the same "index" used by *Forbes* a decade later.

31. S&P, Dow Jones and other market tracking services offered many specific industry indexes for decades prior to 1999, including "new" industries such as computer equipment.

32. Shilling, ed., *International Guide to Securities Market Indices*, 214.

33. Henry Harmon, *New York Stock Exchange Manual, Containing Its Principles, Rules and Its Different Modes of Speculation* (New York: J. F. Trow, 1865), 128.

34. Humphrey B. Neill, *The Inside Story of the Stock Exchange: A Fascinating Saga of the World's Greatest Money Market Place* (New York: B.C. Forbes, 1950), 48.

35. Thomas King, *More Than a Numbers Game: A Brief History of Accounting* (Hoboken, NJ: Wiley, 2006), 15.

36. Huebner, *The Stock Market*, 131.

37. King, *More Than a Numbers Game*, 56–57.

38. As referenced in Gibson's *Simple Principles of Investment* (Garden City, NY: Doubleday, 1919), 128. The American Sugar Refining Company had also furnished a balance sheet and statement of earnings annually since early in the twentieth century.

39. Gibson, *Simple Principles of Investment*, 125.

40. King, *More Than a Numbers Game*, 21.

41. Bevis Longstreth, *Modern Investment Management and the Prudent Man Rule* (Oxford: Oxford University Press, 1987), 69.
42. Clapp & Co., *Weekly Market Letters,* July 28, 1893, 2.
43. As advertised in *Poor's Manual of Industrials*, Vol. 4 (New York: Poor's Railroad Manual Co., 1913), ii–iii.
44. *Investment: A Magazine of Information and Suggestion*, May 1914, 286.
45. Clapp & Co., *Weekly Market Letters* [for 1893] (New York: 1894), 11.
46. As advertised in the *Magazine of Wall Street*, November 11, 1922, 91.
47. Lamar, *Investments*, end pages.
48. *Financial World*, Vol. 47 (January 1, 1927).
49. Quoted in Peter Bernstein, *Capital Ideas: The Improbable Origins of Modern Wall Street* (Hoboken, NJ: Wiley & Sons, 1992), 38.
50. Nancy Regan, CFA Institute, *The Gold Standard: A Fifty-Year History of the CFA Charter* (Charlottesville, VA: CFA Institute, 2012), 4.
51. Thomas Gibson got into the act too, with his *Gibson Manual*, but it covered only a few hundred securities traded in New York.
52. *Poor's Manual of Industrials*, Vol. 4 (1913), 8–9, 327, 336–337, 450–456.
53. Huebner, *The Stock Market*, v.
54. Thomas Gibson, *The Cycles of Speculation* (New York: Moody's Magazine, 1907, 2nd ed., 1909), 4.
55. Gibson, *Cycles of Speculation*, 6, 175.
56. Ott, *When Wall Street Met Main Street*, 130–131.
57. John J. Raskob, "Everybody Ought to Be Rich," *Ladies Home Journal* (August 1929), as reprinted in Charles D. Ellis, ed., *Classics II: Another Investor's Anthology* (Homewood, IL: Business One Irwin, 1991), 75.

58. As little "finance" as there was, there was even less finance "history." It was pretty much a field of one, Alexander Dana Noyes, whose *Thirty Years of American Finance* (New York: Putnam, 1898) and then *Forty Years of American Finance* (New York: Putnam, 1909), followed by *The War Period of American Finance, 1908–1925* (New York: Putnam, 1926), were the standard accounts.

59. Clapp & Co., *Weekly Market Letters*, December 31, 1892, 1, capitals in original.

60. John Moody, *The Art of Wall Street Investing* (New York: Moody Corp.), 61.

61. Benjamin Graham and David Dodd, *Security Analysis* (New York: McGraw-Hill, 1934), 153.

62. The large amount of high-yield, distressed, or emerging market debt that is available in the market today is understood to be different, where significant capital gains or losses will come into play.

63. Huebner, *The Stock Market*, 3.

64. Edgar Lawrence Smith, *Common Stocks as Long Term Investments* (New York: MacMillan Company, 1928, custom reprint 2009 by Kessinger Publishing).

65. The exact origin of the term is unclear. In one version, it comes from the selling of cattle by the pound after they had been bloated with water. See, for instance, B. Mark Smith, *Toward Rational Exuberance: The Evolution of the Modern Stock Market* (New York: Farrar, Straus & Giroux, 2001), 17.

66. Moody, *The Art of Wall Street Investing*, 112–113, 116.

67. Longstreth, 12, citing Shattuck, "The Development of the Prudent Man Rule for Fiduciary Investment in the United States in the Twentieth Century," *Ohio St. Law Journal*, Vol. 12 (1951), 499.

68. Longstreth, 73, citing Lawrence Chamberlain and William W. Hay, *Investment and Speculation* (New York: H. Holt & Co. 1931).

69. Mark Rubinstein, *A History of the Theory of Investments: My Annotated Bibliography* (Hoboken, NJ: Wiley, 2006), 7.

70. *United States Investor*, July 2, 1910, 24.

71. "At par" meaning that when originally issued, the shares had a 5% yield. For instance, shares with a par value of $100 would have an annual dividend of $5. As the shares moved up and down in the marketplace, the yield for new purchasers would fall and rise. An increase in the dividend would often be expressed vis-á-vis its par value, not the current trading value. That is, a change in the above-mentioned dividend to $6 per share annually might be described as an increase to a "6%" dividend, *regardless* of the market price at that time.

72. *United States Investor*, July 2, 1910, 29.

73. Franklin Escher, "How to Judge the Value of a Stock," *Investment: A Magazine of Information and Suggestion*, January 1914, 22–25.

74. Comment by Franklin Escher, *Investment Weekly*, April 13, 1918, 4.

75. *Forbes*, April 15, 1922, 47.

76. *Magazine of Wall Street*, January 6, 1923, 420.

77. *Magazine of Wall Street*, November 11, 1922, 31, 69; February 3, 1923, 609.

78. "My ventures are not in one bottom trusted, Nor to one place; nor is my whole estate upon the fortune of this present year." Act 1 of *The Merchant of Venice*. From a less secular and even earlier source, the Talmud apparently notes a diversification rule of keeping one-third of one's assets in land, one-third in merchandise, and one-third in cash. See Ron Duchin and Haim Levy, "Markowitz Versus the Talmudic Portfolio Diversification Strategies," *Journal of Portfolio Management*, Vol. 35, No. 2 (December 2009), 71–74.

79. Frederick Lownhaupt, *What an Investor Ought to Know* (New York: Magazine of Wall Street, 1913), 26.

80. William N. Goetzmann, *Money Changes Everything: How Finance Made Civilization Possible* (Princeton, NJ: Princeton University Press, 2016), 414–417.

81. Smith, *Common Stocks as Long Term Investments*, 18.

82. Phil Carret, *The Art of Speculation* (1930), as quoted in Ellis, ed., *Classics II*, 175, and reprinted in numerous editions.

83. Harvey Wells, "Essentials in Stock Investment," *Magazine of Wall Street*, February 3, 1923, 605.

84. Huebner, *The Stock Market*, 31, 33, 36–37.

85. Huebner, *The Stock Market*, 33.

86. Goetzmann, *Money Changes Everything*.

87. G. C. Selden, *Psychology of the Stock Market* (New York: Ticker Publishing Company, 1912), 66.

88. Ott, *When Wall Street Met Main Street*, 40, apparently quoting the work of William C. Van Antwerp, a journalist working for the exchange, in his *The Stock Exchange from Within* (Garden City, NY: Doubleday, 1913).

89. William Peter Hamilton, *The Stock Market Barometer* (New York: Harper & Brothers, 1922), 8.

90. See, among others, Richard Thaler, *Misbehaving: The Making of Behavioral Economics* (New York: W. W. Norton, 2015), 87–88.

91. Lownhaupt, *What an Investor Ought to Know*, 155.

92. Selden, *Psychology of the Stock Market*, 3, 29, 55–56, 71, 87, 93. Henry Howard Harper, *The Psychology of Speculation: The Human Element in Stock Market Transactions* (1926), makes the same points, but his work was not widely distributed at the time. I cite it just to make the point that behavioral finance was not created de novo in the postwar period.

93. Lownhaupt, *What an Investor Ought to Know*, 153.

94. *Magazine of Wall Street*, November 25, 1922, 99.

95. Hamilton was the most successful but not the first to try to popularize Dow's view of market trends. See Dow's biographer, George W. Bishop Jr., *Charles H. Dow and the Dow Theory* (New York: Appleton-Century-Crofts, Inc., 1960).

96. Hamilton, *The Stock Market Barometer*, 40.

97. Hamilton, *The Stock Market Barometer*, 24.

98. R. W. Babson, *Business Barometers for Anticipating Conditions*, (Wellesley Hills, MA: 1913) See also Walter A. Friedman, *Fortune Tellers: The Story of America's First Economic Forecasters* (Princeton, NJ: Princeton University Press, 2013).

99. Trustees at the time were governed by the original Prudent Man Rule laid out in an 1830 court ruling from Massachusetts (*Harvard College v. Amory*) whereby trustees were to manage investments "not in regard to speculation, but in regard to the permanent disposition of their funds, considering the probable income, as well as the probable safety of the capital to be investing."

100. Gibson, *Simple Principles of Investment*, 175.

101. Moody, *The Art of Wall Street Investing*, 30.

102. Gibson, *Simple Principles of Investment*, 120.

103. Moody, *The Art of Wall Street Investing*, 105–106.

104. Moody, *The Art of Wall Street Investing*, 32.

Chapter 2

1. John Burr Williams, *The Theory of Investment Value* (Fraser Publishing Company, 1997), reprint of the original published by Harvard University Press in 1938, ix.

2. Benjamin Graham and David Dodd, *Security Analysis* (New York: McGraw-Hill, 1934), 5, 312–313. David Dodd was an instructor in finance at Columbia University and as such a colleague of Graham. He is credited as full coauthor on all the editions of *Security Analysis,* but Graham was the moving force behind the work.

3. Williams, *The Theory of Investment Value*, 114.

4. Graham and Dodd, *Security Analysis*, 429–441, 452, 454.

5. Graham and Dodd, *Security Analysis*, 17–19.

6. Graham and Dodd, *Security Analysis*, 453.

7. Graham and Dodd, *Security Analysis*, 325–338.

8. For this author's screed against the directorate's despotic treatment of shareholders, see Daniel Peris, *The Dividend Imperative* (New York: McGraw Hill, 2013).

9. Graham and Dodd, *Security Analysis*, 451–452.

10. Graham and Dodd, *Security Analysis*, 317, 319–320.

11. Graham and Dodd, *Security Analysis*, vii, 86–87, 317.

12. By the time Keynes wrote *The General Theory* in 1935, he was already among the leading economists of his generation and a well-known public intellectual in England. His passionate objection to the economic terms of the Treaty of Versailles—*The Economic Consequences of the Peace*, written in 1919—foreshadowed what was to happen in the 1920s to the German economy and polity.

13. John Maynard Keynes, *The General Theory of Employment, Interest and Money* (New York: Harcourt, Brace, 1936). GoogleBooks version as of early 2014. Digital version is unpaginated, but Chapter 12 corresponds to pages 124–136 of the downloadable pdf.

14. Keynes, *The General Theory*, 128.

15. Keynes, *The General Theory*, 130.

16. Keynes, *The General Theory*, 129–130.

17. Keynes, *The General Theory*, 134.

18. Numerous sources, citing Williams's memoir, *Fifty Years of Investment Analysis: A Retrospective* (Charlottesville, VA: Financial Analysts Research Foundation, 1959).

19. Williams, *The Theory of Investment Value*, 45–48. For modern audiences, discounted cash flows start with Williams. But in his thirteenth-century work, *Liber Abaci*, Fibonacci of Pisa had also worked out some of the math, as did Edmond Halley in the late seventeenth century. On the premodern efforts at what we now call modern finance, see Mark Rubinstein, *A History of the Theory of Investments* (Hoboken, NJ: Wiley, 2006). For their application, see William N. Goetzmann, *Money Changes Everything* (Princeton, NJ: Princeton University Press, 2016).

20. Williams, *The Theory of Investment Value*, 55.

21. Williams, *The Theory of Investment Value*, viii.

22. Williams, *The Theory of Investment Value*, 6.

23. Williams does acknowledge the contribution of Samuel E. Guild, *Stock Growth and Discount Tables* (Boston: Financial Publishing Company, 1931), for advancing the notion of net present value in a practical manner.

24. Williams, *The Theory of Investment Value*, 6.

25. At first glance, it may not seem that a "rate of risk" needs to be the same as the expected "rate of return." But upon closer examination, they are identical for an asset with a given, reasonable price. If the asset is grossly mispriced or does not have a market price, there is no reason why the figures need be the same as they represent related but separate concepts.

26. Williams, *The Theory of Investment Value*, 59.

27. Williams, *The Theory of Investment Value*, 58–59.

28. Williams, *The Theory of Investment Value*, 67–68.

29. Williams, *The Theory of Investment Value*, chart on 387.

30. Williams, *The Theory of Investment Value*, 406.

31. Williams, *The Theory of Investment Value*, 408.

32. Williams, *The Theory of Investment Value*, 450, 458.

33. Williams, *The Theory of Investment Value*, 158, 187.

34. Williams, *The Theory of Investment Value*, 331.

35. Williams, *The Theory of Investment Value*, 191.

36. Williams, *The Theory of Investment Value*, 68–69, discussing bonds, but the logic would hold for stocks as well, though the return would be above the pure interest rate.

37. Elsewhere Williams was explicit in his disagreements with Keynes in regard to the formation of interest rates and a variety of what would now be called macroeconomic issues.

38. Williams, *The Theory of Investment Value*, 185.

39. The aversion to Keynes comes not from his notions of how the stock market works, but for his ideas about how to stimulate aggregate demand during periods of economic weakness. We have come to know it as deficit spending.

40. Graham ended up reviewing Williams's book, but he struggled to approve the formulaic guidelines within a rational actor context. As cited by James Grant in "Benjamin Graham and *Security Analysis*: The Historical Backdrop," Introduction to *Security Analysis*, 6th ed. (New York: McGraw-Hill, 2009), 18.

41. Graham and Dodd, *Security Analysis*, 3rd ed. (New York: McGraw-Hill, 1951), 16.

42. Graham and Dodd, *Security Analysis*, 3rd ed., 403.

43. Graham and Dodd, *Security Analysis*, 3rd ed., 394.

44. Graham and Dodd, *Security Analysis*, 3rd ed., 493 and asides elsewhere, such as 433.

45. Graham and Dodd, *Security Analysis*, 3rd ed., 16.

46. Graham and Dodd, *Security Analysis*, 3rd ed., 458.

47. Graham and Dodd, *Security Analysis*, 3rd ed., 408.

48. Benjamin Graham, *The Intelligent Investor: The Classic Text on Value Investing* (New York: HarperBusiness, 2005), 55. Reprint of the 1949 original edition.

49. Graham, *The Intelligent Investor*, 55.

50. Graham, *The Intelligent Investor*, 105–106.

51. Graham, *The Intelligent Investor*, 55–56.

52. Graham, *The Intelligent Investor*, 73.

53. Graham, *The Intelligent Investor*, 73.

Chapter 3

1. The history of probability theory as it applies to investments is a rich topic unto itself. For an introduction, see Peter Bernstein, *Capital Ideas: The Improbable Origins of Modern Wall Street* (Hoboken, NJ: Wiley & Sons, 1992), and more recently James Weatherall, *The Physics of Wall Street* (New York: Houghton Mifflin, 2013). See also Rubinstein, *A History of the Theory of Investments: My Annotated Bibliography* (Hoboken, NJ: Wiley, 2006), 17–40.

2. Lord Kelvin (William Thomson), "Electrical Units of Measurement," address from 1883 to the Institute of Civil Engineers, reprinted in his *Popular Lectures and Addresses*, Vol.

1 (London: 1888–1889). Reviewed in a digitally reprinted edition from 2011 by Cambridge University Press. The quote has taken on a life of its own and can be seen in many offhand references.

3. Marshall is actually credited with bringing increased mathematical rigor to the study of economics, but the bar at the time was low, and in his 1890 work, Marshall was keen on making sure the mathematics did not get in the way of a broader understanding of economic processes.

4. Paul Samuelson, *Foundations of Economic Analysis* (1947) and his simply titled textbook *Economics*, first published the following year in 1948. Skipping over Keynes, *The General Theory* (1936), to contrast Marshall (1890) and Samuelson (1947) seems, at first glance, quite unfair to Keynes given his role in creating modern macroeconomics and twentieth-century economic thought in general. No disrespect is intended. I only point out that *The General Theory* does not read like a college textbook. There were, of course, other earlier broad-based treatments of economics, such as Frank Taussig, *Principles of Economics* (1911), in the intervening period, though not necessarily with the impact of the works referenced above.

5. Bernstein, *Capital Ideas*, 33.

6. John Burr Williams, *The Theory of Investment Value* (Fraser Publishing Company, 1997), reprint of the original published by Harvard University Press in 1938, vii.

7. George Goodman, writing as "Adam Smith," *Supermoney* (New York: Random House, 1972), 135–136, citing Graham.

8. Jane Gleeson White, *Double Entry* (London: Allen & Unwin, 2012), 220, paraphrasing Frank Ahrens of the *Washington Post*.

9. Bernstein, *Capital Ideas*, 2, 6–7.

10. http://www.nobelprize.org/nobel_prizes/economic-sciences/laureates/1990/markowitz-bio.html as of September 2014.

11. Markowitz, "Portfolio Selection," *Journal of Finance*, Vol. 7, No. 1 (March 1952), 77.

12. Bernstein, *Capital Ideas*, 49.

13. Bernstein, *Capital Ideas*, 44; Arthur D. Roy, "Safety First and the Holding of Assets," *Econometrica*, Vol. 34 (1952), 431–449. Roy did not pursue this analysis any further, whereas Markowitz did. As a result, Roy is consigned to footnotes in works like this, and we inhabit a Markowitzian world rather than a Royan one.

14. Harry M. Markowitz, *Portfolio Selection: Efficient Diversification of Investments* (New York: John Wiley & Sons, 1959); online edition available through the Cowles Foundation at http://www.cowles.econ.yale.edu/P/cm/m16/index.htm as of October 2014.

15. Markowitz, *Portfolio Selection*, 6.

16. Markowitz, *Portfolio Selection*, 287–297.

17. Markowitz, *Portfolio Selection*, 6.

18. James Tobin, "Liquidity Preference as Behavior Towards Risk," *Review of Economic Studies*, Vol. 25, No. 2 (February 1958), 65–86. Quote from a December 1996 interview with Tobin, http://www.minneapolisfed.org/publications_papers/pub_display.cfm?id=3649&, retrieved October 2014.

19. Markowitz, *Portfolio Selection*, 5, 97.

20. William F. Sharpe, "A Simplified Model for Portfolio Analysis," *Management Science*, Vol. 9, No. 2 (January 1963), 281. Sharpe uses an unspecified "stock market index" as his underlying factor to come up with a portfolio out of 96 randomly chosen industrial stocks from the NYSE which traded from 1940 to 1951. This was prior to the widespread acceptance of the S&P 500 Index as the standard market measure.

21. William F. Sharpe, "Capital Asset Prices: A Theory of Market Equilibrium Under Conditions of Risk," *Journal of Finance*, Vol. 19, No. 3 (September 1964), 425–442.

22. http://www.nobelprize.org/nobel_prizes/economic-sciences/laureates/1990/markowitz-bio.html, retrieved August 2016.

23. Bernstein, *Capital Ideas*, 79.

24. John Lintner, "The Valuation of Risk Assets and the Selection of Risky Investments in Stock Portfolios and Capital Budgets," *Review of Economics and Statistics*, Vol. 47 (1965), 13–37; Jan Mossin, "Equilibrium in a Capital Asset Market, *Econometrica*, Vol. 34, No. 4 (1966), 768–783.

25. Jack Treynor, "Toward a Theory of Market Value of Risky Assets," 1962; "Implications for the Theory of Finance," 1963. Unpublished manuscripts, both widely available on the Internet.

26. For more detailed accounts of CAPM development, see Bernstein, *Capital Ideas*, and Craig W. French, "The Treynor Capital Asset Pricing Model," *Journal of Investment Management*, Vol. 1, No. 2 (2003), 60–72.

27. Holbrook Working, "A Random-Difference Series for Use in the Analysis of Time Series," *Journal of the American Statistical Association*, Vol. 29 (March 1934), 11–24.

28. Maurice Kendall, "The Analysis of Economic Time-Series—Part I: Prices," *Journal of the Royal Statistical Society*, Vol. 116, No. 1 (1953), 11–34, as cited in Bernstein, *Capital Ideas*, 97. See also Justin Fox, *The Myth of the Rational Market* (New York: Collins Business, 2009), 63–64.

29. Kendall, cited in Paul H. Cootner, ed., *The Random Character of Stock Market Prices* (Cambridge, MA: MIT Press, 1964), 85.

30. Brought together in Cootner, ed., *The Random Character of Stock Market Prices*.

31. Rubinstein, *A History of the Theory of Investments*, 49. A leading historian of finance, William Goetzmann places another French stockbroker, Jules Regnault, about a half century prior to Bachelier. Regnault's *Calcul des Chances et Philosophie de la Bourse* came out in 1863 and argued against the possibility of large-scale profitable trading. Regnault based his assertion on the earlier work of Jacob Bernoulli, the seventeenth-century Swiss mathematician, who observed that as the number of events in a data series gets larger, it must

necessarily move toward its central tendency. See Goetzmann, *Money Changes Everything: How Finance Made Civilization Possible* (Princeton, NJ: Princeton University Press, 2016), 278 and thereafter.

32. See Weatherall, *The Physics of Wall Street.*

33. M. F. M. Osborne, "Brownian Motion in the Stock Market," *Operations Research*, Vol. 7 (1959), 145–173.

34. Cootner, ed., *The Random Character of Stock Market Prices*, 100.

35. Fox, *The Myth of the Rational Market*, 69, citing Harry V. Roberts, "Stock-Market Patterns and Financial Analysis: Methodological Suggestions," *Journal of Finance* (March 1959), 1–10.

36. Paul Samuelson, "Proof That Properly Anticipated Prices Fluctuate Randomly," *Industrial Management Review*, Vol. VI (Spring 1965), 41–50, quote from 44.

37. Full list of relevant publications at http://faculty.chicago booth.edu/eugene.fama/vita/VITA.pdf, retrieved as of November 2014. Includes Eugene F. Fama, "Random Walks in Stock Market Prices," *Financial Analyst Journal*, Vol. 21, No. 5 (September–October 1965), 55–59.

38. Eugene F. Fama, "The Behavior of Stock-Market Prices," *Journal of Business*, Vol. 38, No. 1 (January 1965), 90 and 94. Fama has indicated that the *FAJ* article published in 1965 was based on an earlier paper presented to the Graduate School of Business at the University of Chicago. As a practical matter, it appears he started using the term in his own writing in 1964, publishing that work in various journals in 1965 and thereafter. For Mandelbrot's own analysis of commodity prices, see Benoît Mandelbrot, "Forecasts of Future Prices, Unbiased Markets and 'Martingale' Models," *Journal of Business*, Vol. 39, No. 1 (January 1966), 242–255, and his "The Variation of Certain Speculative Prices," *Journal of Business*, Vol. 36, No. 4 (October 1963), 394–419.

39. Eugene F. Fama, "Efficient Capital Markets: A Review of Theory and Empirical Work," *Journal of Finance*, Vol. 25, No. 2 (May 1970), 383–417.

40. Michael C. Jensen, "The Performance of Mutual Funds in the Period, 1945–1964," *Journal of Finance*, Vol. 23, No. 2 (May 1968), 389–416, and Michael C. Jensen, "The Pricing of Capital Assets, and the Evaluation of Investment Portfolios," *Journal of Business*, Vol. 42, No. 2 (April 1969), 167–247.

41. William F. Sharpe, "Mutual Fund Performance," *Journal of Business*, Vol. 39, No. 1 (January 1966), 119–138.

42. Burton Malkiel, *A Random Walk Down Wall Street* (New York: W. W. Norton & Company, 1973), 226. A similar analysis and essentially the same desire was expressed a decade earlier by a University of California finance professor and one of his doctoral students. See Edward Renshaw and Paul Feldstein, "The Case for an Unmanaged Investment Company," *Financial Analyst Journal*, Vol. 16, No. 1 (January–February 1960), 43–46.

43. From an April 7, 2007, interview with Bogle at EconTalk, April 7, 2007, http://www.econtalk.org/archives/2007/04/bogle_on_invest.html#more.

44. Berle was the student of Harvard professor William Ripley, whose *Main Street and Wall Street* from 1926 foreshadowed many of the concerns subsequently expressed by Berle and Means. See Julia C. Ott, *When Wall Street Met Main Street* (Cambridge, MA: Harvard University Press, 2011), 144.

45. Merton H. Miller and Franco Modigliani, "Dividend Policy, Growth and the Valuation of Shares," *Journal of Business*, Vol. 34, No. 4 (October 1961), 411–433. To be clear, M&M did not emerge directly from Berle and Means. They were more directly responding to issues raised by John Burr Williams (1938) and another finance professor, David Durand, who was exploring the issue of how the new corporations financed themselves.

46. Fischer Black, "The Dividend Puzzle," *Journal of Portfolio Management* (Winter 1976), 5–8.
47. Hersch M. Shefrin and Meir Statman, "Explaining Investor Preference for Cash Dividends," *Journal of Financial Economics* (1984), 253–282, and Fox, *The Myth of the Rational Market*, 200.
48. See, for instance, Michael Finke, "It's Time to Get Real About Dividends," *InvestmentNews*, October 2, 2017, 36.
49. Miller and Modigliani, "Dividend Policy, Growth and the Valuation of Shares," 414.
50. As of November 2017.
51. S&P 500 Index data via FactSet Research Systems, 2016.
52. Miller and Modigliani, "Dividend Policy, Growth and the Valuation of Shares," 423.
53. Miller and Modigliani, "Dividend Policy, Growth and the Valuation of Shares," 424.
54. I make this case in greater detail in *The Dividend Imperative* (New York: McGraw-Hill, 2013).
55. Miller and Modigliani, "Dividend Policy, Growth and the Valuation of Shares," 412.
56. Blue chip stocks originally signified such solid and widely held equities that their share prices traded above $100.
57. Carl Roth and John T. McKenzie, *Standard & Poor's Selecting Stocks to Buy for Profit* (New York: Henry Holt and Company, 1956), vii.
58. Winthrop Knowlton, *Growth Opportunities in Common Stocks* (New York: Harper & Row, 1965), 66.
59. Philip A. Fisher, *Common Stocks and Uncommon Profits* (New York: Harper & Brothers, 1958).
60. George Goodman, writing as "Adam Smith," *The Money Game* (New York: Random House, 1967), 16, 20.
61. Goodman, *The Money Game*, 25, 29–30.
62. John Brooks, *The Go-Go Years* (New York: Weybright & Talley, 1973), 135.
63. Brooks, *The Go-Go Years*, 130.

64. Brooks, *The Go-Go Years*, 135.
65. G. E. Kaplan and Chris Welles, eds., *The Money Managers* (New York: Random House, 1969), 20.
66. Brooks, *The Go-Go Years*, 113.
67. The Great Atlantic & Pacific Tea Company, at that time, the largest grocery chain in the United States, and emblematic of postwar, middle-class prosperity.
68. Per a Supreme Court ruling referencing an SEC suit against the Capital Gains Research Bureau, http://www.sec.gov/divisions/investment/capitalgains1963.pdf, retrieved March 13, 2016.
69. As advertised in *Barron's Magazine* in 1965.
70. Gerald Loeb, *The Battle for Investment Survival* (New York: Simon & Schuster, 1957), 31, 118. Originally published in 1935, the book was reprinted numerous times thereafter. It was expanded and revised in 1957 and again in 1965.
71. Fisher, *Common Stocks and Uncommon Profits*, 135, 144.
72. Goodman, *Supermoney*, 192.
73. L. Fisher and J. H. Lorie, "Rates of Return on Investments in Common Stock," *Journal of Business*, Vol. 37, No. 1 (January 1964), 1–21. See also Roger C. Ibbotson and Rex Sinquefeld, *Stocks, Bonds, Bills, and Inflation: Historical Returns (1926–1987)* (Chicago: Dow Jones-Irwin, 1989), and revised thereafter.
74. Richard H. Jenrette, "Portfolio Management: Seven Ways to Improve Performance," in Charles Ellis, ed., *Classics: An Investor's Anthology* (Homewood, IL: Business One Irwin, 1989), 382–391.
75. Robert G. Kirby, "Lessons Learned and Never Learned," *Journal of Portfolio Management*, Vol. 6, No. 1 (Fall 1979), 53.
76. Brooks, *The Go-Go Years*, 305, 348. Also, Arthur Zeikel, "After 50 Years, Nothing New nor Likely," *Journal of Portfolio Management*, Vol. 6, No. 1 (Fall 1979), 27, citing *Financial World*.

77. Bernstein, *Capital Ideas*, 14.
78. Including, among others, the Uniform Management of Institutional Funds Acts of 1972 and IRS Rule 4944 from 1969. See also Bevis Longstreth, *Modern Investment Management and the Prudent Man Rule* (Oxford: Oxford University Press, 1987).
79. Barr Rosenberg, "Extra-Market Components of Covariance in Security Returns," *Journal of Financial and Quantitative Analysis*, Vol. 9, No. 2 (March 1974), 263–274. Consistent with the time, Rosenberg became somewhat of a cult figure, pictured on the cover of *Institutional Investor* in 1978 atop a mountain sitting in the lotus position wearing a robe adorned with flower garlands. Investors in suits are bowing down to him.
80. Interview with Barr Rosenberg, *Journal of Investment Counseling*, Vol. 7, No. 3 (Winter 2005–2006), 12.
81. John Authers, "Factor Investing Has a Way to Go Before It Can Oust a Sector Approach," *Financial Times*, July 30, 2015, 20, citing research by Campbell Harvey of Duke University. The literature on factor analysis is voluminous and present in most issues of most finance journals. An example in book-length form is Richard Grinold and Ronald Kahn, *Active Portfolio Management*, 2nd ed. (New York: McGraw-Hill, 2000).
82. As advertised in the *Financial Times* on May 18, 2015, 15. Current offerings at http://www.scientificbeta.com.
83. Bernstein, *Capital Ideas*, 236.
84. Bernstein, *Capital Ideas*, 247–248.
85. Bernstein, *Capital Ideas*, 262.
86. Goodman, *Supermoney*, 233. See also Bernstein, *Capital Ideas*, 188–189.
87. Bernstein, *Capital Ideas*, 256.
88. *Labor and Investments*, June 1984, 4, as cited in Jerome B. Cohen, Edward D. Zinbarg, and Arthur Zeikel, eds.,

Investment Analysis and Portfolio Management, 5th ed. (Homewood, IL: Irwin, 1987), 185.

89. Robert Hagin, *The Dow Jones-Irwin Guide to Modern Portfolio Theory* (Homewood, IL: Dow Jones-Irwin, 1979), 6.

90. For his own take on the process, see David F. Swenson, *Pioneering Portfolio Management: An Unconventional Approach to Institutional Investment* (New York: Free Press, 2000). Perhaps the most unconventional part of his approach was the inclusion of assets well beyond the traditional stock and bond opportunity set.

Chapter 4

1. For a tour of the "sausage factory" floor, see Jon A. Christopherson, David R. Cariño, and Wayne E. Ferson, *Portfolio Performance Measurement and Benchmarking* (New York: McGraw-Hill, 2009). On investors' continued use of CAPM, whether they know it or not, see Jonathan B. Berk and Jules H. van Binsbergen, "How Do Investors Compute the Discount Rate? They Use the CAPM," *Financial Analysts Journal,* Vol. 73, No. 2 (2017), 25–32.

2. There are some exceptions to the narrow challenges. For example, Robert D. Arnott, "Blinded by Theory?," *Journal of Portfolio Management,* 30th Anniversary Issue (2004), 113–123.

3. Harry M. Markowitz, *Portfolio Selection: Efficient Diversification of Investments* (New York: John Wiley & Sons, 1959), 229.

4. Markowitz, *Portfolio Selection,* 229–230, 274, 302.

5. Markowitz, *Portfolio Selection,* 275.

6. Merton H. Miller and Franco Modigliani, "Dividend Policy, Growth and the Valuation of Shares," *Journal of Business,* Vol. 34, No. 4 (October 1961), 411, 412.

7. Jack Treynor, "Toward a Theory of Market Value of Risky Assets," unpublished 1962 paper, 1–2, widely available on the Internet.

8. John Lintner, "The Valuation of Risk Assets and the Selection of Risky Investments in Stock Portfolios and Capital Budgets," *Review of Economics and Statistics*, Vol. 47, No. 1 (February 1965), 15–16.

9. William F. Sharpe, "Capital Asset Prices: A Theory of Market Equilibrium Under Conditions of Risk," *Journal of Finance*, Vol. 19, No. 3 (September 1964), 434.

10. Markowitz, *Portfolio Selection,* 206.

11. Benoît Mandelbrot and Richard Hudson, *The (Mis)Behavior of Markets: A Fractal View of Risk, Ruin, and Reward* (New York: Basic Books, 2004), 265. Markowitz makes a point of distinguishing between the two "big" assumptions behind the current model. In a recent interview, he asserts, "I never assumed quadratic utility. I never assumed Gaussian distributions. I assume what was then—and still is now, to a great extent—the standard theory of rational decision making in the face of risk and uncertainty." "An Interview with Nobel Laureate Harry M. Markowitz," *Financial Analyst Journal* (Fourth Quarter 2017), 16. Elsewhere he wrote, "I never—at any time!—assumed that return distributions are Gaussian." See Harry M. Markowitz, "Portfolio Theory as I Still See It," *Annual Review of Financial Economics*, 2010, 2.

12. Nassim Nicholas Taleb, *The Black Swan: The Impact of the Highly Improbable* (New York: Random House, 2007), 277.

13. Taleb, *The Black Swan*, 277.

14. Harry Markowitz, "Market Efficiency: A Theoretical Distinction and So What?," *Financial Analysts Journal*, Vol. 61, No. 5 (September/October 2005), 17, 18.

15. For example, Haim Levy, "The CAPM & Beta in an Imperfect Market," *Journal of Portfolio Management*, Vol. 6, No. 2 (Winter 1980), 5.

16. For example, James Ryan and Mark Kritzman, "Catch 500: The Irony of Indexing," *Journal of Portfolio Management*, Vol. 6, No. 2 (Winter 1980), 30–31.

17. Harry Markowitz, "Market Efficiency: A Theoretical Distinction and So What?," *Financial Analysts Journal* Vol. 61, No. 5 (September/October 2005), 29.

18. J. L. Evans and S. H. Archer, "Diversification and the Reduction of Dispersion: An Empirical Analysis," *Journal of Finance*, Vol. 23 (December 1968), 761–767.

19. E. J. Elton and M. J. Gruber, *Modern Portfolio Theory and Investment Analysis*, 2nd ed. (New York: John Wiley & Sons, 1984), 35. See also E. J. Elton and M. J. Gruber, "Risk Reduction and Portfolio Size: An Analytic Solution," *Journal of Business*, Vol. 50, No. 4 (October 1977), 415–437; Meir Statman, "How Many Stocks Make a Diversified Portfolio?," *Journal of Financial and Quantitative Analysis*, Vol. 22, No. 3 (September 1987), 353–363, suggests a range of 30 to 40.

20. Merton H. Miller, "The History of Finance," *Journal of Portfolio Management*, Vol. 25, No. 4 (Summer 1999), 100.

21. This observation was initially based on conversations with companies. I subsequently read Mandelbrot, *The (Mis) Behavior of Markets*, 59–60, referencing academic research that the practice was, in fact, widespread. See John R. Graham and Campbell R. Harvey, "The Theory and Practice of Corporate Finance: Evidence from the Field," *Journal of Financial Economics*, Vol. 60 (2001), 187–243.

22. DowJones Newswire, September 13, 2013.

23. See https://www.sec.gov/litigation/admin/2011/ia-3285.pdf, 2.

24. They are fully cataloged in Justin Fox, *The Myth of the Rational Market* (New York: Collins Business, 2009).

25. Robert J. Shiller, *Irrational Exuberance* (Princeton, NJ: Princeton University Press, 2000). Shiller had previously laid down the gauntlet in an academic article in 1981 highlighting "excess volatility" that could not or should not exist if markets were efficient. His 1987 aside is from Fox, *The Myth of the Rational Market*, 232, citing Barbara Donnelly, "Efficient Market Theorists Are Puzzled by Recent Gyrations in Stock Market," *Wall Street Journal*, October 23, 1987, 7.

26. Roger Lowenstein in a Bloomberg.com commentary (with Max Berley), from October 16, 2013, http://www.bloomberg .com/news/2013-10-16/nobel-needs-grounding-in-reality -based-economics.html.

27. Lowenstein and Berley, Bloomberg.com commentary, October 16, 2013.

28. Jeremy Grantham, *GMO Quarterly Newsletter*, 3Q, 2013, now behind the GMO paywall, but widely reproduced on the Internet.

29. *Quantitative Analysis of Investor Behavior*, for period ending December 31, 2015. DALBAR, Inc., http://www.dalbar. com. According to the company website, "QAIB calculates investor returns as the change in assets, after excluding sales, redemptions, and exchanges. This method of calculation captures realized and unrealized capital gains, dividends, interest, trading costs, sales charges, fees, expenses and any other costs." Updated in *Guide to the Markets* as of December 31, 2017, J.P. Morgan Asset Management, 64.

30. Rubinstein's *A History of the Theory of Investments*, from 2006, does an excellent job chronicling the academic twists and turns of what he calls the "standard model" consisting of MPT, efficient markets, and variants of CAPM, among other elements.

31. Jack L. Treynor and Fischer Black, "How to Use Security Analysis to Improve Portfolio Selection," *Journal of Business*, Vol. 46, No. 1 (January 1973), 66–86. Quote from 74.

32. Robert C. Merton, "An Intertemporal Capital Asset Pricing Model, *Econometrica*, Vol. 41, No. 5 (September 1973), 867–887.

33. Stephen A. Ross, "The Arbitrage Theory of Capital Asset Pricing," *Journal of Economic Theory*, Vol. 13 (December 1976), 341–360, and as developed in numerous other articles where specific factors are introduced. Among many others, see Nai-Fu Chen, Richard Roll, and Stephen A. Ross, "Economic Forces and the Stock Market," *Journal of Business*, Vol. 59,

No. 3 (July 1986), 383–403. Although the CAPM came first, it can be seen as a special-case, single-factor application of the later APT.

34. Eugene Fama and Kenneth French, "The Cross-Section of Expected Stock Returns," *Journal of Finance*, Vol. 47, No. 2 (June 1992), 427–465; Eugene Fama and Kenneth French, "Common Risk Factors in the Returns on Stocks and Bonds," *Journal of Financial Economics*, Vol. 33, No. 1 (February 1993), 3–56; Eugene Fama and Kenneth French, "A Five-Factor Asset Pricing Model," *Journal of Financial Economics*, Vol. 116 (April 2015), 1–22. See also Fama and French, "The Capital Asset Pricing Model: Theory and Evidence," *Journal of Economic Perspectives*, Vol. 18, No. 3 (Summer 2004), 25–46.

35. "What's Working," Evercore ISI, December 26, 2014.

36. Stephen A. Ross, "Factors—Theory, Statistics, and Practice," *Journal of Portfolio Management*, Vol. 43, No. 5 (2017), 1–5.

37. William F. Sharpe, "Factor Models, CAPMs, and the ABT," *Journal of Portfolio Management*, Vol. 11, No. 1 (Fall 1984), 21–25.

38. Mandelbrot, *The (Mis)Behavior of Markets,* 14. See also 82–87 for his critique of the efficient markets component of modern theory.

39. Jason Zweig, *Your Money & Your Brain: How the New Science of Neuroeconomics Can Help Make You Rich* (New York: Simon & Schuster, 2007); Richard H. Thaler, *Misbehaving: The Making of Behavioral Economics* (New York: Norton, 2015); Daniel Kahneman, Amos Tversky, and Paul Slovic, eds., *Judgment Under Uncertainty: Heuristics and Biases* (Cambridge: Cambridge University Press, 1982); Daniel Kahneman, *Thinking, Fast and Slow* (New York: Farrar, Straus and Giroux, 2011); Shiller, *Irrational Exuberance*; James Montier, *The Little Book of Behavioral Investing* (Hoboken, NJ: John Wiley, 2010); Meir Statman, *Finance for Normal People: How Investors and Markets Behave* (Oxford: Oxford University Press, 2017), and his ear-

lier *What Investors Really Want* (New York: McGraw-Hill, 2010). See also Robert J. Shiller, "From Efficient Markets Theory to Behavioral Finance," *Journal of Economic Perspectives*, Vol. 17, No. 1 (Winter 2003), 83–104.

40. See Hersh Shefrin and Meir Statman, "Behavioral Portfolio Theory," *Journal of Financial and Quantitative Analysis*, Vol. 35, No. 2 (June 2000), 127–151. See also Statman, *Finance for Normal People*, 175–218.

41. Laurence B. Siegel, "Read Your Sharpe and Markowitz!," *CFA Institute Magazine*, September–October 2014, 17–19.

42. Eugene Fama and Kenneth French, "The Capital Asset Pricing Model: Theory and Evidence," *Journal of Economic Perspectives*, Vol. 18, No. 3 (Summer 2004), 43 and 44.

Chapter 5

1. Markowitz's explicit axioms—covered in Chapter 2 of his 1959 book—attend to the definition of a rational actor making choices under conditions of uncertainty, but they, like the choices here, represent elections that cannot be reduced any further.

2. Harry M. Markowitz, *Portfolio Selection: Efficient Diversification of Investments* (New York: John Wiley & Sons, 1959), 6, 14.

3. This view is covered in greater detail in Peris, *The Dividend Imperative* (New York: McGraw Hill, 2013).

4. That has not been the case in the past few decades, where share prices and dividend growth have outstripped inflation.

5. Warren Buffett, Chairman's Letter, *Berkshire Hathaway Annual Report for 1987*, as quoted in Charles D. Ellis, ed., *Classics II: Another Investor's Anthology* (Homewood, IL: Business One Irwin, 1991), 273.

6. Irving Fisher, *The Nature of Capital and Income* (New York: MacMillan, 1906), 188.

7. In Bingley's case, the wealth originated in trade. Bingley had inherited a specific amount, 100,000 pounds, that was

invested in government bonds generating 4–5% per year in income.

8. Fisher, *The Nature of Capital and Income*, 324.

9. Frank H. Knight, *Risk, Uncertainty, and Profit* (Boston: Houghton Mifflin, 1921).

10. Peter Bernstein, "The Great Gift of Uncertainty," *Journal of Portfolio Management*, Vol. 22, No. 4 (Summer 1996), 1.

11. David F. Swenson, *Pioneering Portfolio Management: An Unconventional Approach to Institutional Investment*, 2nd ed. (New York: Free Press, 2000), 3.

12. Robert H. Jeffrey, "A New Paradigm for Portfolio Risk," *Journal of Portfolio Management*, Vol. 11, No. 1 (Fall 1984), 33–40.

13. For instance, Jerome B. Cohen, Edward D. Zinbarg, and Arthur Zeikel, *Investment Analysis and Portfolio Management*, 5th ed. (Homewood, IL: Irwin, 1987), 135.

14. For instance, Ashvin B. Chhabra, "Beyond Markowitz: A Comprehensive Wealth Allocation Framework for Individual Investors," *Journal of Wealth Management*, Vol. 7, No. 4 (Spring 2005), 8–34.

15. For example, Lewis D. Johnson, "Equity Duration: Another Look," *Financial Analyst Journal*, Vol. 45, No. 2 (March–April 1989), 73–75; Paul Bostock, Paul Woolley, and Martin Duffy, "Duration-Based Asset Allocation," *Financial Analysts Journal*, Vol. 45, No. 1 (January–February 1989), 53–60, 80. See also William F. Sharpe and Ronald Lanstein, "Duration and Security Risk," *Journal of Financial and Quantitative Analysis*, Vol. 13, No. 4 (November 1978), 653–668.

16. See Patricia M. Dechow, Richard G. Sloan, and Mark T. Soliman, "Implied Equity Duration: A New Measure of Equity Risk," *Review of Accounting Studies*, Vol. 9 (2004), 197–228. As an exception to the general U.S. indifference, I would also point to a working paper by my Federated colleague Michael Granito, "The Equity Term Structure," 2018, and Oscar Varela, "The Stock as a Portfolio of Durations:

Solving Black's Dividend Puzzle Using Black's Criteria," *Journal of Portfolio Management* (Summer 2015), 122–132.

17. Geoff Considine, "Do Income-Oriented Portfolios Reduce Safe Withdrawal Rates?," http://www.AdvisorPerspectives.com as of August 27, 2013.

18. John Maynard Keynes, *The General Theory of Employment, Interest and Money* (New York: Harcourt, Brace, 1936), Chap. 12, Sec. V, para. 7, online edition.

19. Stephen A. Ross, "The Arbitrage Theory of Capital Asset Pricing," *Journal of Economic Theory*, Vol. 13 (1976), 341–360, and Nai-Fu Chen, Richard Roll, and Stephen A. Ross, "Economic Forces and the Stock Market," *Journal of Business*, Vol. 59, No. 3 (July 1986), 383–403.

20. DCFs are not ignored by the textbook writers. While the present work focuses on cashflows to shareholders in the form of dividends—the dividend discount model (DDM)—other approaches include free cashflow to the firm (FCFF) or free cashflow to equity (FCFE). All are subsets of the generalized DCF model. Residual income approaches—where an equity cost-of-capital charge is made against company profits—are also theoretically robust but little encountered in the marketplace.

21. For instance, Howard M. Schilit, Jeremy Perler, and Yoni Engelhart, *Financial Shenanigans: How to Detect Accounting Gimmicks & Fraud in Financial Reports*, 4th ed. (New York: McGraw-Hill Education, 2018).

22. The flaws in using P/E ratios as a valuation tool are addressed in greater detail in Peris, *The Dividend Imperative*, 6–33.

23. In the current system, "mispricing" is usually defined in terms of higher or lower P/E multiples or estimates of future EPS. In a cashflow–based system, the questions will concern the expected growth rate of the distributions or the discount rate. If the actual discount rate turns out to be greater than the expected rate of return, or the growth rate lower, then the value of the asset is a lot lower than the quoted price.

Short sellers seek out these opportunities. At the other end of the spectrum, too high a discount rate applied to the cash stream, or much greater than expected growth, and you have an opportunity for capital appreciation. Many investors seek out these "undervalued" stocks.

24. Fisher, *The Nature of Capital and Income*, 230–231.
25. Fisher, *The Nature of Capital and Income*, 224.
26. See Shanthi Rexaline, "Class of 1997: 2 Decades After Their IPOs, Where Are These Companies Now?," May 16, 2017, http://www.Benzinga.com as of January 2, 2018.
27. That equates to 630 of 856 IPOs in 1999–2000. Private correspondence with Jay Ritter, University of Florida professor of finance, who follows the IPO market. See his online database at https://site.warrington.ufl.edu/ritter/ipo-data/.
28. "The Global Income Investor Slide Pack," April 2017, Société Générale Cross Asset Research, 52.
29. Markowitz, *Portfolio Selection*, 8.
30. Note that the sample sizes are slightly different, 21 for total return and stock return and 20 for the growth in income, due to the need for a base year. To highlight the structurally lower standard deviation of the income return, we ran an analysis involving all the companies of the S&P 1500 that paid dividends consistently from 1996 through 2017. Two REITs (WY and PCH) were excluded because they were not REITs through the entire period and made large stock and cash distributions at the time of their conversions. The final list included 474 securities, from which 125,000 unique random portfolios were generated, and the total return and standard deviation data for each were gathered and compared. In the scenario where dividends were being reinvested, the gap in the total return and income median standard deviation was 3.6% (17.1% versus 13.5%). Where the dividends were not being reinvested, the gap was similar at 3.7% (17.1% versus 13.4%). Source: Federated Investors and FactSet Research Systems, Inc., 2018.

31. Richard H. Thaler and Cass Sunstein, *Nudge: Improving Decisions About Health, Wealth, and Happiness*, rev. and expanded ed. (New York: Penguin Books, 2009).

32. William P. Lloyd and Richard Haney, Jr., "Time Diversification: Surest Route to Lower Risk," *Journal of Portfolio Management,* Vol. 6, No. 3 (Spring 1980), 5–9.

33. Peris, *The Dividend Imperative.*

34. "Harvard College Versus Amory," in Ellis, ed., *Classics II*, 10–18. Original source: Octavius Pickering, *Reports of Cases Argued and Determined in the Supreme Judicial Court of Massachusetts*, Vol. 9 (Boston: 1831), 461.

35. Markowitz, *Portfolio Selection*, 207.

36. This silo could, with some tweaking, be set up to have roughly equal income streams from its constituent members at the beginning of any measurement period. If bonds or other "flat" coupon ventures were included in the mix, however, any periodic rebalance would need to be done with care, lest the weight drift toward bonds and away from stocks as the latter raised their dividends.

37. Keynes, *General Theory*, Chap. 12, Sec. 6, para. 1, as reproduced widely on the Internet.

38. Hersh Shefrin and Meir Statman, "Behavioral Portfolio Theory," *Journal of Financial and Quantitative Analysis*, Vol. 35, No. 2 (June 2000), 128, 141. Further elaboration of BPT can be found in Chapter 8 of Statman's *Finance for Normal People: How Investors and Markets Behave* (Oxford: Oxford University Press, 2017).

39. Robert G. Kirby, "Lessons Learned and Never Learned," *Journal of Portfolio Management*, Vol. 6, No. 1 (Fall 1979), 54.

40. David Blanchett and Hal Ratner, "Building Efficient Income Portfolios," *Journal of Portfolio Management*, Vol. 41, No. 3 (Spring 2015), 117–125.

41. This is above and beyond the more basic problem of the double taxation of equity dividends, first at the corporate level

and then again at the investor level. Because interest payments on debt are generally deductible for corporations, the entire U.S. corporate capital structure leans more in the direction of debt than it otherwise would.

42. Widely quoted on the Internet and popular media. Specific citation from http://www.tcm.com/tcmdb/person/14740%7C73253/Irving-Berlin/ as of July 14, 2016. See also Susanna McCorkle, "Always: A Singer's Journey Through the Life of Irving Berlin," *American Heritage*, Vol. 49, No. 7 (November 1998).

43. Paul A. Samuelson, "Challenge to Judgment," *Journal of Portfolio Management*, Vol. 1, No. 1 (Fall 1974), 18.

44. Both holding figures as of June 30, 2017, as reported on SEC form 13-F.

Conclusion

1. Mark Rubinstein, "Markowitz's 'Portfolio Selection': A Fifty Year Retrospective," *Journal of Finance*, Vol. LVII, No. 3 (June 2002), 1044.

2. Paul Cootner, *The Random Character of Stock Prices* (Cambridge, MA: MIT Press, 1964), 337.

3. Merton H. Miller, "Behavioral Rationality in Finance: The Case of Dividends," *Journal of Business*, Vol. 59, No. 4, Pt. 2 (October 1986), S467.

Suggested Further Reading

The following list excludes academic articles and textbooks in favor of books that individual investors and financial advisors may find of more general interest. It includes recently published accounts or the current editions of classic texts. Most but not all are referenced in the endnotes.

Peter Bernstein, *Capital Ideas: The Improbable Origins of Modern Wall Street* (Hoboken, NJ: Wiley & Sons, 1992).

Justin Fox, *The Myth of the Rational Market* (New York: CollinsBusiness, 2009).

William N. Goetzmann, *Money Changes Everything: How Finance Made Civilization Possible* (Princeton, NJ: Princeton University Press, 2016).

Benjamin Graham, *The Intelligent Investor: A Book of Practical Counsel*, rev. ed. (New York: HarperCollins, 2013). While this work references the first edition (1949) in order to establish the historical context, the most current edition is listed here.

Benjamin Graham and David Dodd, *Security Analysis*, 6th ed. (New York: McGraw-Hill, 2009). While this work references the first and third editions (1934 and 1951) in order to establish the historical context, the most current edition is listed here.

Daniel Kahneman, *Thinking, Fast and Slow* (New York: Farrar, Straus and Giroux, 2011).

Benoît Mandelbrot and Richard Hudson, *The (Mis)Behavior of Markets: A Fractal View of Risk, Ruin, and Reward* (New York: Basic Books, 2004).

James Montier, *The Little Book of Behavioral Investing* (Hoboken, NJ: Wiley, 2010).

Howard M. Schilit, Jeremy Perler, and Yoni Engelhart, *Financial Shenanigans: How to Detect Accounting Gimmicks and Fraud in Financial Reports*, 4th ed. (New York: McGraw-Hill Education, 2018).

Robert J. Shiller, *Irrational Exuberance: Revised and Expanded Third Edition* (Princeton, NJ: Princeton University Press, 2015).

Meir Statman, *Finance for Normal People: How Investors and Markets Behave* (Oxford: Oxford University Press, 2017).

Nassim Nicholas Taleb, *The Black Swan: The Impact of the Highly Improbable, Second Edition* (New York: Random House, 2010).

Richard H. Thaler, *Misbehaving: The Making of Behavioral Economics* (New York: Norton, 2015).

James Weatherall, *The Physics of Wall Street* (New York: Houghton Mifflin, 2013).

Paul Wilmott and David Orrell, *The Money Formula: Dodgy Finance, Pseudo Science, and How Mathematicians Took Over the Markets* (Chichester, West Sussex: John Wiley & Sons, 2017).

Jason Zweig, *Your Money and Your Brain* (New York: Simon & Schuster, 2007).

Index

About the Author

Daniel Peris is Senior Vice President at Federated Investors in Pittsburgh, where he oversees dividend-focused portfolios. He is the author of two prior books on investing, *The Strategic Dividend Investor* (2011) and *The Dividend Imperative* (2013). Prior to transitioning into asset management, Peris was a historian of modern Russia and the author of a book and several articles on Soviet political culture in the 1920s and 1930s.